Lessons for Dylan

This Large Print Book carries the
Seal of Approval of N.A.V.H.

Lessons for Dylan

From Father to Son

Joel Siegel

Thorndike Press • Waterville, Maine

Published in 2003 by arrangement with Public Affairs, a member of Perseus Books, LLC.

Thorndike Press® Large Print Biography.

The tree indicium is a trademark of Thorndike Press.

The text of this Large Print edition is unabridged. Other aspects of the book may vary from the original edition.

Set in 16 pt. Plantin by Ramona Watson.

Printed in the United States on permanent paper.

Library of Congress Cataloging-in-Publication Data

Siegel, Joel, 1943–
    Lessons for Dylan : from father to son / Joel Siegel.
       p. cm.
    Originally published: New York : Public Affairs, 2003.
    ISBN 0-7862-5816-0 (lg. print : hc : alk. paper)
    1. Siegel, Joel, 1943–   2. Film critics — United States — Biography.   3. Conduct of life.   4. Large type books.
I. Title.
PN1998.3.S495A3 2003b
791.43′.092—dc212
   [B]   2003056351

TO DYLAN

Of course

As the Founder/CEO of NAVH, the only national health agency solely devoted to those who, although not totally blind, have an eye disease which could lead to serious visual impairment, I am pleased to recognize Thorndike Press* as one of the leading publishers in the large print field.

Founded in 1954 in San Francisco to prepare large print textbooks for partially seeing children, NAVH became the pioneer and standard setting agency in the preparation of large type.

Today, those publishers who meet our standards carry the prestigious "Seal of Approval" indicating high quality large print. We are delighted that Thorndike Press is one of the publishers whose titles meet these standards. We are also pleased to recognize the significant contribution Thorndike Press is making in this important and growing field.

Lorraine H. Marchi, L.H.D.
Founder/CEO
NAVH

* Thorndike Press encompasses the following imprints: Thorndike, Wheeler, Walker and Large Print Press.

Contents

Introduction

One morning while I was shaving, looking into the mirror, squinting through the soap and the steam, I thought about putting my glasses on, the better to see my face. Of course that is a dumb idea: Would I shave over or under the stems? And the steam that fogged the mirror would fog the lenses even worse. But I bet a couple of million guys have tried it. The thought made me smile. And, squinting the other way through the steam and the smoke, I saw my father smiling back. I knew it wasn't my memory of my father that was smiling back at me — it was the part of my father that lives inside me.

My father has been gone for more than twenty years. I knew him pretty well; I was almost forty when he died. But my son, Dylan, may not get to know me. I was in my fifties when Dylan was born, so even in the best of times I couldn't expect more

11

than a score or so of years with him. And it hasn't been the best of times, not with three cancer surgeries and chemo and CAT scans and six months of radiation in the past five years.

My doctors are optimistic, and, honestly, they have every reason to be. Not one of *them* has shown so much as a single symptom of anything even like cancer in the five years since my original diagnosis. I haven't been that lucky. That's why I'm writing this book.

The book is not chronological. It begins with my fight against cancer because that is where my life with Dylan began. Dylan will have his own memories of some of those times; I want him to know mine.

In the book there are letters I've written to Dylan, things I've done I want to share with him, and a series of my side of the conversations Dylan and I might never get to have about things like college, drugs, baseball, even about his mom.

One of the unspeakable joys of watching your children grow up is watching them experience things for the first time. The first time we went to Disneyland, Dylan was three. His favorite thing about our trip was meeting Mickey Mouse. His second favorite was pulling leaves off a bush, dropping them, and watching them float to the ground. It was winter in New York, and when we left for Disneyland the trees there had been bare. A few months before, when there had been leaves on bushes and trees in New York, he hadn't been old enough, or his motor skills weren't fine-tuned enough, or he couldn't reach high enough to accomplish this feat. He must have spent half an hour at the ice cream store on Main Street dropping leaves and watching them fall. He was more interested in the leaves than he was in the ice cream (this tendency must have been inherited from his mom's side of the family). And I watched him discover that they'd float a little longer if he stood on his tiptoes and held his arm up as high as he could before he let the leaves go.

I've written about some other things I'd like to watch Dylan experience for the first time, some places I want to take him, some movies I want to watch him watch, some things I did with my dad that I want to do with him.

I know Dylan will take different things from these stories at different times in his life. It's taken me decades to understand the real meanings of things that have happened to me.

When I was about nine or ten and a smart-ass kid to boot, I asked my grandfather, my father's father, why we Jews couldn't mix milk and meat.

"Because it says in the Bible, 'Thou shalt not seethe a kid in its mother's milk,'" or something like that, was my grandfather's answer.

Now, I knew that answer. I'd asked that question before, I'd heard that answer before. But I didn't ask the question to learn the answer. The question was a trap. A setup. I told you I was a smart-ass kid.

"OK," I pretended to puzzle out. "But if it's wrong to eat animals in their mother's milk, which does sound awfully cruel, why can't we eat chicken and milk? Chickens don't give milk."

My grandfather answered me the best way he knew how. He smacked me, hard, across the cheek with the back of his hand.

The lesson I learned that day was: Careful what you say to Grandpa, he might lose his temper and smack you across the head.

It took me forty years to figure out that the real lesson was: Never dis your grandfather by asking him a question he doesn't know the answer to.

I still haven't figured out the answers to

other questions life has forced me to ask myself. Like, why have I been married so many times?

Much of the time Dylan and I spend together we spend trying to make each other laugh. Playing hide-and-seek or being the monster or telling the most blatant, outrageous lies, especially about whether we've already eaten dessert, or sneaking up on me when I'm reading the paper — which, to Dylan, I must always seem to be doing — and shooting it out of my hands with an explosive push and a huge, loud scream. Scares the hell out of me every time.

I asked Dylan if he could help come up with a title for this book. He thought for a second, then motioned me close with his finger.

"I need to whisper it," he whispered.

I moved in to hear him and he shpritzed a Bronx cheer, a loud, wet "PFFFFFFT!" right into my ear, and laughed.

"Hmm," I nodded, thoughtfully. "Not bad, but how do you spell it?"

He thought for a second and shpritzed me with four quicker, quieter Bronx cheers: "Pfft, pfft, pfft, pfft." Not bad for four and a half years old. And I had no idea PFFFFFFT was a four-letter word.

I write about my triumphs so that Dylan will know the things I did well, and some flops so he'll know the things I didn't do so well. And I've tried to keep him laughing through both.

I don't think Dylan will mind my sharing our story with you. This is something I decided to do after we went public on *Good Morning America* and I received thousands of e-mails. Dylan and I aren't the only parent and child who are afraid they may never get to know each other well enough, and my storytelling might help some of the others.

And, no, this isn't an autobiography; I've left a lot out. It was never intended to be complete. After all, I have to save something for the sequel. What if I live?

PART 1

I Don't Have Good News

1

I Don't Have Good News

Dear Dylan,
They are words you don't easily forget — "I don't have good news." Especially when they're said by a doctor who's just finished giving you a colonoscopy.

It was the summer of 1997. One week before, we'd had very good news. The *in vitro* had taken. Ena, your mother, my wife of one year, was now officially pregnant. The baby, that's you, Dylan, was due in February. The American Cancer Society's web site said that, all things considered, I had a 70 percent chance of being alive to witness the birth.

I had surgery one week after the diagnosis. It was supposed to be easy. It wasn't. The lesion (the word even looks like a euphemism) was lower than the doctors anticipated. To lose the cancer, they had to tie off my colon. They gave me a colostomy. There were nodes; the cancer might have spread. The treatment protocol would now include simultaneous radiation and chemotherapy. The odds of my seeing you born dropped to 60 percent.

One day as Ena was leaving my hospital room I noticed, for the first time, that she was starting to show. I started to cry.

I remember looking out the hospital window at a tree, a tree that had somehow managed to grow large and lush even though its seed had somehow taken root on a two-foot wide spit of land between the FDR Drive, one of the busiest highways in America, and the East River, one of the most polluted bodies of water in the world. I remember thinking about the impossible coincidences that come together to create the miracle of life. I began charting the coincidences that had brought me, in the words of a Jewish prayer, to this season. I thought of the things I'd been able to do, the places I'd been able to see. My grandmother had crossed this same river each day to work in a sweatshop, and I'd been invited to the White House and met three presidents — and hadn't voted for any of them. If whoever had given this to me wanted to take it back, I decided, I could do it: I could give it back. And somehow knowing that I was able to give life up gave me the strength to hold on. As for miracles, until I saw you being born, Dylan, I didn't have a clue.

I missed a lot when your mom was pregnant. We didn't do Lamaze, I barely read the books. I was there for your first sonogram, but I was too sick to pay much attention to you or your mom. Your profile on the black-and-white printout looked exactly like the special effect of the God-like baby from the movie *2001*. I didn't think it was real. I thought they printed these up and gave the same one to all the parents.

The morning you were born, Dylan, maybe because we're used to machine-age hard edges, polished steel, and right angles, I wasn't ready for the glop and the imperfections and the organicness of it all. "My God," I muttered under my breath, "it's just like the movies." And, of course, it is: the slap, the cry, the pride, the kitchy-kooing.

A woman in labor produces a hormone that allows her to forget the intense pain. But she doesn't forget much of anything else. A few days later Ena frowned and said, "Just like the movies?!"

Almost thirty years of doing live television has taught me to edit myself. I didn't tell Ena till months later that what I came very close to saying was, "My God, it's just like *Alien!*"

When you were born, I did a quick count: hands, arms, legs, fingers, and toes. Two, two, two, ten, ten. And your profile looked exactly like the sonogram. It still does.

I told my friend, Rabbi Larry Raphael, whom I've known since he was your age, "I have no secret ambitions for Dylan to star in the NBA or win a Nobel prize. I just want him to be normal."

"Normal," Larry corrected me, "but not average."

He also told me, about kids, "The days take forever, but the years go by in a minute."

He's right, of course. But when you're reminded of your own mortality every morning when you watch your hair fall out in clumps, days that take forever aren't so bad. And average would be OK, too.

The day we took you home from the hospital was my last day of chemotherapy. There's a picture of me carrying you. I look like shit — ten years older than I look today, and because it was five years ago I should look five years younger.

OK, I'm old. I'll be sixty-eight at your Bar Mitzvah, seventy-three when you graduate from high school. My dad was forty-two when I graduated from high school, and for all he related to me, he might as well have been seventy-three. Age is not a liability. In fact, old age can be an asset. When I'd ask my dad for money he'd pretend not to hear me. But he was in his forties. When you're old enough to ask me for money, I really won't be able to hear you.

I had no idea what my mom meant when she would look at an infant and say, "She looks just like so-and-so," when so-and-so was close to fifty and even closer to 300 pounds. When you were a newborn and looked just like my baby pictures, I finally understood. She didn't mean the baby looked like so-and-so looks now, she meant the baby looks like so-and-so did then. The tough part is that, when I finally did figure out what she meant, my mother wasn't here for me to tell her.

Because you were an *in vitro* baby, we actually have a picture of you when you were six cells old. I have no idea how you'll be able to assimilate that when you see it and realize what it is. But every time I look at that picture I can hear my mother say, "Looks just like cousin Shirley." And I hear the punch line to the Thermos bottle joke: "It's the greatest invention ever, better than fire, better than the wheel. Keeps hot things hot, cold things cold — how does it know?"

How did those cells know to become you and not a tree or an Oldsmobile? And what I really hear is astronaut John Glenn when he looked down at the Earth from space and said, "It's impossible to look at this and not believe in God."

August 1997

The first thing I saw after I came to was this huge Lichtenstein pop art poster. If it had been a Raphael Madonna, I might have thought I'd died and gone to heaven. But Lichtenstein? I died and went to the Museum of Modern Art?

It was the recovery room at New York Hospital, I figured out. There was a clock near the poster, and it must've been a big clock, because I could read the time without my glasses: 4:25, it said, and I wondered, "Where is everybody?"

Save for some guy at a computer terminal at the opposite end of the room, I was the only person there. "I've had the only surgery in New York Hospital?" I thought to myself. "Will they still charge me extra for a private room if I'm the only patient?" I really did think these things.

I was bandaged and belted in. There were tubes coming into my nostrils and clear liquid being pumped into my arm. I could barely move, and I wasn't sure I wanted to. I did wiggle my toes and they wiggled back, which is the reason this book isn't called *Where's the Rest of Me?*

"Hey," I shouted at the guy at the computer terminal. "Where is everybody?"

Where, I wondered, was my wife, Ena? My cousin Ronnie the Doctor, an LA gastroenterologist who flew to New York to make sure they took good care of me? My friend Jerry Imber, a plastic surgeon on the staff of New York Hospital, who promised to come by and make sure the scar didn't show?

"I'll tell 'em you're up," he said.

"My wife should be in the next room," I said. One of my wife, Jane's, first memories coming out of brain surgery twenty years

25

before in this same hospital was hearing the recovery room nurses buzzing about Joel Siegel waiting in the hallway. Three years later, Jane would die in this hospital when her tumor came back. I tried not to think about that.

"Nobody waiting," the guy grumbled and went back to his book.

He could have told me it was 4:25 in the morning.

I'd gone in at 7:00 the morning before, for what was supposed to be routine colon cancer surgery. Snip out the bad stuff, check the nodes, glue the two pieces of the colon together, and go home in a few days as good as new.

Ena and Ronnie and Imber had been there, waiting, at 5:00 in the afternoon when my surgeon stumbled in, stoop-shouldered and exhausted, after six hours of surgery.

The lesion was on the cusp between the colon and the rectum. There was barely enough tissue left to staple the clean ends together. To give me time to heal, he had to, as they say, cut me a new asshole, a temporary colostomy two inches due right of my belly button. The lymph nodes had been affected, evidence that cancer cells had escaped the initial site and might have been and probably were roaming through my vital organs, looking for a vacancy sign. If these cells grow and metastasize, the cancer would then spread, most likely to my lungs, my liver, or my brain. Cancer metastasizes to organs that use a lot of blood — and the lungs, the liver, and the brain fill the bill. The heart isn't an organ, it's a muscle, which is why we're spared heart cancer. Chemotherapy and radiation are the guns oncologists use to kill these rogue cells to keep them from spreading. Suddenly, things weren't so simple.

I learned later, much later, that the surgeon told Imber he would have to make the colostomy permanent, that he wasn't sure he could leave a large enough margin of cancer-free tissue to reverse it. Imber urged him to do his best, give it another try, work a little harder. He did. Thank God. It pays to have friends in low places.

Cancer is infantilizing. You're no longer a grown-up. You can't take care of yourself.

After surgery, while living with the side effects of chemo or radiation or both, you need help walking, dressing yourself, even feeding yourself. You lose control of bodily functions you'd learned to control when you were a child. Your hair falls out, your muscles give up, you grow decades older in weeks or months. (I kept thinking of those pictures of FDR taken during his presidency, how old he got from 1932 to 1945, and how he never got younger.) And, on top of all of that, no one can tell you with any certainty how long you have to live.

I don't remember how or when I was told about the colostomy. I was on a morphine drip, felt no pain, and don't remember much of anything. I do remember meeting the colostomy nurse a few days later. This has got to be the worst job in the hospital. Maybe in the world. I remember a scene from a *Shaft* kind of movie where the tough gang leader gets shafted, and as they're dragging him, bullet-ridden, into the emergency room, he's screaming, "Don't give me the bag, Doc! Kill me before you give me the bag!"

I got the bag.

A colostomy is an ingenious idea. They really do cut you a new opening, called a *stoma,* somewhere to the right of your navel. They glue a kind of Tupperware ring around it — they come in a series of sizes, lined up in the department of your drugstore you've glanced at ever since you were a kid and prayed you'd never have to buy anything there. You glue the ring to your skin, skin-tight, you hope. You attach the bag to the ring, air-tight, you hope.

Before plastics, they made the bags of silk, raincoat material, all kinds of things, and tried to hold them in place with metal and bone. They didn't work well, and it wasn't just the smell and the leakage. This is an open wound, prone to infection. Colostomies are much safer since antibiotics were developed, and the appliances really do work like Tupperware: you press till you hear the "snap." They sell reusable bags that you wash out between uses. They also sell, at a much higher price, disposable bags you only use once. I figured, go for broke, I'll allow myself this little indulgence. Hugh Downs tells a story that when he was a page at the NBC radio station in Chicago back in the 1940s, Paul Reimer, who wrote *Vic 'N Sade*, a comedy so big it ran on two different radio networks at the same time, was walking down a hallway one day eating a Milky Way. As he passed young Downs, Reimer saluted him with the half-eaten candy bar and said, "I make big, I spend big." That was going to be my answer if anyone asked about the disposable bags.

My aunt Barbara, a longtime colon cancer survivor, sent me some issues of a magazine for colostomy patients filled with fun-in-the-sun-even-though articles and colostomy bag fashion spreads. Honest. Al Geiberger, it turns out, played the PGA tour wearing a colostomy bag, giving new meaning to the phrase "hole in one," something I truly did not want to know. I believed my doctors when they told me that this was temporary for me, not a life-style change, and I was helped by the reporter's syndrome: disassociation. Every reporter I know has done things he or she would never do in real life, because when you're reporting, you're the perfect observer. You watch, and you make notes, but the real you isn't there; it's just watching. That's how reporters can ask ridiculous questions of people in obvious pain, and insult world leaders and would-be presidents. I once spent half an hour sitting on a foot-wide ledge, thirty stories above Times Square. In real life I'm afraid of heights, but Joel Siegel, reporter, fears nothing.

Shrinks call this "denial." My shrink, Olga Silverstein, said to me, "No wonder you're doing so well, you're in complete denial."

I answered so quickly I stepped on her last word, "No, I'm not."

OK, I was, and probably still am, but it works. I learned to change the bag, of course. You're supposed to pull off the ring that holds the bag and clean the stoma once every two weeks. That I wouldn't do. I went back to New York Hospital and had the colostomy nurse do it. I hired private-duty nurses to do it. In Connecticut, where we have a weekend home in a town called Lakeville, I hired the visiting nurse service. I didn't want to look at it, I didn't want to know from it, and that went on for months.

I learned that two old friends had gone through similar experiences — both because of diverticulitis and not cancer — two friends I'd known since Louis Pasteur Junior High in West LA: Bill Ginsberg — yes, that Bill Ginsberg, Monica Lewinsky's lawyer — and Chuck Plotkin, whose work you know even if you don't know his name; he's Bruce Springsteen's record producer. Both had had colostomies, both had had them reversed, both had survived. Chuck is one of the calmest, most centered, most competent people I know — he always was, even when he was eleven — and he, just by being himself, gave me the confidence to know that I could live with this thing. Bill, it turned out, knew an awful lot about shitting in a bag, perhaps because his legal specialty is medical malpractice. What helped most was having friends I could laugh with. The worst, we agreed, was changing your bag in an airplane. You become a member of a very different kind of Mile High Club. We also agreed there was no best.

There's no feeling in the stoma. There aren't any nerve endings there, so the only way you can tell if you're going is by feeling the bag. I developed a nervous habit: my right hand would brush against the bag to see how full it was, the way my left hand tends, unconsciously, to brush against the bridge of my nose to make sure my glasses haven't slipped. If I hadn't become a movie critic, I could've been a hell of a third-base coach.

One morning, on page six of the *New York Post*, in the tabloid's gossip column, I read that I'd thrown a tantrum at a movie screening, demanding an aisle seat and threatening to walk out if I didn't get one. Richard Johnson, who writes the column, had called me the day before to check the item, an awfully nice thing for a gossip columnist to do. I'd told him that the studio people caused the fuss, there was no aisle seat available but I'd offered to stand while

I watched the film, which was the truth, but he didn't believe me and ran the item anyway. What I didn't tell him was that the reason I needed an aisle seat was that I was afraid my bag would fill and, as I was pushing my way out of the middle of the row in a crowded theater, would jar itself loose. If Oliver Wendell Holmes convinced the Supreme Court that it's dangerous to shout "Fire!" in a crowded theater, what would he have to say about the riot *that* would cause?

I traveled with a kit: baggies, wipes, paper towels, Lysol spray. You know how they say, "After a while you get used to it?" After a while you get used to it. It becomes the new normal and it's no big deal; it's what you do to get by.

One of my first days doing the news, in 1972 on hippie-radio KMET-FM, 94.7 in Los Angeles, I read a story that came over the wire about a so-called enema bandit in Springfield, Illinois. He would tie up women, give them enemas, and leave them in their bathrooms. The last line of the story: "He has yet to leave a clue or a trail behind him." I thought of that story every time I cleaned up the trail I left behind me.

The colostomy, it turned out, was the easy part, one of the side effects of the disease. The hard part is the cure. If you're not careful, or a little lucky, the cure'll kill you before the disease will.

I liked my oncologist right off. Dr. Jeffrey Tepler. My cancer was common enough that I didn't need cutting-edge treatment. Thousands of people every year got what I got, and, I knew, when the year was over some lived, some died. What Dr. Tepler had going for him was that he genuinely seemed to care which of the two would happen to me.

In his book-filled office, plastered with watercolors his kids had painted, Tepler recommended a course of radiation at the initial site and chemotherapy to kill any of the rogue cells that might have traveled past my lymph nodes.

The chemotherapy of choice for grade 3 colorectal cancer is 5-FU (5-fluorouracil) with leucovorin: 5-FU is the chemical that kills the cancer cells, leucovorin is a vitamin that amplifies the kill rate. It had been the chemotherapy of choice for ten years, which, my reporter's instinct told me, was a good thing. There are few arenas as cutthroat or as competitive as the search for a cancer cure. Every once in a while a scientist trying to cure cancer will get caught lying in a paper or keeping a second set of books in his lab and make the front pages, the stakes are that high. The prize they're fighting for isn't grant money or even the Nobel prize in medicine; the real battle is for immortality. Salk, Einstein, Newton, Galileo — how many scientists' names does the average person know? Find the cure for cancer, you're on humanity's shortlist for a thousand years. So, I figured, if the finest minds of my generation couldn't find anything better than 5-FU with leucovorin in ten years of research, that was the stuff for me.

The way it seems to work best is through infusion. My surgeon had dug a port into my chest, plastic tubing connected the port to a pouch about the size of a box of Grape-Nuts I would have to live with 24/7; it was, literally, part of me. Inside the pouch, a computer-controlled, battery-powered pump would dribble just the right amount of chemical through the tubing and into the port which connected to my jugular vein. The pouch even had a belt loop, so I could attach it to my slacks and hide it with a sportcoat, I'd been told. But it was a bit too bulky for that, and the plastic tube would kink if I ran it under my shirt, so I ended up running the tube up my shirtsleeve and carrying the pouch full of chemo in my left hand like an attaché case from hell. That's the way I went to work, that's the way I interviewed Brad Pitt, that's the way I interviewed the stars of *The Lion King*, that's the way I appeared on network television. I have no idea how I did it.

Two nurses came to our apartment to hook me up to the chemo. They pried open the layer of skin that covered the port with a rather large needle and pumped it with saline to make sure I wasn't backed up like an overused drain. They told me that if something should happen and the chemo should leak or spill, DO NOT, UNDER ANY CIRCUMSTANCES, TOUCH THE CHEMICALS!

They gave me twenty-four-hour emergency numbers to call. They would come and clean up the mess, it's that toxic. And that's on the outside. What was it doing to my inside? I found out fifteen minutes after they hooked me up. I got sick.

I ran a fever, I was nauseous, I had diarrhea. All expected, they assured me (assured me?), though not usually this quickly. One of my mantras is that pain is God's way of telling me I'm not dead yet.

Somehow I learned to sleep on my right side, the chemo pumping into the port on my left, and three mornings a week I dutifully showed up at Memorial Sloan Kettering for radiation.

I'd gone through this when they treated my wife Jane's brain tumor. They irradiated her brain, they irradiated my tushie; the symbolism did not escape me. First they did a dry run, focusing three green lasers at me, and they built a computer model from which craftsmen molded a three-dimensional plasticine copy of my backside. The overwhelming majority of colorectal cancer reoccurrences happen at or near the initial site, and radiation is the best way to ethnic-cleanse the area so that there's no cancer left to come back. Because it was a dry run, I could watch them line me up and see my tushie take shape in green parabolic arches on the computer monitor. It looked amazingly like the computer models I'd seen while I was doing behind-the-scenes stories on the use of computer animation in *Toy Story* and *Beauty and the Beast*.

"That's right," said my radiologist, the world-renowned Dr. Bruce Minsky. "The same people developed this for us. First." Dr. Minsky really is world renowned. And he was right about the computer program. A year or so later, I interviewed the president of Pixar for a behind-the-scenes story on *Toy Story 2,* and he confirmed it.

"We couldn't get any money to make any movies, so we looked around for other applications and created a program to make 3-D models from CAT scans." He was very flip about it, couldn't care less that he might have saved my ass, movies obviously being the important part of his business.

Once the model building was done, Dr. Minsky marked the model exactly where the radiation needed to hit. I never saw the model, and never wanted to (hey, I'm glad I can't walk behind me). But a couple times a year, I'm solicited for personal items for celebrity auctions and I think about calling Dr. Minsky.

Next step, he duplicated the mark on my real tushie and gave me three tiny tattoos he'd use to pinpoint the lasers. A perfect idea except for one small detail: Jews aren't allowed to have tattoos. There's a nice reason for this, really. Because we're all equal in God's eyes, we're all supposed to leave this world exactly the way we came into it. No jewelry, no signs of worldly wealth. Orthodox Jewish coffins are held together with wooden pegs; there's no metal on them. That's a European affectation, I think, because in Israel there aren't any coffins; Jews are wrapped in a shroud and slid into the sand — which is why there are no "Treasures of King Solomon" exhibits paralleling the "Treasures of King Tut." No mummies, no gold, no treasure, no tattoos.

Lenny Bruce used to do a routine about how his mother screamed at him when he came home from the Navy with a tattoo on his arm.

"Now you can't be buried in a Jewish cemetery!" she screamed.

"OK," Bruce went on. "I'll be buried in a Jewish cemetery, they can bury my arm in a Catholic cemetery."

Look for my tushie next to Lenny Bruce's arm.

The major side effect of radiation is exhaustion, and the effects are cumulative. At first I was kind of peppy about the whole thing, smiling my way through it even though it took me a long time to get dressed and undressed, because I had to loop my clothing around the chemo tube that was attached to my chest. Once the lead doors slammed shut and the humming of the X-rays started, I had to lie as motionless as possible for twenty minutes. I didn't move, the X-ray tube moved, computer-controlled to come at me from three different angles.

Joanna Bull had been Gilda Radner's therapist when Gilda was fighting cancer. Joanna studies Eastern religions, and she taught me the Zen trick of self-hypnosis. She told me to create a picture in my mind of something beautiful, positive, serene, something that would protect me, make me smile. It's not hard, once you unclutter your mind, and I recommend this technique. It kept me positive and serene through days of discomfort.

I pictured my grandmother. I'd see her face, I'd try to feel her hands, her long fingers, wrinkled as if she'd spent too much time in the pool. She, too, had colon cancer. She was diagnosed at eighty, had ten great, garrulous years — perhaps because most of them were spent without my grandfather — and died at ninety.

My cousin Ron was her attending physician when she died; in my family "family doctors" are just that. He was on staff at Saint Johns, a Catholic hospital in Santa Monica and told me Grandma "knew she was going to die and was very philosophical about the whole thing and very calm." He remembers a large crucifix in front of her bed positioned so she had to look at it her every waking moment.

"Also the nuns would come in every day

to see how she was and to pray for her. They said extra prayers because they knew she was my grandmother. One day I walked in to see her and pointed to the cross and asked her what she thought about it. She smiled this beatific smile and looked at me and said, 'I need all the help I can get!' "

She had told her eldest son, Ronnie's dad, Herman, that she wanted to be buried with her glasses on. "In case I meet God," she told him. "I want to recognize him."

I hope you got some of those genes, Dylan. I hope I did, too.

But not even Grandma's help was enough to keep my exhaustion from beginning to show. I had prepared for the worst — at least I thought I had. I remember a friend, Michelle Cossack, who died of breast cancer, telling me about the depths of the chemical depression caused by chemo.

"No matter how depressed I am knowing I have breast cancer, knowing I've lost my breasts, knowing I might die," she told me, "the chemical depression is worse."

The exhaustion caused by the chemo and radiation is also unimaginable. I have one memory of lying on our couch, staring at a glass of water. I really wanted that glass of water. *Really* wanted that glass of water. I was on the couch, it was on the coffee table, maybe a foot away. I could've reached it easily, all I had to do was extend my arm, and I probably wouldn't even have had to extend it all the way. But I couldn't do it. I couldn't even lift my arm. I was too tired.

I'd been warned that chemo and radiation would also cause me to lose my appetite.

I write "chemo and radiation" because as each symptom developed, my oncologist would assure me it was caused by the radiation, and Dr. Minsky would assure me it was the chemo.

But I didn't just lose my appetite, food became demonized. Another scene out of a movie, and this time not a very good movie. I was living on rice pudding, supermarket rice pudding, bland, sweet, comfort food everybody I ever knew who had AIDS lived on. And the kernels of rice became like maggots in my mouth. When I spit them out I could see them writhe.

Eating dry toast was like biting into a two-by-four. Like chewing sand. They had given me pills for nausea — $40 a pill. I had pills for diarrhea. I would put my colostomy bags in baggies, and put the baggies in a garbage bag. One morning I weighed the previous day's output. Ten pounds. When the pills didn't stop it, they prescribed tincture of opium.

"If you'd given me this thirty years ago," I told Dr. Tepler, "I could've paid for my entire college education. And bought a car."

When rice pudding turns to maggots in your mouth, the last thing you want to do is experiment with opium. I followed the prescription to a T. It didn't work. I knew what would.

I called my friend Jerry Della Femina.

"Jerry, is there any reason for you to think your phone might be tapped?"

"No," he said. I think he thought this was the setup to a joke like "Do you have Prince Albert in the can? Well let him out, Queen Victoria's horny!"

"I don't think my phone is tapped either," I said. "I need some marijuana."

"I'll be right over."

Jerry Della Femina is, of course, the advertising genius. Part of his *tummling* has always been how the kids in his agency get stoned in the bathroom. I called him on it. An hour or so after the call, Jerry showed up with three very tightly rolled joints and a caveat: "This shit is a lot stronger than the stuff from the '60s."

I waited until the nausea hit and tried some. Two hits, the nausea was gone. I had some toast and tea and a bowl of cereal, put on my Grateful Dead albums, turned the stereo up to a Spinal Tap 11, ordered a pizza, baked a batch of brownies, tie-dyed my T-shirt, and spray-painted "Free Huey Newton" on the side of my apartment building.

No, I didn't. But the nausea was gone, and I could down the toast and tea and the cereal. It's also an antidepressant, and that helped too. But the stuff *was* an awful lot stronger than stuff from the '60s. Like so much of everything else, innocence has disappeared, even from dope smoking. In the '60s, everybody was an amateur. Even Owsley, who permeated Berkeley with five-dollar drops of pure LSD on blotter-paper called "Owsley blue," wasn't in it for the money. Today's dope farmers hybridize seeds and titrate percentages of THC, and the stuff has become dangerously strong and, because of that, not so much fun. But it worked for the nausea.

I had radiation the next morning. Radiation is an interesting concept: Lie here motionless, we're going to burn your insides, make you sicker than you've ever been in your life, zap your gonads with so much poison that if you are able to have children they'll look like the Creature from the Black Lagoon, and we expect you to wake up early, hail a cab, and come in every Monday, Wednesday, and Friday for the privilege.

That morning I told Dr. Minsky about the marijuana.

"You know," he told me. "The laws of the state of New York don't allow me to mention marijuana, but it is the best drug we know about for the side effects of chemo and radiation."

I smoked it only when I needed it. I'd lost so much control over my body — my hair was falling out, I couldn't control my bowels — I didn't want to give up any more. In fact, I never finished the three joints.

The second time I smoked dope the phone rang and it was my cousin Felice. Felice works for the government, she carries a gun, she and her husband are building a log cabin in the high desert south of Tucson. You didn't think nice Jewish girls did this, did you? In the family we call her "Felice de Police." I've never asked her exactly what she does but, well, she was raised in East LA with a bunch of kids who speak Mexican Spanish, she's

45

dark complected, she lives near the Mexican border, you figure it out.

I talk to Felice maybe once every couple of years, and I was stoned out of my mind when I picked up the phone. When I heard, "Joel, it's your cousin Felice," it was all I could do to keep from shouting, "It was Jerry Della Femina! It was Jerry Della Femina!"

Then I got too sick. I don't know how Ena got me off to radiation or to Dr. Tepler's, but both doctors agreed that it was dangerous for me to continue treatment. Tepler took me off the chemo; the pouch was gone, but they kept the port "just in case." (Just in case, even in my altered state I understood, they ever needed immediate access to my jugular vein.) Minsky told me I needed a few weeks away from radiation. I wasn't so worried about that. The radiation schedule had built-in hiatuses; the docs and technicians would take Labor Day and Thanksgiving and Christmas off. Minsky showed me the numbers; a significant number of patients needed time off, and taking it didn't seem to affect the cure rate. But the chemo was something else. Tepler had told me that it would be easy; he'd told me that many people got through it with no side effects, that the odds were my hair wouldn't even fall out. So I figured, My God, I'm too sick for the treatment, I'm going to die. When he about-faced and tried to convince me that my reactions to the chemo were normal, I not only got mad, I got an apology.

"Just tell me the truth," I told him.

"Look, if you were climbing Mount Everest, would you want the sherpas to tell you, 'This isn't as hard as it seems. If you can do two miles on a treadmill you'll make it easy'? Or would you want them to tell you, 'This is probably the hardest thing you've ever done but we've been here before, so listen to us and we'll help you make it'?"

Then he 'fessed up to the almost random, very unscientific way the medical community decides how much chemotherapy over how long a time a patient should receive. You really can't do a large placebo-controlled double-blind study, because that would mean people with cancer would get placebos and die. So, Tepler told me, they try out a new drug on a small sample — in the case of 5-FU with leucovorin, it was fewer than twenty — and they give them as much of the stuff as they can stand until they get so sick they can't stand it anymore, and that becomes the standard dose. Which means the doctors and the pharmaceutical firms and the Food and Drug Administration have no idea how small a dosage can stop the cancer. They do keep lists of how many people live or die, so they know, at least for the first few years after the treatment has ended, how much chemo you have to ingest for it to be effective. Tepler showed me that I was still on the plus side. After a few weeks off, he told me, they'd restart the 5-FU, dripping it into my arm in his office, one hour a shot, three times a week.

Of course this entire time, Ena was pregnant with Dylan. I made very bad jokes about not knowing which of us was throwing up more. I was not a good dad-to-be. We found a *dula:* someone who'd be there at the birth to do what the daddy should do: she knew when Ena should walk, when she should stand, when she should push, when to head for the hospital. The difference was that the *dula* had assisted at hundreds of births and new daddies hadn't assisted at any. And I was completely useless. I was too sick.

The *dula* timed things so perfectly that Ena came within minutes of giving birth to Dylan in the entryway to New York Hospital. (If they had a Frequent Patient program, we could all get our appendixes taken out free).

The day we took Dylan home from the hospital was my last day of chemotherapy. It should have been a cause for a double celebration, but stopping the chemicals didn't stop the side effects. My hair had begun to fall out in earnest. I didn't go completely bald, but it came out by the handful and got so thin that the best coiffure I could've done on my own was a half Giuliani. I found a great wigmaker, Broadway's best; if you've seen *Hairspray* you've seen his work — the work the folks who wear 'em don't mind you knowing about. You wouldn't believe the folks who wear his stuff who don't want it known. I won't tell, and you can't tell.

When I did a pre-Oscar interview with Billy Crystal, whom I've known for years, his manager, whom I've known almost as long but hadn't seen in years, looked me over and said, "At least you've kept your hair."

"Do you want it?" I asked, taking off my piece, gray, bushy, and perfect, and handing it to him.

I did an interview with Chuck Close, whom I consider America's finest living artist, at his one-man show at MOMA. He uses a wheelchair — he's paralyzed from the waist down and has virtually no movement of his hands below his wrists, and he's still America's finest living artist. He's bald as a rock. He did want to give it a try, so after the interview I took off my rug and put it on his head. What we shared was the camaraderie of people forced to live lives they never imagined they could, and surviving in spite of it, getting on with the pieces of our lives that are still whole.

In 1968 I did a story for the *Los Angeles Times* Sunday magazine on Mickey Mouse's fortieth birthday. I interviewed Ward Kimball, one of Disney's "nine old men," one of the original animators of *Snow White*. He created Jiminy Cricket, among other things.

"You can recognize my house," he told me when he gave me driving directions. "There's a railroad car out in front."

I was expecting a cast-iron caboose with geraniums growing out of it, a two-foot tall planter behind a white picket fence. It was a full-sized railroad car. He also had two working steam engines in the back, a mile of track, and a guest house filled with toy Mickeys and Plutos and The Goof (old-time Disney people always call him "The Goof").

I took my friend Terry Gilliam, who was interested in learning about animation — this was long before Monty Python — and the first thing Ward showed us was how to get a cat looped on marijuana. If you're interested, you put the cat in a paper shopping bag, blow some smoke into the bag and crunch up the opening.

He told us about Walt (old-time Disney people always call him "Walt").

"He wasn't much of an artist," Kimball said. "In fact, he couldn't even sign his name. Not the stylized way it was drawn on the cartoons and the comic books."

When kids would ask for his autograph, he told us, Walt would say, wait, I'll do you one better, and he'd get a photo of him and Mickey that one of his artists had signed.

Of course I put this bit of trivia into the story, and Kimball got into all kinds of trouble for it. I don't know, but I got the feeling that if he hadn't been the guy who created Jiminy Cricket, he might have gotten fired. This is the kind of family secret you just don't tell the *LA Times*. I ended up writing a note saying I messed up, just because I felt bad and didn't want anything to happen on my account to this very nice man who'd created Jiminy Cricket.

Kimball said that Walt's genius was as an editor and a storyteller. This is true. When they brought *Snow White* back for a fiftieth-anniversary release, I saw it twice on the same day, something I've never done before or since. I just couldn't believe it was as good as I thought it was. It is. The storytelling is so perfect that Disney cut *The Soup Song*, a very funny bit that's one of the add-ons on the DVD. The song is funny, a Bavarian drinking song about soup instead of beer, and the animation — almost complete, everything but cleaned and colored — is even funnier (Kimball directed the animation). It was guaranteed to get laughs, and the easy decision would have been to finish it and keep it in. But Disney, under incredible pressure and close to bankruptcy, had the courage to cut it because he knew it hurt the story.

"I remember story conferences," Kimball said. "Walt would act out all the parts, do all the voices." Disney's secret to great storytelling? Kimball knew the exact words: " 'Just when things are going well,' he told us, 'bring back the witch.' "

I had about three great months. My hair came back. Darker. My colostomy was reversed. That was nice. It took major surgery, and I had to figure out a new diet and relearn muscle control. Easter Sunday visiting friends, I ran out of my diapers and had to borrow one of Dylan's. But still, life was getting better. My CAT scans were clean, and I was getting better.

When Dylan was nine months old, Ena had her first one-person show, at the Robert Miller Gallery, one of the top New York galleries. The *New York Times* called her work "exceptional." The *New Yorker*, very impressed, described her delicate images of flowers and fauna as "the last things Ophelia might have seen."

Dylan was learning to walk and to talk. One thing I noticed, when I was able to notice, was that he didn't have much baby fat. He was long. He was the first person in my family, including second and third cousins and people who died in Pinsk whose pictures I'd seen but whom I'd never met, who could be called "lanky."

Dylan was happy and gurgling. Ena was painting. I was feeling good. Things were going well.

And the witch came back.

2

The Witch Comes Back

Dear Dylan,

I have a memory of standing on a bench in a small room off the kitchen at my bubbie's house, my mother's mother. Had I come from classier stock, they would have called the room the pantry. But we come from hearty peasant stock, and we called it the service porch.

That was where my bubbie and *zaideh* (my grandfather) kept their phone. One phone. For the whole house. Oh, the hardships we endured back when I was your age. And it was a heavy phone, made of metal, too big for me to lift, with a rotary dial there was no way my little-boy fingers could turn. Not that anyone in my family would let me try. A toll call cost five cents a minute. "Who do you think you are,

Rockefeller's *eynik'l* (grandchild)?"

I remember my bubbie holding the phone up to my ear and hearing my mother's voice on the other end, then my dad's. They were calling from San Francisco. It would be the first time I'd spend a night away from my parents. I don't remember what they said, and I don't remember it being traumatic, but it must have been, if just a little, because I remember it. And this was before my sister, Phyllis, was born, so I was probably three years old. Younger than you are now. The fact that I remember this scares the hell out of me, because it means that one day, fifty years from now, you'll probably remember bits and patches of things we are doing with you today.

One of those things — maybe triggered by a photograph, or a sense memory of a texture or a color — may be the soft, gray cashmere sweater I bought for you for your second birthday. As an adult you may wonder, "What kind of schmuck buys a cashmere sweater for a two-year-old?"

The answer is "a schmuck who tempts fate."

February 2000

I was feeling great. We were just back from Florida, where Dylan had made his first trip ever into the ocean, giggling and laughing, bouncing on his mother's hip.

We took him to Sea World, and at the exact instant the killer whale leaped out of the pool, jumped through the hoop, and grabbed a fish out of the trainer's hand, Dylan, three rows back in the amphitheater, fell fast asleep. We'd shlepped him 2,000 miles for the unforgettable thrill of waiting in line.

He'd already charmed Will Smith, who was staying with his family at the same hotel we were. Two years later, when Smith's film *Ali* was released and Smith looked like a sure thing for an Oscar nomination, I threatened to release the picture we'd taken of Dylan on Will Smith's lap unless Smith gave me an interview. "You tell him I get the interview," I told the guy who does his press, "or I slap him with the biggest paternity suit of all time."

I had a February tan, which always makes one feel great in New York City when everybody else's face is prison-pallor yellow or tattle-tale gray. I was up to two and a half miles on my treadmill, four or five times a week. My clothes fit, even the Ralph Lauren chinos with the ripped rear pocket that had ripped when they didn't fit so well.

I was always a fat kid, and even when I wasn't, I always thought of myself as a fat kid. It was easier for me to make jokes about how I couldn't do things than to try to do them, so I was never very athletic. Even in the army, I managed to get myself through basic training only when I discovered that a hematoma (a bruise) was nothing but loose blood floating under the skin. One of Ronnie the Doctor's med school buddies happened to be stationed where I was, at Fort Bliss, Texas, just outside El Paso. I asked him what would happen if he took 5 cc's of blood out of my arm and shot it into my ankle. We gave it a try. The extra fluid turned my ankle puffy, and the loose blood made it look like a rainbow. I pretended to limp to sick call and was officially waived from having to run a mile in fatigues and combat boots in under eight minutes. I couldn't *see* a mile in under eight minutes.

One day the drill sergeant asked us, "All you guys who hate Texas, step forward."

I'd been warned never to volunteer for anything, but after six weeks of being yelled at and pulling KP and marching in the desert sun, I couldn't help myself. I stepped forward. So did everybody else. We also screamed and cheered a little, too. And that day we got to march to New Mexico.

That time I made it. And I wasn't the last guy in, either, in spite of what on the other side of the nearby international border would be called Montezuma's Revenge. I gave one guy my backpack, another guy carried my helmet; it was just me, my entrenching tool (in the army they don't call a spade a spade), and the toilet paper they thoughtfully pack in every case of K rations. And I still made it.

"I don't know, Siegel," Drill Sergeant Langley shook his head. "Every time I looked back all I saw was your big white ass flappin' in the wind."

After Jane died, just after she died, I spent two weeks at a health spa in San Diego. The days were structured, I had places I had to be, I wasn't alone, it was a good choice for me, I didn't know what else to do. After that, I started taking care of myself. I started playing tennis and played regularly and, eventually, not badly. I lifted free weights and did the treadmill when I didn't play tennis. It's possible, even likely, that on that February after-noon, at age fifty-six, minus a foot and a half of lower intestine, two and a half years past my initial diagnosis, I was in the best physical shape of my life. And, because of Dylan, a week away from his second birthday, talking, laughing, at that amazing age when everything from the taste of ice cream to the texture of a soap bubble is a miraculous surprise, I was probably the happiest I had ever been in my life.

Dr. Tepler had prescribed a whole bat-tery of tests, and I was passing 'em all. My latest colonoscopy was clean. The blood test that measures cancer antigens showed negative. Zero. *Bupkes.* I had an MRI, an even stranger experience than a CAT scan, just to be sure. The machine looks the same — you are conveyored through a huge plastic doughnut; but with this one, you hear the magnetic field resonating. It sounds like Sonar, ping-ping-pinging, and it takes longer than a CAT scan and is even more claustrophobic. It does a better job of imaging certain kinds of tissue, and it was what the doctor ordered. I was standing on Fifth Avenue in front of the Baby Gap Luxe, incredibly expensive clothing for incredibly insane parents, when my cell phone rang. It was Tepler.

The MRI I'd had that morning was clean as a whistle. I walked in and bought Dylan a cashmere sweater.

I knew it was a stupid thing to buy a two-year-old, but I was feeling so good that if the call had come when I was walking down Park Avenue in front of the Mercedes place, I would've walked in and bought Dylan a car.

The next day a CAT scan showed a small black spot on the lower lobe of my left lung.

I don't remember being surprised. When Jane's brain tumor reoccurred and almost simultaneously developed into an inoperable glioblastoma, her doctor told me that all it took was one cell — one — that the cobalt missed or that his knife had missed. My lymph nodes had been infected with cancer cells; I wasn't expecting to get off scot-free. Her doctor also told us that if the cancer reoccurred, it would take about two and a half years. It did for Jane. And it did for me. Almost to the day.

I did think hard about whether I'd go through another round of chemotherapy, and Ena and I talked about it. This is the kind of hypothetical conversation you have in college when you're pulling an all-nighter, not something you discuss for real with your spouse while your two-year-old is tickling his Elmo in the next room.

I decided against chemo.

"I'd rather die."

A stark phrase when you mean it.

I'm not lucky. I don't think of myself as lucky. I know how hard I've worked for things to happen that other folks might think of as lucky. So part of me knew the witch would come back. My private nightmare — and it scares me to write it, to make it public, because this is the curse of the Bambino, the mention of the name of the Scottish play curse, the forget to say break-a-leg jinx, the thing that will make it come true — is liver cancer, a favorite place for colon cancer to spread. It hurts, and for a long time. And there's no cure. You shrink and shrivel and your skin turns black. (James Earl Ray, the guy who shot Martin Luther King, died of liver cancer. If his skin turned black, that's justice.)

Meanwhile, my doctors were trying to boost my courage with their optimism.

The spot was small, very small. Smaller than two centimeters in diameter (which doctors and only doctors pronounce *saunt-i-meters*). So small it wouldn't have shown up on anything but the brand-new spiral CAT scan. Because I had smoked (though

61

I hadn't in eighteen years), they were hoping this was a new cancer, not related at all to my colon cancer. There is a more than 90 percent cure rate with primary lung cancers when they are discovered and removed when they are this small.

A quick anatomy lesson: the right lung has three lobes, which expand and contract as we breathe, and the left lung has two, which leaves room for the heart. Individual lobes are expendable. We're designed that way. Lose half your left lung, the remaining half learns to expand to fill the void.

The tumor was on the lower lobe of my left lung. Less than a week after they found the cancer, they removed the lobe. They call this a lobectomy, obviously a word Mel Brooks made up.

Writer Budd Schulberg's father, B.P., ran Paramount in the 1920s, Hollywood's heady days. Schulberg, who wrote *On The Waterfront* and *The Disenchanted* (about working with F. Scott Fitzgerald), wrote a wonderful short story about how he knew his father was falling out of favor by the annual shrinking circumference of gifts he'd find around their Christmas tree. I thought of that story in my hospital room. After the first surgery, the room was filled with flowers, boxes, candies, stuffed toys. I got so many orchids, Ena hates them to this day. But this time, I got almost nothing. Of course I had asked friends not to send anything, but why, I wondered, did they believe me?

A good sign, part of me hoped. My friends didn't think I was going to die, so they didn't have to bother.

A bad sign, another part of me knew. My friends knew I was going to die, so . . . why bother?

The second day out, my friend, Andy Bergman, one of the guys in the group I've lunched with every Wednesday since Jane died, came to visit. I hadn't had any solid food. The only thing I'd had to drink was cranberry juice, and I hadn't had much of that. But my body reacted anyway. I started to vomit. I went ballistic. It shot out of my body. There wasn't any bile. There wasn't any smell. Dyed pink by the cranberry juice, it looked like Day-Glo.

All I had near me was the eight-ounce Dixie cup the nurse had brought the cranberry juice in. That got filled up with the first burst. I have no idea where this stuff was coming from, but it wouldn't stop. I must've barfed a gallon. Over my robe. My bed. The metal table. The *New York Times*.

When I was finally finished, Andy raised

his right hand and said, "Check please."

Somewhere in New Jersey there is a warehouse where they keep cancer cells removed from thousands of New York Hospital patients. This is an idea Kafka couldn't conceive of.

Do they store them alphabetically? By patient, doctor, or body part? Do they use the Dewey Decimal system? Old-fashioned diner slang? Two on a raft and float 'em! Hold the chicken and make it pea!

They found the cells from my original cancer and matched them with cells taken from my lung. A perfect match. It wasn't a new cancer with a survival rate of more than 90 percent. It was metastatic colon cancer, the kind of distant metastasis for which the American Cancer Society's Web site lists a survival rate of less than 10 percent.

My doctors were crestfallen. I'd known it all the time. Just one node in my lung was infected. Was it the node the cancer rode in on? Or the node a cell or two rode out on to attack some other organ?

Fuck you and the node you rode in on.

Four months later I had another CAT scan. I should have known better.

3

The Witch Comes Back Again

June 2000

Did you ever hit something empty and metal like a fifty-five-gallon steel drum, hard with a hammer? Do you know that resonating, ringing "GONG, GONG, GONG" that sounds like what the church bells must've sounded like to Quasimodo? That's pretty close to the way I feel the day before a CAT scan.

This day, a Sunday, was a beautiful start-of-summer's day. We were in Connecticut. Dylan, now almost two and a half, and I were outside. He was playing, I was churning, when Dylan handed me his well-chewed copy of *The Runaway Bunny* and asked me to read it to him.

Once there was a little bunny who wanted to run away.

So he said to his mother, "I am running away."

"If you run away," said his mother, "I will run after you.

"For you are my little bunny."

I looked up at the sky, dark gray cumulus clouds, beams of sunlight, the kind of sky where you expect to see God's finger appear from behind one of the clouds and touch Michelangelo's.

"Can't I catch a break?" I asked.

Back in the city the next morning, I'd been scheduled to do my movie review on *Good Morning America* at 7:36 a.m. At 6:45 I woke up the driver of the black Lincoln parked in front of our apartment. (For the first week or two I was on the show, I thought they sent a car for me because they liked me; then I figured out they send a car to make sure I'll get there.)

"Wow, you're early," the driver said.

"Early? I'm on at 7:30." Pause. These things have been known to happen. "Aren't I?"

"8:30." He showed me a note. Someone was scheduled to call me at 7:00 to tell me they weren't going to pick me up at 6:45. Talk about signs.

The review went fine, but the washing

machine broke. When I got off the air and called home, Ena told me a hose had pulled out and there was water everywhere.

I checked my voice mail. There was a message from my ex-wife, Melissa, who'd heard a Randy Newman tune on the radio that she knew was a favorite of mine, so she was thinking of me. The song was "I Think It's Going to Rain Today."

At 10:00 a.m. I had a meeting with an ABC lawyer who'd flown up from Washington. I'm being sued for using four seconds of a movie called *The Curse of the Living Brain* in a story I did on alien life forms. It was a neat story. I interviewed a Columbia University astrophysics professor who theorized that life forms on planets like Jupiter would be short and slow moving, maybe self-propelled hockey pucks, because the severe gravity wouldn't allow for human-like spinal columns. I hadn't thought about that. He wondered why aliens in science fiction movies are always portrayed as some kind of humanoid bipedal beings. I had thought about that: "So the actors can fit into the costumes," I told him. At least he didn't sue.

My CAT scan was set for 2:00 p.m. I have no idea what possessed me, but as a virtual guarantee I'd jinx it into reading positive, I brought along an ABC crew. Katie Couric had just had a colonoscopy live on network television on that other network, so the least we could do was run a videotape of a CAT scan.

It's not that I'm superstitious, it's that cancer *makes* you superstitious. Grown-ups not stepping on cracks on the sidewalk, counting the steps on every stairway, prompting their friends to say "Bless you" after every sneeze.

My thing is bums. I've grown convinced that God has come down to Earth disguised as a panhandler in order to test me, to see if I'm worthy of being saved.

I'm nice to bums.

And just in case God has come down as a New York cabdriver, I'm nice to them, too. Which is harder.

(Of course if Jupiter is heaven, then God may have come down as a hockey puck. In which case I'm nice to the New York Rangers. And Don Rickles.)

Al Gagliardi, a good guy I've known for twenty years, was our cameraman, and Cari Strassberg, who's become a very close friend, was my producer. I did *shtick* drinking the half gallon of cranberry juice and iodine the CAT scan reads. I waved as

I closed the door to the dressing room, had Al start shooting as I opened the door and runway-modeled the hospital robes.

When we were ushered into the room where the CAT scan lives, I pointed out, tour guide style, the heavy, lead doors, the leaded glass, the room done in the lovely earth tones of beige and taupe. I asked the radiologist a few leading questions, and he sketched out how the scan works, what it sees, and how the image it produces is read. Then Al left the room, and I waved good-bye. TV works that way. We'll edit twenty minutes down to one or two minutes, painting broad strokes, putting up billboards, writing headlines. The audience, raised on television, adds the brush strokes, fills in the detail, intuits the fine print.

Alone with the doctor on my right and the cold CAT scan everywhere else, even I couldn't stay in denial any longer.

Veins have a tendency to go floppy after chemotherapy. We can't imagine our veins having a learning curve, but maybe they do. Remember the kids' stunt of holding your arm straight out for a while, then dropping it and watching it while it slowly lifts, all on its own? My veins had always been an easy target for a blood test, until I

69

finished chemo. Then, after six months of being poked and stuck unmercifully, they'd learned to run and hide when they sensed a needle coming. As I lay feet-first on the CAT scan's platform, it took the radiologist five very painful tries before he struck blood and hooked up the IV tracer. More signs. I started to think about cabbies I hadn't overtipped: none recently. And bums I hadn't shmeared: only the bums who panhandle sitting down. Is this a New York thing, bums who won't even stand up when they ask you for money? I refuse to give any money to anyone who won't even bother to stand up when he begs, even if He is God.

I know one guy who works the northeast corner of Sixty-eighth and Columbus who panhandles sitting down on the stoop of a Korean deli. He knows my name. He watches my reviews. What, he's made so much money bumming quarters he bought a TV set?

That's the thought I was wrestling with when I heard the door clang open and sensed Al walking his camera backwards, aimed at the doctor, who was walking into the room. The doctor explained that as far as he could tell there was no reoccurrence in my left lung, and he was certain that my colon was clean, there was no reoccurrence at the original site. The scans would have to be studied, and we'd know for sure later that day.

In the crew car, driving back to ABC, I got a call on my cell phone. It was the radiologist. The scan showed a black dot on the middle lobe of my right lung, even smaller than the one that had just been removed from my left lung. They weren't sure what it was.

There are three obvious elements to any story: a beginning, a middle, and an end. Because television stories, especially news stories, are told in shorthand, there's usually only time for two of the elements. A beginning and an ending works. If it's an old story, a presidential scandal that's been in the news for weeks, you figure the audience knows the beginning, so you can leave it out, and a middle and an ending works. But a beginning and a middle is angry-making. Unsatisfying. The tape we shot that day is on a shelf in an ABC News warehouse, unwatched and uncut. The piece never made air. A story, even a forty-five-second rip and read, needs an ending, and this story didn't have one. And wouldn't for more than a year.

One of the problems with new technology is that there's no model, no body of empirical evidence to give context to new information; it's like giving out football scores for just one team. Because doctors hadn't been able to see anything this small on a human lung before this spiral scan was invented, they truly had no idea what it was they had found.

One more time, my doctors tried to Mary Baker Eddy me.

"We think it's scar tissue," they told me.

"From what?" I asked.

"Could be almost anything. Most likely an undiagnosed bout of pneumonia you might have had even when you were a child."

Well, that was possible — though, I knew, not likely. The spot hadn't been there three months before, when they found the larger spot on my left lung. But the doctors' optimism, though not contagious, did prevail.

"Let's watch it," they said, as if they were talking about a Jets game.

And watch it they did. Chips and dips, who ordered the Buffalo wings? Who wanted pepperoni? And CAT scans every three months. For the first three scans it didn't grow, it didn't move. Every time I'd look up, I'd see this sword hanging over me, hanging from a very narrow thread. Every time I listened hard I could hear the sound of water dripping on my forehead, drop by drop, one *s l o w d r o p* at a time.

"Can't you do some kind of biopsy?" I asked. "Just so we know what this thing is?"

My oncologist asked the thoracic surgeon, a "right stuff" guy named Nasser Altorki.

"Nasser Altorki?" you are saying to yourself.

"Do you know how good a guy named Nasser Altorki has to be," I said to myself and I'll say to you, "to be hired by New York Hospital? And to be recommended by doctors named Steinberg and Imber to patients named Siegel?"

They do needle biopsies now, using a CAT scan like a road map to follow the needle as it heads for the lesion. But after he checked the scans one last time, Altorki decided that this spot was in an impossible place to do a needle biopsy. The spot was on the wrong side of the lung, and the surgery to do the biopsy would be the same as if he were performing a lobectomy — and that, even I agreed, wasn't such a good idea. I was running out of lobes.

After the third scan, in March, they convinced me. The spot hadn't grown. Not a millimeter. I learned the word for this kind of scar tissue: *granuloma.* Dr. Tepler, his desk a foot deep in files and papers and journals, sat me down.

Doctors really don't know how long certain cancer cells can remain in the body, undetected, without growing. They don't know how long, and they don't know why. What they do know, from years and years of record keeping, is how long it takes to be reasonably certain that the cancer won't show up again. With most cancers it's five years. That's why if you have been colon- or lung- or prostate-cancer free for five years, the American Cancer Society considers you "cured."

It had been almost four years since my original diagnosis, a long time for a cancer cell to lie dormant. The spot hadn't grown. It was in the other lung, and most metastatic reoccurrences would happen in the same lung. And it was in a place where microscopic lumps of scar tissue are common.

He convinced me.

He was wrong.

My next scan was in June. I was fine. I was fine checking in at East River Imaging, and I was fine drinking the ionized Seabreeze, and

I was fine until the lead doors clanged shut and I heard the doctor, safe in his radiation-free room, shout, "Don't breathe!" over the loudspeaker like the voice of God.

I wasn't surprised. I was ready for it: The spot had grown. Lung cancer. The middle lobe of the other lung. There was only one option: cut it out.

4

If It Weren't for the Downside

Dear Dylan,

I had to wait for my surgeon to come back from vacation, a very unpleasant two weeks. Dr. Nasser Altorki, an Egyptian, could be a Muslim, could be Coptic Christian, I didn't want to ask. I did ask him where he went on his vacation.

"Saudi Arabia," he told me. This might have been the only time in my life that, when someone told me where they'd gone on their vacation, I didn't wish for a second that I'd gone along.

I waited for Dr. Altorki because I liked his no-nonsense, "right stuff" confidence. And, because he'd done the lobectomy on my left lung, he knew the neighborhood. But this surgery was different for two very important reasons: one was you. You were becoming a person, a real person, with a distinct personality, serious likes and dislikes. "Day-Blue," a color you named yourself, was your favorite color. Cell phones had taken over from vacuum cleaners as your new favorite thing, and you were on your way to knowing everything about them. You knew the names of the songs of the various rings: Camptown Races, Yankee Doodle, Fur Elise. You even knew how to get different kinds of phones to play their different rings. When I couldn't figure out how to get my new phone to play all of its rings, you told me which buttons to push to change the rings.

You were ready to learn to read — you were memorizing the symbols for Sprint and Verizon phones and Mercedes and BMW cars.

Watching you grow is in some way like watching human culture develop. At three and a half you're able to read signs and symbols; that's hieroglyphics, picto-writing. One day soon you'll discover an alphabet is a much better way to express things, the way people did when they came in contact with the Phoenicians. Ena and I, we're pretty sure, were doing the right thing by letting you discover these things for yourself. If we taught you to read, and we probably could, it would be for us, a party trick, not for you. We were doing our best to let you be three and a half for as long as you could. It won't be long enough. One morning, very soon, no matter what we do, you're going to wake up and be four.

I wanted to make sure that whatever happened to me in the hospital wouldn't hurt you or cause you pain or steal even a day away from your childhood.

The second reason this surgery was different from the other two? This time I really thought I was going to die.

When I was a kid nobody got cancer. Certainly nobody in my family. Not only did nobody get cancer, nobody *said* "cancer." Ever. Not out loud. If the word had to be used — and it was only used about people we didn't know personally — it was whispered.

"Oh, yeah," my mother or aunt or grandfather would say at full volume (and believe me in my house and my aunts' and my grandparents' houses, we talked at full volume), "she's got . . ." Then a whisper. Toscanini couldn't conduct the New York

Philharmonic and get this kind of dynamic range. *"Cancer . . ."* would be whispered, the last syllable only mouthed, not audible at all.

If someone was cured of *"cancer . . ."* or, more likely in those days, misdiagnosed, the word would be followed by a curse-curing *"Kinneinhora,"* a word meant to ward off the evil eye, and this was always followed by Pinsk insurance: three *"Ptews!"* mock-spit through the second and third fingers of the right hand.

These superstitions, sometimes so deeply ingrained we have to be told they're superstitions, die hard. I was in a cab with an Egyptian cabdriver from Alexandria, who had seen Dylan on *Good Morning America* and commented on all his hair.

"It's a Jewish tradition," I said, "not to give a first-born boy a haircut until his first birthday."

"In Egypt I was three before I had my first haircut," the cabbie said. And he knew why. "So if the angel of death comes he'll think it's a girl."

Well, I thought, Egyptians have had more experience with angels of death taking first-born sons than the rest of us, maybe they know something.

The cabbie was Coptic Christian. I don't mind asking cabbies what their religion is, or telling them mine. It's guys who carry knives and wear masks whose religion I don't want to know about. What, we have to be afraid of terrorist taxi drivers? Al Qaeda cabbies? Hamas suicide cabdrivers driving like madmen through the streets of Manhattan, willing to give up their own lives, pulling out to pass into oncoming traffic, swerving into lanes where there is no room, gunning yellow lights, running red ones, putting their passengers and thousands of pedestrians smack in the middle of harm's way? I don't think so. Besides, as Dorothy Parker once said (in a very different context), "How could they tell?"

Gilda Radner died of uterine cancer because no one in her family had told her that it was in her family. Had she known, she would have been diagnosed months or maybe years earlier, and an early diagnosis most likely would have been the difference between life and death.

I found out in the hospital, recovering from my first surgery, that my Auntie Annie had colon cancer. And I found it out from my Auntie Annie, who also told me that two of my mother's first cousins also had colon cancer. This is not a good secret to keep.

My generation is different about cancer. When Jane was dying, our friends came to visit. We'd go out for Chinese food, a party of twelve. Jane, a vegetarian, would order mu shu pork, hold the pork. In New York, people don't just "drop by"; it isn't done. But after Jane was diagnosed, and especially when she was undergoing radiation or recuperating from surgery, friends — hers and mine — started dropping by with pizza or pastries or Chinese food as if they'd been in the neighborhood anyway. No one stayed away.

Three weeks before she died, on New Year's Eve, 1982, Robert Klein, the comedian, who'd lived in our building, invited us to his party at his new Fifth Avenue digs. His wife, Brenda Boozer, was close to Jane. She was a mezzo-soprano; she sung with the Met, and she'd sing at Jane's funeral. A few days before, when we were going out, Jane had put mascara and eye shadow on just one of her eyes and announced, very girlishly, that she was ready to go. She didn't notice she'd only made-up one of her eyes. This time, I'd asked one of the ABC make-up artists to come over to do Jane's make-up.

Marvin Hamlisch was at the party. He asked if we had a song, and said he'd play it on the piano for us to dance to. I can't dance at all. Jane wasn't much better. But each New Year's Eve we'd been together, we danced to Nat "King" Cole, "When I Fall in Love, It Will Be Forever." Marvin played it, beautifully. Jane and I danced. The room applauded when we finished. Marvin and Robert still remember. So do I.

We're different, my generation. We've learned from our parents.

I didn't want to hide my cancer from Dylan, but I knew that telling him I had cancer would be meaningless. And the word "dead" is something he only thinks he understands, using unassailable three-year-old logic.

Earlier that summer, in the country, I saw a butterfly on the lawn and "Shhhh'd" Dylan, and the two of us tiptoed over to try to capture it.

"Oh," I said. "It's dead." And I handed it to him.

"Why is it dead?" he asked.

"Butterflies don't live very long," I told him. "That's why they fly all the time they're alive."

A few months later, after he'd figured out which numbers to push on my cell phone to call his mother, he asked me why I never called my mother. I went through a hundred reasons in my mind, thought about saying, "She's in heaven," but I don't believe that and I don't want to burden him with that. So I said, "My mommy can't talk. She's dead. She died a long time ago, before you were born. She's buried in Los Angeles. And next time we go there we can go visit her."

I thought that was the right thing to say. When Ena came in a few minutes later, Dylan, who still calls us by our first names, told her "Joel's mommy is buried in Los Angeles," and went on to other things.

The next day, Ena told me, Dylan opened his mouth and grunted a few times.

"I'm dead," he announced. "Dead people can't talk."

Three and a half is not the age for a metaphysical discussion, no matter how honest we want to be about our life-threatening illnesses. But I didn't want to lie to him. I'm going into the hospital, he's old enough to notice I'll be gone, maybe even old enough to remember.

When I come home I'll be tired, weak, sick, uncomfortable, and kvetching; I won't be able to lift him, he certainly won't be able to bounce on my stomach, and I won't be able to carry him on my shoulders or roll with him on the floor. What do I tell him?

My first thought was to talk with Ann Pleshette Murphy, who does the kid psychology pieces on *GMA*. She's neat, she's a friend, and I knew that she would understand that this is serious enough business that if she didn't know the best things for me to do, she'd find someone who did. She knew.

"Is this for a story, or is this for you?" she asked.

"For me."

"There are a lot of things you can do," she said, and started cataloguing them — her mind works that way.

She brought in some books, and I found some others. We changed Dylan's nighty-night reading from *Goodnight, Moon* to *A Visit to the Sesame Street Hospital*. Grover had a sore throat. Dylan could identify. Grover's mommy told him he had to go to the hospital to get his tonsils out. Dylan didn't have a clue.

"Daddy has a boo-boo. Inside. Way inside. I've got to go to the hospital where a doctor will take my boo-boo out." I knew he couldn't understand the idea, but I also knew he would understand the emotions, so I said it as matter-of-factly as I could.

84

Dylan looked at me and asked, "Can Mommy and me go with you?"

And I thought if I were going through this, there must be hundreds of thousands of parents and grandparents who have gone through or who will go through the same ordeal. Why not do it on television?

I know you've had this metaphor mixed more ways than one of Wolfgang Puck's sauces, but we really are family at *GMA*. And I don't mean a TV sitcom family, *Hi Mom! Hi Dad! Hi Dave! Hi Rick!* Full of false friendship, where the real Rick resents his father for keeping him out of college and the real Mom, Harriet Nelson herself, really told me, years after Ozzie's death, years after Ricky's death, how angry she was that she couldn't get work in Hollywood because she'd been typecast as a mom.

No, we are a real family. Loud, broad, loving, real. Some of us hate each other. Some of us haven't spoken to each other in years. We don't necessarily socialize; for one, the work is too hard, and for two, we're on different schedules — and, come on, you've got cousins and uncles and maybe even brothers or sisters you wouldn't have dinner with on a dare. Just like us. I work nights, going to the movies.

The crew is in at 4:00 a.m. The producers work nights *and* are in at 4:00 a.m. It's happened to me: sometimes we don't know what religion one of our coworkers is until we go to a funeral. And we go. Just like family.

Dr. Tim, Tim Johnson, is the only on-air person who's been on *GMA* longer than I have. But there must be a dozen camera and technical people who were already veterans when Pat Collins gave up her gig as movie critic and suggested I fill in. That's how I started on *Good Morning America*. I was reviewing movies for *Eyewitness News*, and still am. Pat took a leave of absence and suggested to ABC that I fill in for her. I did. Twenty-one years ago. And Pat never came back.

The official reason was that she wanted to spend more time with her family, which was true. She did have two very young children, and we all assumed, the way family does, they were the reason she was taking time off. Doing the math, though, I figured out long afterward that her husband, songwriter Joe Raposo, must have been diagnosed with lymphoma at about that time, and he was the family she needed to spend more time with. She'd later tell me that her infant son was also ill and he and Joe were on different floors at Lenox Hill Hospital. She'd virtually moved into the hospital and slept catnapping on the elevator going from the cancer floor to pediatrics. She didn't tell anyone then.

I understand that everybody has their own way of dealing with this kind of crisis. Pat and Joe's way was to keep it to themselves.

Pat is still a friend. She helped Gene Wilder and Joanna Bull and me and Ann Moore of *People* magazine get Gilda's Clubs going; support groups for people with cancer named for comedian Gilda Radner. Pat's second husband, Bill Sarnoff, headed the board that took us national. Joe was as big and warm and fuzzy and the characters he wrote songs for, the Muppets. He wrote the "Sesame Street Theme" and "C is for Cookie" and "It Isn't Easy Being Green," and it isn't easy for me to hear Dylan sing that song.

It wasn't until just days before Joe died that we found out about his cancer. I know I couldn't let that happen to me. I couldn't live like that. I'm with Abe Lincoln. Tell the truth; you don't have to remember anything. This is good advice for me because I have a rotten memory.

A "tell" is a word poker players use. A

guy pulling on his ear when he's bluffing, or stacking and restacking his chips when his hole-card has you beat — those are "tells." My face is one big tell. If I anchored the news instead of covering Hollywood, you could tell before I started to talk whether the news was good or bad.

1945. Lower East Side. The day Franklin Roosevelt died.

"Did you hear the news?" one old Jewish lady asks another.

"What do I have to hear for? I can see it on everybody's face."

I've got one of those faces.

I never kept my cancer a secret, but there is a difference between acknowledging something and broadcasting it, literally, on network television.

I still remember a couple of books I didn't buy at Collector's Books on Hollywood Boulevard (a first edition of *Seduction of the Innocent*, the catalyst for comic book reform, and a Whitman copy of *Tom Swift and His Giant Telescope*, if you must know). I remember not bidding on a Jasper Johns number 9 with the Mona Lisa peeking out of it that went for all of $400 at Sotheby's when it was still Sotheby's Parke-Benet and the LA branch was on Beverly Boulevard near the Pan Pacific, which was still there, too. And, of course, I remember all the times I didn't say "I love you" to women I did.

Just some of the lessons I learned in "It isn't the things you do, it's the things you don't do that haunt you the rest of your life" 101.

And at the bottom of it all was the nagging truth that if I had known there was colon cancer on my mother's side as well as my father's, I certainly would have told my doctors, and they, acting prudently, would have made certain I'd had colonoscopies years before my fifty-fourth birthday. With early diagnosis, the odds were heavy that I could have avoided the colostomy, the chemo, the radiation, and the metastases to both my lungs.

I walked into Shelley Ross's office, our executive producer, to suggest the story. When you tell a rabbi you want to convert to Judaism he is obligated by Jewish law to tell you "No" and throw you out of his office three times. If you come back a fourth time, he knows you're serious. Shelley didn't exactly throw me out of her office three times, but she did give me the third-degree, making sure I knew exactly what I was getting into and that I really did want to get into it. That's what family does and

Shelley is a friend and, also, family, too, in that cockamamie, dysfunctional way.

This is as good a place as any to tell you how the people I work for reacted to my initial diagnosis. The truth is, they could not have been better. I'd had a total of one conversation and a couple of nods in the hallway with David Westin, the president of ABC News and my ultimate boss, before I called his office and made an appointment to see him. He couldn't possibly have known what I wanted to talk to him about, because I hadn't told anyone at work. No one.

"I have bad news," I began, riffing on an early refrain. "I have cancer."

I think he was about to cry. He could not have been more supportive.

When I told Charlie Gibson, I think he did cry. We're friends.

This third round, when I talked with Charlie about going public, he wanted to do the interview. And I was fine the morning we went on the air, revving my psyche into high denial when, in the green room waiting to go on, I heard Charlie tease the interview.

"Coming next, our own Joel Siegel tells us what he's going to tell his three-year-old son, Dylan, when Joel goes into the hospital next week for lung cancer surgery, his third cancer operation. Stay tuned."

That's when it hit me. This wasn't my friend, Charlie Gibson, quick to laugh, bragging on his daughters, bemoaning the Baltimore Orioles. This was Charles Gibson, ABC News, *Good Morning America*'s host for the past ten years. That was the voice I heard. Three cancer operations? When do we hear Charles Gibson give that kind of read? When somebody is going to die, that's when.

How many people do you know who've had three cancer surgeries in four years and are still around? Then I didn't know any. Now I know one.

During the chemo and the radiation, I was so sick I figured that if I was going to die, it would be from the cure. I had always understood the intellectual possibility that the cancer might kill me. But that morning, hearing Charles Gibson announce my illness over network television, I was scared for the first time since that first doctor said, "I don't have good news."

We talked about Dylan, Charlie and I, about being a first-time father at fifty-four, about how much Dylan meant to me, about why I would tell him. And what I would tell him. And how.

"I don't mind if Dylan sees me cry," was one of the things I said. "But I don't want him to know I'm afraid."

I received 3,000 pieces of e-mail after the broadcast. To put that figure in some kind of perspective, when I was writing for the *LA Times* Sunday magazine back in the early '70s, one of my pieces, an LA shopping guide, set a record for most mail. The *LA Times* sold a million copies every Sunday. I got 150 letters.

I got an e-mail from China, from a couple to whom English was probably a third or fourth language. "Tell him. We will pray for you."

I was sent mass cards — Catholics who'd lit candles for me. I cannot tell you how moving that was, to be prayed for by people who didn't know much more about me than to know I wasn't Catholic.

I got dozens of letters, more than fifty, from grown-ups who hadn't been told their parents had cancer when they were kids. Some had a parent who had died, who went someplace, they were never told where, and never came home. They never forgave not being told and never forgot not being able to say good-bye.

I think, via e-mail, I was able to answer most of the 3,000. If I didn't answer yours, I'm sorry. I did try.

We followed Ann's advice and started reading *Sesame Street Goes to the Hospital*, about Grover's sore throat and how he needs his tonsils out, and *Curious George Goes to the Hospital*, where George swallows a piece of jigsaw puzzle. We told Dylan that daddy had a different kind of boo-boo and would have to go to the hospital too.

I was scheduled to be in the hospital for five days, and Ann had another great idea, a paper chain. Ena made a chain of five links, large circles of different colored construction paper stapled into circles. It looked like the Olympics symbol. If they only gave medals for *tsoris*.

Each night I was gone, she and Dylan would tear one link from the chain. He could count, but it's hard to know if he had any idea what the numbers meant. At four, he still hasn't quite figured out which day "tomorrow" is and why "tomorrow" is never "today." A tough concept, tomorrow. But he could see and touch and hold five paper links and watch them become four and three and two as daddy came closer and closer to coming home.

The morning of my surgery, Dylan brought me two books — *Jenny's in the*

Hospital and *Curious George Goes to the Hospital.* "Before you go, can you read me these?" he asked.

I'm glad I was on the record as having said I didn't mind if Dylan saw me cry.

The surgery was straightforward. An hour and a half in and out. The next morning I couldn't believe I felt as good as I did. I was even able to walk a little. I was still attached to the IV, but the machines that ring and ping and monitored my heart and pulse had been disconnected. Dylan was healthy — there is a greater fear that a toddler will bring an infection into a hospital than take one home — so he could come to visit. I'm not sure if it was better for him to see me or for me to see him.

He walked in wearing his baby scrubs like a two-foot-tall chief of surgery making morning rounds — no fear, no surprise.

People did a story about me and Dylan. They ran a still of Diane Sawyer sitting next to me on the *GMA* set. She was interviewing me, we were talking about Dylan and about cancer and if you look carefully you can see that she's holding my hand. Now you don't hold someone's hand when you interview them, you just don't. But we're family and Diane knows when that takes precedence over what we learn in journalism school. That is why she is so good at what she does.

They had a photographer follow me to New York Hospital and ran another still of Dr. Altorki taking out my stitches. Topless in *People* magazine. The cover of that issue read "Sexy at Any Age" — but that story wasn't about me. (They did a follow-up in their year-end issue, "The Year's 50 Most Fascinating People." That story wasn't about me either.)

I told *People*, "Cancer changes your life. You learn what's important, you learn to prioritize, you learn not to waste your time. My friend Gilda Radner used to say, 'If it weren't for the downside, everyone would want to have it.' If it weren't for the downside."

My downside was my marriage. A month after I came home from this third surgery, Ena threw me out of the house.

Ena had told *People*, "Our whole marriage has been defined by cancer." She'd told friends, "It's as if we spent our honeymoon at New York Hospital."

Pretty close.

When we got married, I was in my fifties, Ena had just turned forty; we knew we were getting a late start, so we were in a hurry to get everything done. We bought a loft, sold my apartment, moved into temporary digs half a block from Carnegie Hall, hired an architect, started construction, flooded our downstairs neighbor's bedroom, fired an architect, found a new architect, tried to get pregnant and failed, tried to get pregnant and succeeded, Ena had her first solo art exhibition, *and* I got cancer all in less than a year.

Ena started the *in vitro* fertilization process, which is a hell of a thing for a woman to go through — shots every day, tremendous hormonal changes. The first time through, it didn't take, so after a few weeks' rest, she did it all over again. (Anne Heche was on *Good Morning America* when Dylan was an infant. She and Ellen DeGeneres had just come out, and there were all kinds of rumors about one or the other wanting to get pregnant, wanting to have a child. I proselytize for parenthood, and told Anne that it is absolutely none of my business if they have a child, but it is the greatest thing in the world. We went through *in vitro,* I told her, and because I'm fairly liberated about such things, I told her that we had to go through it not because of Ena, but because of me: I have a low sperm count, I said. Without missing as much as one beat, Anne replied, "Not as low as Ellen's.")

Any of those things would test a new marriage. All of those things were a test we just couldn't pass.

I'm sensitive to drugs. This is something I never thought about because I never had reason to think about it. But five minutes after the chemo hit my bloodstream, I started to show symptoms. I'd overreacted to an allergy drug a few years before. I found myself waking up at three and four in the morning, sitting bolt upright in bed and seriously wondering if I should wake up and watch TV, try to go back to sleep, or jump out my bedroom window (I lived on the sixteenth floor), and none of the three seemed any better or any worse than the other two.

I knew I was depressed, and I knew, because this was five years after my father, my wife, my dog, and my Broadway play died within six months of each other, I knew I didn't have any real reason to be depressed. The only change in my life had been the allergy medicine. When I asked my doctor about side effects, he listed half a dozen things I didn't have and said, "Oh, yes, some people get clinically depressed."

I took myself off the pills.

After my first lung surgery, the lobectomy on my left lung, I was told that I would be given Percodan as a painkiller. They gave it a trial run the day before I was discharged, taking me off the morphine and putting me on the pills to see if I could tolerate it. I was fine. No pain. I checked out on a holiday weekend, filled the prescription on our way home — but it was for a different drug. Some kind of fancy Advil. A call to Ronnie the Doctor confirmed my worst suspicions: they'd given me the wrong stuff. "Almost the same," the doctor on call confessed.

And Rome, Italy, is almost the same as Rome, New York.

Never check in or out of a hospital on a holiday weekend is one more lesson I learned. The resident who wrote the prescription was either too busy to fill out the necessary forms to prescribe a narcotic or wasn't qualified to prescribe the narcotic in the first place. I'm all in favor of education. But not when I'm in pain. It's Mel Brooks's life lesson, the difference between comedy and tragedy. Comedy is when somebody else is walking down the street and a safe falls out of a window forty stories high and flattens him into a pancake. Tragedy is when *I* have a hangnail. This time I made sure I got the right stuff. Maybe too right.

I grew up in your very normal, very average, very loud, roiling, ethnic family. Once when I told Olga, my therapist, how proud I was that I hadn't yelled at my mother in a whole month, Olga's response was "But how does she know you love her?"

Ena had heard her father get angry once. Exactly once. In forty years.

She could never understand why I never used terms of endearment like "Darling," or "Honey," or "Sweetie"; in my house "Darling" or "Honey" or "Sweetie" dripped with so much sarcasm that they weren't endearments, they were euphemisms for words my parents were afraid to call each other.

We spoke different languages, Ena and I, and we never learned to understand each other's.

They'd prescribed a new painkiller this time, one, it seems, that numbs *your* pain but causes pain in everybody around you. I was still taking it when the news started running stories about it. I was on a derivative of a high-powered pain killer that had been known to cause irrational and even violent behavior in junkies who were using it as a heroin substitute. I quit. But not soon enough.

I'd had an episode. Lost my temper. Dis-associated. In layman's terms, I went fucking nuts. While it was happening, it was like an out-of-body experience. That wasn't me; it was a play starring me, a movie with me in it. I wasn't doing it, I was watching it happen. It was very scary. It scared Ena even more than it scared me.

"Look," she said, angry, frightened (and, in retrospect even I understand). "Either you move out or I'm taking Dylan and I'm leaving." I couldn't do that to Dylan. I moved. Into a hotel at first.

I hadn't fully recovered from my surgery, I was still in pain, and I was shlepping luggage around Manhattan. It took a week for me to get up the nerve to tell my friends, who of-fered places to stay. Nice places. And I saw Dylan every day. Dylan, you were great.

We went, I'm not sure if it was before I moved out or long enough after that Ena and I were getting along, but we went and bought Dylan a big-boy bed. A fire-engine-red big-boy bed in the shape of a fire-engine.

I was at the wheel, Dylan was in his car seat, and Ena and a kid from Toys "Я"Us were trying to fit the bed into the back of our car. I explained to Dylan that I couldn't help move the bed because of my boo-boo.

Dylan thought about it and asked, "Are you well enough to drive?"

I did go back on the air. As I explained to friends, I only had to watch the movies, I didn't have to lift them. The work was a kind of ritual that helped me get through it all. The work and Dr. Wager. Everybody who gets sick needs a Dr. Wager, a psychiatrist, which means he's an M.D. Dr. Wager's specialty is psychopharmacology, how drugs make us behave — not just individual drugs, but how they work in concert.

I was on three categories of drugs: antidepressants, painkillers, and antidiarrheals to help me cope with having a foot and a half less lower intestine than God intended. Different drugs prescribed by three different doctors. The drugs met, perhaps for the first time anywhere, in my bloodstream. And they made me nuts.

Wager asked questions, weighed the responses, explained the difference between "anxious" and "irritable," helped me understand that although, in laymen's terms, I *went* fucking nuts doesn't mean I *was* fucking nuts. The cocktail of drugs I was taking, Wager explained, can have the same effect as having a few drinks too many; your inhibition level just drops.

I saw Wager alone and with Ena. He changed my meds, helped me monitor their effects. I still see him, every three months or so. He's a Godsend.

So was Joanna Bull, who has helped hundreds of cancer patients.

"How are you doing?" she asked a few months after this last go 'round.

"I'm doing OK," I said. "I'm going to make it. But I don't think my marriage is going to."

"It won't be the first," she said.

PART 2

Who You Are

5

Dylan Thomas Jefferson
Swansea Siegel

I made a deal with your mom just before you were born: I'd get to pick your last name, she'd get to pick all the others. I had no idea she'd pick so many.

Dylan would have been her name if she'd been a boy. When she wasn't, her folks had no idea what to call her so her mom, your grandmommy Charleen, found Dylan Thomas's widow, who lived in the town of Swansea in Wales, and *she* named your mother Ena. And Ena named you Dylan Thomas. And added your second middle-name, Jefferson, after the first member of the Swansea family to be born in America who was named Thomas Jefferson to honor the President.

I'm sure you know all this, but what you don't know is that you also have a secret name.

It is Rachmeal Lev ben Yoel Ha'Levi. I

gave you that name at your bris. It is your Hebrew name. One day it will be carved on your tombstone in ancient Hebrew letters. It is your name between you and me and God.

I always check cabbies' names, it's a great New York game, and one day a few years ago I had a cabbie whose hack license had "NFN" where his first name should have been.

"Excuse me," I asked, "is your first name Nefen?"

"No," he answered. He was a very large Samoan-looking guy, like he was bred to be an NFL lineman. "It means 'No First Name.' On my island, nobody has first names."

"Aha," I answered and, remembering my college anthropology, knew he was lying. Of course he had a first name. It's just that you had to belong to his tribe to know what it was.

Our names are kind of like that. You don't have to belong to our tribe to know what it is, but you do have to belong to our tribe to have one. All Jews do. Mine is Yoel Schlomo ben Rachmeal Ha'Levi. Jesus' was Yoshua ben Yosef. King Solomon's was Schlomo ben David. We've been doing this a long, long time.

Your middle name, Lev, is for your great-grandmother, Lena. I look a little like her, and so do you, and a lot of what I like about myself I see in my memories of her; like the way she never seemed to be afraid of new things and, especially, her sense of humor.

She came to America in 1906 from a town in Romania called Botosani. A few years before, her older brother, Jack, had come to New York, got a job in a sweat-shop, and, like millions of other first-born immigrants to America, saved every coin he could to send for the rest of his family. Grandma was the next oldest, so she was the next to come. She lived to be ninety, and I was in my thirties when she died, so I was able to ask her about our family's story and her story.

She was sixteen when she came to America. She remembered Ellis Island. She remembered looking up at all the people who seemed to be staring down at her from the balcony in the Great Hall and not seeing her brother. The balcony — you can see it when you visit Ellis Island, it's all been restored — was reserved for immigration officers and public health officials, but she didn't know that. She was sure she'd be alone in America.

When you exit the Great Hall and walk down the steps, turn to your left. That's where Jack met her, where they cried and embraced, where they boarded the ferry to New York, where she started your life.

She was wearing a straw hat, she told me, all the rage in Botosani, and carrying a straw suitcase. Jack threw the suitcase away. She wouldn't let him throw away her hat.

"Only greenhorns dress like that," he told her. As if the awe in her eyes and the fact that she didn't speak one word of English weren't enough to give her away.

Jack took her to lunch at a restaurant on the Bowery. Grandma had never seen anything like it. Crowded, long tables, loud noises, three walls of red flocked velvet, and a fourth wall that was all mirror, though she didn't know it.

"Why do you say only greenhorns wear clothes like this?" she asked her brother and, pointing at herself in the mirror said, "There's a girl right over there dressed just like me."

On her way to New York, she told me, she'd spent an hour staring at the mannequins in the windows of a Bucharest department store, waiting to watch them move.

Grandma had to be smuggled out of Romania in the back of a wagon filled with dry goods. She remembered a border guard jabbing at the *shmattehs* with a long wooden pole, looking for contraband. She was the contraband. That's as good a metaphor as any for the Jewish experience in Eastern Europe: they didn't want us while we were there, and they wouldn't let us leave.

Of course America was different. This was something she sensed instantly, riding the subway to Delancey Street. Not only was there a subway, but there were people on it reading Yiddish, the newspapers, in public, without fear.

We have a picture, you'll be able to find it, of my grandmother seated in what looks like a boat that's flying an American flag. Look carefully and you'll see that the lighthouse in the background and the waves on the lower right are painted, not real. The picture was taken in a photo studio on Coney Island on her first Sunday in America. That's a forty-six-star American flag.

"Where did you live when you first came?" I asked her.

"Allen Street," she answered. I'd done a lot of reading about the Lower East Side.

Allen Street was mostly Romanian and Turkish and Syrian Jews.

"Where was the bathroom?" I asked. A personal question, but I was curious and she was my grandmother.

"In the back, outside," she said. "And when I had to go at night, Jack would go with me to make sure nothing happened."

What could possibly happen, I thought to myself. I wondered what kind of *bubbemeyse* would she tell me. That, in fact, was exactly what I knew *bubbemeyse* to mean: "Grandmother's tale."

So I did some research and learned that immigrant girls and their families feared the "white slave" trade. Young girls would be kidnaped and sold into prostitution. Moral codes were so strict, especially for women, that even a hint of transgression would result in the family's sitting *shiva* for their daughter as if she were dead — even if that transgression wasn't her fault.

A few blocks west, in the Italian Lower East Side, a similar unforgiving ethic and the same white slave trade were at work. They met on the Bowery. Jewish houses of prostitution lined the east side of the street, and Italian houses of prostitution lined the west. There are contemporary accounts of girls shouting out the windows in

Yiddish and Sicilian and Neapolitan Italian at their own fathers, who refused to recognize their own daughters because, to them, they were already dead.

That's why Uncle Jack walked Grandma to the toilet.

But escaping white slavery or even escaping Romania wasn't her greatest escape.

She got a job in a sweatshop. She was very pretty, and her boss asked her to model the clothes she was sewing for some buyers. "You'll have to bring your lunch," he told her.

Well, "lunch," in her newly learned English, sounded very much like "lounge," which is what she slept on. She thought that meant she would have to sleep with the boss to keep her job. She quit on the spot.

She got a job at the Triangle Shirtwaist Factory, and this was a family story I really never believed until the first time I came to New York. My apartment was on Washington Place in Greenwich Village, and every morning, two buildings to the right, I'd walk past the NYU psych department on my way to the subway. One morning I read the plaque on the corner: *Site of the Triangle Shirtwaist Factory Fire, March 25, 1911.*

On my next trip to LA, where the family had moved in the 19-teens, I asked her about it.

She had worked on the tenth floor. Her job was cleaning, cutting, and trimming loose threads from the shirtwaists, which were Victorian vests every woman wore, and which the factory produced. To prevent them from stealing thread and fabric — and to make sure the girls stayed at their stations — the doors were locked from the outside, including the fire doors. When fire broke out one day, there was no escape. The New York Fire Department got there in a hurry, but their ladders could only reach four stories high. Girls jumped, some were caught by firefighters, but so many weren't that the sidewalks cracked from the force of being hit by so many bodies. Almost 200 workers died, almost all women, almost all teenage girls.

My grandmother remembered the fire, she remembered her friends, and sixty-five years later, she remembered two girls' names. She remembered the city in mourning, the funerals. She didn't know about the sea change in labor laws the Triangle Shirtwaist Fire helped to create: Al Smith and Frances Perkins and the New York State Legislature passed the first real work-safety legislation.

Grandma missed the fire because she didn't go to work that day. That was the family myth — and it was true.

"Why didn't you go to work?" I asked her.

"Grandpa didn't want me to."

They had met two years before, when her brother Jack married another Botosani girl, grandpa's older sister, Yettie. Now they too were engaged to be married. It was Saturday, *Shabbos,* and he had a day off; he had a gold pocket watch; he had a pretty girlfriend; he didn't want her working, and he wanted to show her off.

Go know.

(OK, the pocket watch isn't gold, it's gold-filled. Grandpa gave it to me to give to you. It's in the leather collar-case in my closet where I keep my cuff links and wristwatches. You can pop the back with your fingernail. The picture is of my father, Rachmeal.)

My earliest memory of my father, Rachmeal ben Ephraim Ha'Levi, was when I was three and a half, even younger than you are now. I spend a lot of time at the movies, and it was a scene in a movie that brought back that first memory of my dad. In Stephen Spielberg's *1941,* he has a shot of Hollywood Boulevard just before Pearl Harbor Day, the streetlamps hung with Christmas lights. My father was an electrician, all of twenty-eight years old when I was three and a half, and I have a memory of my mom taking me to Hollywood Boulevard to watch my dad hang those lights. He was high up in a yellow cherry picker, the tallest man in the world, lighting up Los Angeles.

Your grandfather was a mechanical wizard. He was an electrician and a contractor, he'd been a radio amateur, and there wasn't anything he couldn't fix or put together. He made sure there wasn't anything *his* son, me, *could* fix or put together. He'd see me twisting wires or building a model airplane or putting together a crystal set, he'd grab it from me and do it himself, cursing the whole time. He made damn sure I went to college.

Still, I learned a few things just hanging around.

After I hung a fixture in our den, and did a pretty good job, my wife, Jane, called my father.

"And as soon as he got up on the ladder," she said, "he started to curse."

"That's right," my father said proudly. "That's just how I taught him."

I wish I'd learned a few more things about my dad.

He never went to college. He graduated from Jefferson High School in 1934, in the middle of the Great Depression. His older brother, Herman, was on his way to medical school, and there wasn't anywhere near enough money for two boys in the family to go to college. Besides, in 1934, there weren't any jobs. The best thing he could do for his family was to take care of himself, so he and his best friend rode the rails, became hobos. "A hobo," he explained to me, "was a migrant worker. A tramp was a migrant nonworker, and a bum was a nonmigrant nonworker."

My dad left LA with $5 in his pocket, picked fruit in the San Joaquin Valley, got shot at by a farmer when he tried to steal a melon from the farmer's watermelon patch, and came back to LA a year later with $5 in his pocket. I wish I'd known that when I was in high school and wanted to hitchhike across the country. Maybe he would've let me.

There's something else I wish I'd known about. When he was eight he ran a garden hose into his father's Model T. And turned the water on, of course. Henry Ford built his cars watertight, so when his father, my grandfather, Frank, opened the door, a tidal wave knocked him over. My dad had pumped three feet of water inside that car. If I'd known about that when I was a kid, I think I could've gotten away with anything.

There is a picture of that Model T. It shows Grandma driving. Jane, who was an artist like Ena — a family weakness — made a drawing of the old photograph. It's framed; you'll find it too.

A few days after the picture was taken, Grandma was driving a car full of her kids and their cousins, her nephews and nieces, through the hills near San Gabriel, east of LA, where they owned a momma-poppa grocery store, to a family dinner. Grandma was bringing borscht. It was one of the first times she drove — this was probably 1920 — and she flipped the car into a drainage ditch. One of the neighbors ran into Grandma and Grandpa's store shouting, "Mr. Siegel, Mr. Siegel, your wife crashed the car! There is blood everywhere!"

Grandpa ran, in tears, half the town following him. It wasn't blood, it was borscht. No one was hurt. Grandma never drove again.

Another famous family story: The one time someone tried to rob their little store,

Grandma came at the guy, flicking her dishtowel at him and cursing him in Yiddish. She chased him away; he never got a cent. My uncle Herman, Ronnie's dad, heard the whole thing from the storeroom. The would-be burglar had a gun, but it was no match for Grandma's dishtowel.

My folks met at a Workmen's Circle meeting. The Workmen's Circle was a Yiddish/non-religious/Eugene Debs socialist club that still exists. Dylan, our Seder plate comes from the Workmen's Circle store; so does the photograph of Frank Sinatra and Spencer Tracy reading the *Yiddish Forward*.

There was a war on, and they wanted to have kids as quickly as possible. They got pregnant soon after they got married, but not with me. My mother had an almost full-term miscarriage. No one hid that story from me growing up. I was always told I would have had an older brother. As I grew up, I understood had he lived (he was a boy) I would never have been.

He would have been born the summer of '42; I was born the summer of '43. Two things kept my dad out of the army during World War II: me and his defense job, wiring up Liberty Ships at the San Pedro shipyards. He worked the "lobster shift," overnight, and after I was born he wanted

117

more regular hours, so he tried to quit and take a day job he'd been offered at a different shipyard. But you couldn't quit war work, and his boss wouldn't let him go. One day — and his days were in the middle of the night — he fell asleep in front of the door to his boss's office. His boss tripped over him when he went outside and shouted, "Siegel, you're fired!" before he knew what he was saying. Before he could change his mind, my dad ran to the other job.

One day a Russian tanker came in for repairs. Its hold was filled with what were exactly the size, shape, and weight of ten-pound canned hams. No one could read the Russian writing, but so what? Everybody left the shipyard that day with two cans under his coat, my father told me. Everybody but the Jewish guys.

The next morning everybody was pissed. Everybody had carefully and painstakingly stolen twenty pounds of drinking water.

Everybody but the Jewish guys.

One of the worst fights my parents ever had was when my mother crossed a picket line. I was an infant, and she needed something for me at the grocery store, but my father was furious. I grew up going to union Christmas parties and got an IBEW scholarship (the International Brotherhood of Electrical Workers) to help pay my college tuition.

I never crossed a picket line.

Until 1974. I was at WCBS-TV, my first job in television.

"Dad, I got bad news. I crossed my first picket line today."

Silence.

"It's film editors and studio technicians, their contract ran out, but our contract is in effect and my union said I had to cross the line."

Silence.

"I talked to my union's lawyer, and he told me if I didn't cross the line I would probably be sued for breach of contract because I have a personal contract with CBS, and he told me my union would refuse to support me."

Silence.

"And the worst thing is, the union that's on strike is your union. The IBEW."

More silence. Finally, my father said: "You send your boy to college . . ."

After the war my father got the first black electrician and the first Mexican-American electrician into the union.

"They must've been hanging around the local, looking for a journeyman electrician to apprentice for and your father said yes," a cousin who'd also apprenticed for my dad told me, long after my father had died.

I was a little kid and I knew them both, Jose Sandoval and Leroy, whose last name I can't remember and there's no one I know left alive who does. When my father would get real mad at me he'd call me Jose or Leroy — that's when I knew I probably shouldn't come home for a few hours — but I had no idea they were the first of anything. I didn't find out till after my father had died.

The best friend he rode the rails with during the Depression was a black kid. I didn't know that, either, until after my father died. I'm not so sure my father would have thought of himself as a pioneer. He just liked people. And, as a Jew, he knew what it was like to be different, or to be thought of as different.

Now you know a little bit about the Rachmeal and Lev part of your name.

Ben Yoel means you're my son. Literally. It means "Son of Joel." And Ha'Levi is our tribe. It really is. Africans know their tribe, and Native Americans and Scotsmen — old MacDonald had a tribe — and us.

We are Levites, descendants of Moses. The name *Siegel* is a Hebrew acronym for

S'Gai Levi, sons of Levi. When the Temple stood in Jerusalem, we Levites played a part in the Temple rituals, helping the *Cohenim,* the priests, who are the descendants of Moses' brother, Aaron. The line has been passed, male to male, like I am passing it on to you, for more than 3,000 years. Our Israeli cousin, Ze'ev Meshel, a renowned archaeologist who has taught at Harvard and Oxford, tells me he believes that tribal traditions like these are true because "it is too important and too serious not to be."

We are survivors, Dylan. Not just you and me, all Jews. None of our biblical contemporaries, none of the peoples we met and married or conquered or were conquered by are still here. But we are.

The Babylonians captured us, enslaved us, marched us a thousand miles to their capital. They're history. We're here.

Philistines? Put a fork in 'em.

Chaldeans? Hittites? Spread jelly on 'em.

OK, there are Egyptians, people born in that place called Egypt. But you can't find any Egyptians who still worship the pharaoh or send their kids to Egyptian school where they learn to read hieroglyphics.

Yes, there are Romans. And, yes, a lot of 'em still speak Latin. And roads and buildings and art and architecture and even their alphabet survives. And so does a copy of a decree from Julius Caesar granting Jews "the freedom to practice their ancient religion" throughout his empire.

Two thousand years ago we were already an ancient religion. We've survived, Dylan, and I'm not sure how. Or why.

Some Jews believe it's because God chose us.

I'm more inclined to believe it's because we chose God.

But I do know that for the past 1,500 years the lives of each one of our ancestors would have been easier had he or she just stopped being Jewish. That's fifty generations. Line 'em up: your father, my father, his father, his father before him, fifty times. Their lives and their families' lives would have been better had they converted to Christianity or accepted Islam or just quit making such a big deal about it and melted into the mainstream.

But no. Not us. And we're still here.

Fifteen hundred years ago, Caesar's decree had run its course. So had his empire. It was about then that Constantine had converted to Christianity, which called itself "the one true religion," and set about converting everyone to his beliefs. This was something we Jews had never done.

"But why should we become Christians," pagan skeptics would ask, "when Jesus Himself was a Jew and the Jews won't become Christians?"

This question did not have an easy answer. St. Augustine figured that these Jews, this wandering, impoverished people, were God's example to the rest of humanity: here is what happens if you don't accept Christ.

For that prophecy to come true, Jews had to be kept poor and wandering, and there were always those in the gentile world who did their part to make sure we were. We were ghettoized, forced to wear dunce caps or yellow stars, kept from getting good jobs or secular educations, even kept from growing anything but root vegetables (that's why Eastern European Jewish cooking uses potatoes and carrots and onions and garlic and on Passover we don't eat anything leavened and we don't eat anything green).

When the Crusades marched through Europe to free the holy land from the infidel, who should they find on their way to Jerusalem but infidels of their own? Our ancestors. Jews. And the Jews didn't have any armies, so we couldn't fight back.

More than once, in cities and towns where Jews had lived for centuries, men, women, children, whole communities were locked into their synagogues and the synagogues were set on fire. It happened in France, in Germany, even in England.

In Lincoln, where most of England's Jews lived, the townspeople herded their Jews into the synagogue and set it on fire. In York, the Jews beat them to the punch.

"In the days before Easter of 1190," James Reston, Jr. wrote in his history of the Crusades, *Warriors of God*, "the Christians of York drove some 500 Jews into the tower where they committed mass suicide."

When I was a little boy, in the early days of television, the football games we'd get on TV were the Ivy League and New England games. My favorite team was the Holy Cross Crusaders. I liked the dashing name. I loved their helmet, with a wide, white stripe. When my Grandma asked me were I wanted to go to college when I was five or six, I told her, without hesitation, "Holy Cross." This was an answer she wasn't expecting. The voyage hasn't been easy, but New York is a long, long way from old York.

"In every generation . . ." the Hagadah

has been teaching us for generations, there were pogroms and inquisitions. When the bubonic plague spread through Europe, no one knew it was spread by fleas that lived on rats; they blamed the Jews. And we're still here.

One of our most important commandments is for a parent to teach his children. I may not be alive to teach you, so I'd like you to promise me that you'll learn without me if you have to. You don't have to promise you'll believe, just learn.

On Yom Kippur we read the story of Abraham and Isaac, of how Abraham heard the voice of God telling him to sacrifice his son. It was always a story to me. A good story, real drama, a message, a story worth telling and retelling, but, to me, just a story.

I've always appreciated debating the story, the way Jews do, holding it up to the light and inspecting every single facet. Even from the point of view, in a beautiful retelling written by one rabbi, of the ram who watched Abraham and Isaac from a nearby thicket and, a completely innocent bystander, happened to get his foot caught just at the moment that God, understanding that Abraham really would sacrifice his son, saved Isaac and provided a substitute.

"What did I do?" the ram asked himself. "Why me?"

But, Dylan, the story was no more than a story to me, until you were born. Then the story came to life. I understood how much Abraham must have loved God and believed in God even to think about harming his son, let alone sacrificing him. I'm not sure I believe God really spoke to Abraham, but I'm certain Abraham believed He did.

These are the things I was thinking about the Yom Kippur before last, when you and your mom came to services to meet me for the break fast. Her timing was perfect. The memorial Yizkor service was just about over, and when you found me, the whole congregation was standing and singing the Schma.

It's not the most sacred prayer in the Hebrew liturgy. I don't think we have that kind of hierarchy. But it must be one of the oldest, because the words define our religion: "Hear, O Israel, the Lord Our God, the Lord is One."

One God, not three, so for 1,500 years the Catholics in Europe gave us no peace. And one, not two, so for 700 years the Muslims have chased us through the Middle East. And we sing the Schma triumphantly, because we're still here. And I watched your face while I sang, and I watched your face light up with the thrill of recognition, and I recognized what was happening, too.

When you learn about songs watching *Sesame Street*, when the song is over, everybody applauds. So, as the congregation sang "Adonai echad!" and noisily sat down, your face broke into this huge smile. You'd never seen anything like 500 people standing and singing but, suddenly, you knew exactly what to do. You clapped your hands and shouted "Yeah!" at the top of your little lungs.

I can't ask for any more than for you to one day sing the Schma yourself. But, when you finish, think about applauding on the inside.

PART 3

Who I Am

6

How to Decide
What to Be When You Grow Up?
Don't.

Dear Dylan,

It seems to me that as good a metaphor as any for growing up is walking down a hallway, closing doors behind you. When I was in high school, all the doors were open. I could have been anything. I was a terrific math student, and I really loved math and physics and chemistry until I took calculus as a high school senior. It stopped being interesting, my passion was gone, and that closed the doors that led to engineering — very big in those post-Sputnik days — as well as to astronomy and chemistry and the technical side of radio and television which had fascinated me as a little kid. It also closed the doors that led to medical school, which had interested my mom an awful lot.

In college, at UCLA, I majored in

American history, because as a history major I could take fewer courses I didn't want to take than in any other major. What I did was close as few doors as possible while I tested the waters and tried to figure out whether I could actually make a living doing what I really loved. Of course, first I had to find out what I really loved.

I did. I could. I have. I hope the same for you.

7

Joel Siegel: Critic

I think the first thing I wanted to be when I grew up was a fruit man like Albert. Not *that* kind of fruit, man. A peddler. Jane, in Pittsburgh, grew up calling them "hucksters."

When I was three or four, Albert would pull up in his truck, which was filled with produce, and honk his horn. My mom would smile and we'd walk down the steep steps and then down the hill to meet him. Back then, you could only buy what was in season: no apricots in February, no oranges in July. Albert got to weigh everything on this scale that was big enough to weigh me, and sometimes he did weigh me, and I could read the numbers, and I thought, "This is the job for me."

When I was five or six, I told Art Linkletter that I wanted to be a composer. I had actually written a tune or two by then. "Fourth of July Is Here," I titled my first song, with arpeggios in triplets representing the fireworks. I could read and write music before I could read and write English, and when I played the song for my mom, she smiled and was encouraging. Two weeks later she walked by my room and heard me playing the same song note for note — she was shell-shocked.

When I was in the first grade at the Harrison Street School in City Terrace, East LA, I remember being called to the principal's office and telling the teacher that yes, I knew where it was, and feeling very small walking down this long hallway with impossibly tall ceilings, past the quiet classrooms where the fifth- and sixth-graders were, and thinking, "I wonder what I did wrong."

Actually, I'd done something right. I'd somehow impressed my first-grade teacher enough to recommend me as one of the schoolkids who would appear on the *Art Linkletter Show*. This was a national CBS talk and chat show where, as one of the regular features, Linkletter, a very pleasant man who, as I recall, did spit a little when he spoke, would interview five schoolkids from the greater LA area and feed us straight lines in hopes that we'd say a "darndest thing," which is what he'd later call the TV series and the books he'd write: *Kids Say the Darndest Things*. This was my first media appearance. Radio. Before television.

They picked us kids up in front of the school in a limousine: a 1946 or '47 Cadillac with jump seats and an inside window behind the chauffeur, who wore a black cap with a patent-leather visor. I wore my best clothes: brown slacks and a Hopalong Cassidy brown shirt with a tan country-western yoke. My mom must've spent half an hour slicking down my pompadour.

We all drove together, five kids from the first grade and a producer/chaperone who took us to lunch at a restaurant called Nickodell's. It was the first time I'd been in a restaurant without my mom, and the first time I'd ever been in a restaurant that had cloth napkins. I ordered a hamburger. (Nickodell's survived until the 1990s. It used to be on the edge of the old RKO Pictures lot. I must've driven by it a thousand times, but never went back in.)

The producer — Linkletter called her a "schoolteacher," but a mere fifty-three years later I figured out otherwise — kept asking us questions. "Can you name something that grows and grows?" she asked.

And she pressed. And she suggested, in a very friendly way, some answers. "A bald spot on a man's head," was one of the answers she fed us. "A big fishing story," was another.

When the show began and we went on the air, in front of a studio audience, with a live band playing "School Days," lo and behold, Art Linkletter himself asked those same questions.

Dylan, there's a transcription of that show, a real transcription disc, a one-of-a-kind 78 rpm record with peeling acetate on an aluminum disc. It's in a green sleeve, it's labeled *Art Linkletter* 1949. If you find someone who can play that recording (How do you play a sixty-year-old acetate transcription disc? Very carefully) you'll hear Linkletter ask all us kids to name something that grows and grows, and Lucy, the teacher's pet, on whom I had my first crush, says, "A bald spot on a man's head" and gets a very big laugh. I say, "A fishing story," and get no laugh at all. Art has to explain it: "Oh, you mean how the fish somebody caught gets bigger and bigger each time he tells the story. . . ." He didn't get much of a laugh either.

After that I always did my own material.

We got prizes for being on the air, but in

those days before television, the prizes weren't worth very much. I got a flashlight that glowed in the dark that I kept until I was in college and stale D batteries had oozed green acid all over the inside, and a record album — when they really were albums that opened like books and had two or three or four heavy 7-inch 78 rpm records in individual sleeves — of songs about the circus.

There was a professional musician in the family who led the band at the Biltmore Bowl in downtown LA. Unfortunately, he played the accordion. I say unfortunately, because that was the instrument I chose to play, and an accordion is little more than a musical toy, not much more difficult than playing a stereo. (Though Lawrence Welk, who once announced, reading the cue cards, "And now Alice Lon and the champagne music-makers will sing a medley of songs made famous during World War Eye . . . ," couldn't even play the accordion well.) The Hollywood definition of an optimist is "an accordion player with a beeper." As a little kid I learned which buttons made which chords but didn't learn anything about music more serious than how to play a melody. When I was in my fifties I told my mom,

"You know, if you'd given me piano lessons or violin lessons, today I could've been an out-of-work musician." She didn't get it.

When I told Art Linkletter I wanted to be a composer, I wasn't lying. But even at five and six, I didn't want to be *only* a composer. The world was just too interesting.

Who figured out what toys I'd get in a Cracker Jacks box? Who made it sound like fires were burning or horses were running or doors were creaking open on the radio shows I'd listen to? Who made those silly silent movies — even then called old-time movies — that my dad and I would laugh so hard at?

My first-grade teacher kept a file of 3" by 5" index cards with bold-printed words we kids didn't know how to spell. I told her I couldn't spell "electrician." A few days later when it was my turn to pick a card and she asked if I'd learned to spell it I proudly announced "Yes, I have." And I spelled the hell out of "electrician."

The truth is I lied. I could spell "electrician," it was my daddy's job. I didn't know any words I didn't know how to spell. I also didn't know it then but my life's ambition was chosen for me that day in the first grade of the Harrison Street School: Show-off.

Although computers and the Web have made it obsolete, when I was in high school and in college, the *Reader's Guide to Periodical Literature* was a very big deal. This was a series of tall, thin, quarto-sized green volumes that was the LexisNexis of its day. Look up a topic, look up a name, and the *Reader's Guide* listed every magazine piece, every article in every major newspaper by that person, on that subject. That became another ambition: I wanted to be listed as an author in the *Reader's Guide*. Once I did, I figured, my name would be in every library in America. My name would live forever. I'd be immortal.

I was all of twenty-two when one of my magazine pieces made it into the *Reader's Guide*. I can't remember if it was a book review I did for *Sports Illustrated* or a piece for the *LA Times*, but there it was. And I looked at my name, which, in print, always, even now, looks like it belongs to somebody else, and thought, "All that for this?!"

On the letdowns scale, it was almost up there with the time, a year before, I'd met my one honest-to-God childhood hero, Harvey Kurtzman.

Harvey Kurtzman started *Mad Comics*. From the moment my Uncle Mickey gave me a beat-up copy of the issue with Lena the Hyena on the cover and Flesh Garden on the inside, I wanted to be Harvey Kurtzman.

Harvey Kurtzman's job was *to make fun of things!* He got *paid* for making fun of things. He was *famous* for making fun of things. What could be better than that?

My first trip to New York, 1964, I interviewed Harvey for the UCLA humor magazine. "You're going to college," Harvey said to me. "I wish I'd been able to go to college."

It was as if Mickey Mantle pushed away a nine-year-old kid's autograph book, shook his head "No," and told him, "Forget about this baseball stuff. Study hard in school, maybe one day you can be an accountant. A CPA. That's something to dream for."

No, I never wanted to be a critic. What kind of kid *wants* to be a critic? Can you imagine a seven-year-old kid at the dinner table clearing his throat and announcing, "Well, mom, the meat loaf tonight lacks its usual insouciant bite, the green beans just sat there panting like a dog in August, the gravy doesn't come close to the gravy on Thursday's hot beef sandwiches, and no one and I mean no one will be writing mash notes to these potatoes."

If there are seven-year-olds who do that, we don't know about them because their parents don't let them live to be eight.

I started reviewing movies absolutely by accident. Jane, a film editor who loved film and hated critics, was opposed to it. We went to see a Jewish-Canadian movie, a sentimental mess about a little boy and his Yiddish-speaking *zaideh*. I was crying my eyes out when the movie was over.

"How would you review that movie?" Jane asked.

"It stunk," I sobbed.

The problem was that the other stuff I was doing, feature reporting, was turning out to be a dead end. There is a reason the cliché of an old reporter is of an old drunk. You do the same story over and over and over again. How many different ways can you cover a fire, or, in my case, Thanksgiving and Purim and Valentine's Day? I did a story on an all-nun rock-and-roll band that played dances at Catholic school sock hops. "And you thought Guy Lombardo played the sweetest music this side of heaven." That should have been enough, like Ted Williams retiring on a home run.

"Great line, Siegel," the news director should've said. "We're retiring your number. You did it so well you'll never have to do it again."

I was too smart, the stories were getting too easy, I found myself creating obstacles to make the stories more interesting: I'll write in rhyme. I won't start on my script till 4:15. A story on how they wash chain mail and suits of armor at the Met? I'll start it with "In days of old when knights were bold . . ."

I really was ready to quit when a guy named Bob Salmaggi introduced himself to me in the *Eyewitness News* room one afternoon.

He was the movie critic on Group W's radio stations, and I listened to him all the time.

"What are you doing here?"

"They're auditioning movie critics."

"Ah," I said. "Good luck," I lied.

I walked into Ron Tindiglia's office. Ron was our news director. He'd smuggled me over to Channel 7 from Channel 2. He was a friend and a fan.

"Why don't you audition me?" I asked.

He thought about it for about five seconds.

"I don't have to audition you. You want the job? You got the job." And this is a great job. Warm in the winter, cool in the summer, different every day, different every movie, I get to use my writing chops, and I get to stump for my secret agenda: getting people to be nice to each other.

When Tindiglia said I had the job, what he didn't say was that I had the job for one shot, one movie, one day. Everything was on his side. If I could do it, he wouldn't have to hire anybody and would save some money. If I stunk, big deal, he lost a day or two.

The movie was *Magic*, starring an unknown, unlikely-looking British actor named Anthony Hopkins. He played a ventriloquist whose dummy was committing all these murders. This was an old idea; I'd seen Eric von Stroheim's *Gabbo the Great*, of which this was an unremarkable rip-off.

On TV, a lesson everyone who has ever been on TV more than once has learned, the most important part of the job is to keep people from turning you off. The second most important part is to end on time, and the third most important is to start on time. If the audience learns anything in the time in between, that's sheer serendipity. And if anybody tunes in to watch you, just you, the next day on your dressing room they'll hang a star.

That's the Joel Siegel "How to Stay on TV" rule: If you buy a newspaper, you can read some of it, or none of it, or all of it, and you still bought the paper: the *Times* still has your seventy-five cents. But if you're watching TV news and you never go to the movies and I come on and you turn me off, you're gone forever — and so, as soon as my boss finds out, am I. The folks who cover hard news have something going for 'em I don't: the audience prima facie wants to know about a murder or a jewel heist. I have to convince them that my little piece is worth sticking around for because it's fun. And because television is a medium that works in close-up, I have to convince them without letting them know I'm trying.

It's a great George Burns line. When he was asked to what he owed his great success in the show business, he'd answer, "Sincerity. Once you learn to fake that, you can do anything."

One of the first things I learned about television is that you can't fake it. I also decided early on that I didn't want to fake it. I don't want a job where I have to go to work every day and *lie*.

When I show my audience something I'm pretty sure they don't know, I'm excited about letting them in on a behind-the-scenes secret because I genuinely am.

Or I'm matter-of-fact about it, never condescending. Sure, I know the brighter the light, the smaller the f-stop, the greater the depth of field, it's no big deal, it's what I do, I go to the movies. Same way if you're a plumber or in the *shmatteh* business you're going to know things about sinks and shirtwaists I don't know.

I reviewed *Magic* with my own ventriloquist's dummy. I stole a gag from Albert Brooks. The dummy drank a glass of water while I talked. I taped the review so I could dub in the dummy's voice so he could talk without me moving my lips. I didn't like the movie, the dummy loved it. I had the job.

There's a greeting card definition: "Luck is when preparation meets opportunity." This is the kind of crap football coaches pin up on locker room walls and the kind of crap people who believe the key to life's mysteries can be told in six words believe.

I was prepared. I'd taken film history courses at UCLA. I have a genuine fascination with American pop culture and how what is great and unique about America doesn't trickle down from the top but rises up from the bottom of our culture. We vote for hit films, I wrote in one paper, the way we vote for presidents and political agendas. I also love going to the movies.

I took screen and playwriting courses, too, which help me as a critic, but I took them because I thought, with a little luck, I might actually end up writing scripts for films and TV.

I'd always wanted to be a writer of something. When I was nine or ten, we lived at 3222 Oakhurst Avenue. I was very excited about starting a newspaper, *The Oakhurst Express.* I even dummied up a front page, but, trying to fill in the blanks, I realized I had no news to report.

Dylan, there's an Indian pot in the country with a couple of tchotchkes in it: a bear fetish the Zuni believe will keep you healthy (bear eat roots, and many roots are medicinal), a good-luck coin given to me by Hopalong Cassidy himself at the May Co. in downtown LA in 1950, a sales tag from a Navajo rug, and a brass sheriff's badge that says "Lone Ranger" on the front.

The Lone Ranger is one more piece of my childhood you'll probably never know from. That's a shame. I like the very American mythology of the western, and the Lone Ranger was this straight-shooting mythic hero who, on radio and TV, taught a couple of generations of American kids to be honest and loyal and to stand up for their beliefs.

Come with us now to the thrilling days of yesteryear, this is from memory, *a puff of smoke, a cloud of dust and a hearty HI-YO SILVER, AWAYYYYYYY! The Lone Ranger rides again!*

The Lone Ranger's theme song was Rossini's William Tell Overture (Rossini was dead and they didn't have to pay royalties). One test of an intellectual, when I was a kid, was someone who could listen to the William Tell Overture and *not* think of the Lone Ranger. (A better test is someone who's asked to name the James Brothers and says "William and Henry," and not "Jesse and Frank.")

His horse's name was Silver. His sidekick was an Indian named Tonto. The reason heroes have sidekicks? On the radio you couldn't see what the heroes were up to. For the listeners to follow the action, they needed someone to *tell* what they were going to do.

"You stay here, Tonto. I'll sneak around behind those rocks."

"Ugh, Kimosabe!" Pronounced key-mo-SAH-bay.

Tonto's lines were so unimportant, when the folks at WXYZ radio in Detroit spun the Lone Ranger off into another kids' series, Sergeant Preston of the Yukon — *On King, on you huskies!* — they used the same scripts for both shows, just changed the names. And they gave Tonto's lines to Preston's dog, Yukon King. Instead of "Ugh, Kimosabe," it was "ruff, ruff, ruff, pant pant pant."

John Reid was a Texas Ranger, ambushed by Butch Cavendish and his Hole-in-the-Wall gang, rescued by Tonto and nursed back to health.

"Where are the other Rangers?" he asked.

Tonto answered, "Other Rangers dead. You Lone Ranger now."

The Lone Ranger Deputy Sheriff's badge, mine since I was eight or nine, was purchased for ten cents and a boxtop from Cheerios, the Ranger's longtime sponsor. This is a special Lone Ranger Deputy Sheriff's badge with a secret compartment. A top secret compartment. Slide the pin on the back ever so slightly and reveal a small space, just big enough for a tiny piece of paper. I had the badge. I had the secret compartment. What I didn't have was secrets.

Well, I had one. I wanted to be a writer. But could someone actually make a living doing something they liked? My father didn't go to *play* early every morning, and he sure didn't come home from *play* dirty and sweaty every night. Work is what you're supposed to do, and it's not supposed to be fun. ("OK," Woody Allen tells his cast and crew, when they have to hunker down to do something they might not want to do. "That's why it's called show *business*. If it were all fun it would be called show *show!*")

The Call Comes

I was one of half a dozen guys in LA actually making a living as a freelance writer when the call came. I wasn't making much of a living, but I didn't need much. It was the mid-'60s, rent was a couple of hundred dollars a month for half a bungalow half a block from the Pacific in Ocean Park. Mine was one of the small houses that had been built as vacation cottages in the teens and twenties when the Ocean Park and Venice piers were summer resorts with carnival rides and dance bands and ballrooms. The merry-go-round in *The Sting* is on the Santa Monica pier, the third and smallest of the west-side piers and the only one that has survived.

When I moved in, the neighborhood had run way down, the Ocean Park pier had been abandoned, there was great surfing between the rotten pilings and, when the surf was down, the local kids, who called the neighborhood near Main and Pier "Dogtown," would drive through Santa Monica looking for "For Sale" signs on fancy houses. They'd find a vacant one and try to recreate ocean surfing in empty swimming pools on half-sized boards with roller skates nailed to the bottoms, and that is how skateboarding was invented. If the pool looked promising and wasn't empty, they'd empty it.

The Ocean Park cottages were barely winterized, but this was Los Angeles and it was barely winter. I'd bought a new BMW for $3,300 out the door. I still had my Bar Mitzvah money in the bank, $400, just in case. All I needed to live on was $600 a month, and I could do that. The *LA Times* was paying me a grand a story. If I could sell them six stories a year I was that close to home. And I could, I knew I could. And if the *Times* said "Sorry," I'd get a $500 kill fee and could turn around and sell the story to *Los Angeles Magazine* or to the *Playbill* that you got at the Music Center and the Hollywood Bowl for a couple of hundred bucks and free tickets.

I could've made more money if I'd stayed in advertising, but, a kid in my twenties, I understood that what I needed was time, not money. I was so free, I flew.

I wrote anything which is, of course, what freelance writers do. I'd written the side of the Blue Cheer box during my New York summer internship at Young & Rubicam Advertising, and the back of the Brillo box ("A new pot free if Brillo fails to clean") when, fresh out of college, I got my first real job at Carson/Roberts Advertising in LA. This side of writing recruiting posters for the Aryan Nation was it possible to sell out more than that?

A month ago I was in an ice cream store in Maui, and their special of the day was "German Chocolate Cake Ice Cream."

"Hey," I muttered to the haoli behind the counter. "I invented German Chocolate Cake ice cream." He was either stoned on drugs or in some kind of insulin-induced ecstasy, but even he stopped smiling and gave me a look.

But I did invent German Chocolate Cake ice cream. Baskin-Robbins was a Carson/Roberts client and I also invented Peaches and Cream and Pralines and

Cream and Strawberry Cheesecake and Blueberry Cheesecake and Red, White and Blueberry for the Fourth of July and Green Cheesecake when we landed on the moon, and Chilly Burgers, Baskin-Robbins speak for ice cream sandwiches. It usually takes some kind of personal crisis and a little bit of time for a freelance writer to compromise his or her standards for a paycheck. I was doing it before I started.

I did a cover story for the *LA Times*'s Sunday magazine on Mickey Mouse. Another one on Earl "Madman" Muntz, the king of the used car dealers. And, ultimately a piece on LA trivia ("Where was the hot fudge sundae invented?" "Who invented the Hamburger Size?"). The *Times* ran an "about our authors" picture of me wearing a giant Jewfro and a very furry face, with a note that said I also broadcast the news on hippie-rock-radio KMET-FM.

Local news on TV was expanding to an hour around the country, and they needed stories to fill out the broadcast. Sam Zelman was kind of a talent scout for CBS. The news director in New York had told him to look out for someone who could cover rock and roll and the counterculture. On his quest Sam read my piece in the *LA Times* Sunday magazine, saw a picture of a guy with hair all over his face, tuned into KMET, and figured, what the hell, it's worth a phone call.

I'd ended up on KMET, writing, reading, and producing a ten-minute newscast three days a week for $25 a day, through a different chain of coincidences. I had a big collection of old radio shows and ended up on LA's first free-form radio station, KPPC-FM, as Uncle Joel playing kids' shows on Saturday mornings and his demonic twin, Uncle Noel, playing *Suspense* and *The Shadow* (Kent Allard, not Lamont Cranston, was the Shadow's real name) and *Lights Out* late Sunday nights, scaring the bejeebers out of stoned hippies.

It was fun. And the $100 a month paid for gas. And I got to be part of this rock-and-roll culture that was changing America. Then we all got fired. The general manager, who was the money guy, managed to convince the station's owner, William Buckley, that us creative guys had too much control. The inmates were taking over the asylum. Which was true. But in the heady mid-'60s (pun intended) it was an asset when the inmates took over the asylum.

Most of us hooked up with the station that had been our rock-and-roll rival,

KMET. The news on KPPC had been done by The Credibility Gap, a three-guy comedy team that consisted of my old roommate, Harry Shearer, and the two guys who'd later become Lenny and Squiggy on the sitcom *Laverne and Shirley*, Michael McKean and David L. Lander. They were doing great radio — brilliant, satirical, highly produced, great radio. They did one bit on a record that is one of the funniest things I have ever heard. A rock-and-roll promoter (Harry) is trying to explain this concert he's promoting to a superstraight ad salesman for the *LA Times* (David L. Lander, who would become Squiggy).

Three groups. The Who. Guess Who. And Yes.

"OK," Lander says, "Who's on first."

"Guess Who," Harry says.

"I don't know anything about these rock-and-roll groups. Who's on second?"

"Yes!" Harry says, "Who's on third."

Genius.

But KMET wouldn't pay three guys to do the news, and The Credibility Gap wouldn't break up their act. Somebody, probably Harry, said "Let Siegel try."

They did.

I loved it. When George Wallace got

shot, I ran the story, intercutting witnesses and reactions over three different versions of The Band's "The Night They Drove Old Dixie Down." I'd done politics, and so had Harry, so I invited him to do analysis with me the night of the 1972 California primary. I said something about secrecy being the tenor of the Nixon administration, and he said, "I thought Dennis Day was the tenor of the Nixon administration," and I laughed for fifteen minutes.

My future plans? I didn't have any. I was having too much fun. I didn't need any future plans. I was a kid in my twenties learning my craft. Unintentionally. Doors were closing behind me, but I was unaware of them. Looking back, it's a straight line from college and the humor magazine through advertising and radio to writing, producing, and performing film reviews. But I didn't know it then. My aim certainly wasn't network television. "TV movie critic" wasn't even a job category back then. What I wanted from life, my dream of dreams, was to be able to do what I loved doing for as long as I could.

I am one of the few truly lucky people, careerwise; I'm still doing what I loved and I still love it.

When Sam Zelman called, I was sure it

was Harry disguising his voice. People who looked like me weren't on television news. I was too fat. I was too Jewish. I wore glasses. My voice was too high.

I told none of these things to Sam Zelman.

"Write a story for air, come down to KNXT and we'll tape you and see how it looks," he said.

That was easy enough. KNXT was at Sunset and Gower. Built as CBS Radio's West Coast headquarters, it was where I'd gone to appear on the Art Linkletter show.

When I got there, Clete Roberts, who'd been on television news for as long as there had been television news, who wasn't fat, or Jewish, who was born in a trench coat, was in the next studio taping a response to a letter from an irate viewer: Blanche Bettington of Brentwood. My Blanche Bettington: my favorite high school teacher. Who had lost her job in Canoga Park in 1942 when they took the Japanese students away and she went batshit. Blanche Bettington, who, when they kicked me out of Hamilton High and sent me across town to University High, told me, "Nobody chases you if you don't run."

How many omens does a fat, Jewish, superstitious guy with glasses and a high voice need?

I didn't hear from Sam for a month.
Finally I called him.

"I was just going to call you," Sam said. "The news director in New York liked your tape. He wants you to fly out for an audition."

I bought a suit. My audition story was on a Times Square bar where it was Christmas every day.

"It's 95 outside, 99 percent humidity, but inside it's Christmas in July."

I had never done anything like this before. Sitting on a barstool, talking into a camera. I don't think I'd ever sat on a barstool before. My technique was to mimic the guys who were on the news, and to get on the cameraman's good side and do everything he told me.

The bartender wore a Santa Claus outfit.

"It's the middle of July, right?" I asked him.

"What does your dry cleaner say when you go to pick up the suit?"

I don't remember the answer. I think it was the question that got me the job.

That and the fact that Ed Joyce, the news director (who'd later get into a mess of trouble when he downsized CBS News), was a rock-and-roll music fan and figured he'd take a chance. It was a cheap chance — my first contract was for three years at $22,000, $24,000, and $26,000. I was doing better as a freelance writer in LA. I took a pay cut to be on television, but I was betting on my future. And it turned out to be a good bet. I became the first person to regularly cover rock music on any television news station.

I didn't know if I could do it or if I would like it, but I didn't know anybody in New York, so if I failed I'd at least be failing out of town.

My first night in New York, I saw Patsy Kelley in *No, No, Nanette* on Broadway and, at intermission, ran like a maniac to Nathan's Times Square for two franks (I still called them hot dogs) and an order of fries. The hot dogs were amazing. How did Nathan's figure out how to pour six ounces of fat into a four-ounce hot dog? But it was the fries that sold me — crisp, crinkly, perfect. I'd found a home. The next day I walked from CBS to the 400 deli on Ninth and Fifty-seventh for lunch. Among the old Jewish waiters and young Puerto Rican busboys, I was the tallest person in the room. Job or no job, TV or no TV, I was going to stay in New York City.

Ten years later, our technical director,

Mike Zyderko, told me a story that ce-mented my love affair with this city. His daughter was in the third grade at Ethical Culture, an Upper West Side private school. At home they were playing Trivial Pursuit, junior edition, and her question was, "What is the most common last name in America?"

She thought and thought, Zyderko (who's Ukrainian) told me. Finally she brightened up and shouted, "I know, Siegel!"

I don't think so, Zyderko said. He turned the card over and showed her. The correct answer was Smith.

His daughter got angry, and started to cry. "But I don't know *anybody* named Smith!"

I love New York.

(Another why-I-love-New York story: A mother and her eight-year-old daughter had moved downtown and were audi-tioning synagogues, trying to decide which one to join. They visited an Orthodox syn-agogue where men and women do not sit together — the women's section is usually behind a curtain in the back of the sanc-tuary or up in the balcony. After the ser-vice the mother asked the daughter if she liked it, and the daughter answered, "No.

159

The only people who get to sit together are the gay couples.")

I was falling in love with New York, but I knew I didn't know much about it, so I haunted the used books stores on Fourth Avenue and read A. J. Liebling and Herbert Asbury and E. B. White, and Gay Talese's *Serendipiter's Journey*. Dylan, if you want to be a writer, make sure you read Liebling and Talese.

I learned that Shyster was a New York lawyer. Typhoid Mary had been a New York maid. Yellow journalism. Take me to the Garden. *You provide pictures, I provide war.* Kiehl's Pharmacy down on Third Avenue still sold live leeches.

The Flatiron Building, at Twenty-third and Fifth, was the tallest building in the world at the start of the twentieth century. Wind rushing off the rivers also made that the windiest corner in town, and mashers and nogoodniks would hang out there hoping to catch a glimpse of ankle or even thigh when a young woman's wide dress would catch the breeze.

"23 Skidoo!" is what they'd holler when the cops would chase them away.

The plan was that I'd spend a month in the newsroom, learning the ropes, and bank a dozen or so stories so that once I went on the air I could be on every day. My first day, during my first meeting with Ed Joyce, the assignment editor, Marv Friedman, ran in waving a paper and shouting: "We've got our lead story! We've got our lead story! A woman in Queens just smothered her three children. Penza's on his way!" (Meaning Ralph Penza, their lead reporter. It should also be noted that Marvin was smiling, ear to ear, when he got to the "smothered her three children" part.)

Welcome to the news.

I had banked a story on a Brooklyn Heights store called the Warlock Shop, a place that specialized in witch's supplies, something you'd expect to find on Harry Potter's Diagon Alley. With Liebling and Talese as my mentors and my fat man's please-like-me insecurity firmly in my corner, my TV technique was to add pictures to a New Journalism read. I listed ingredients, the stranger the better, gave recipes for spells and love potions and the cure for the common cold.

Then somebody held up the Warlock Shop, and instead of a month and a dozen stories on the bank, I went on the air after less than a week.

My tag, live: "If only he'd been attacked

with eye of newt or dragon's teeth, he would have known just what to do. Instead the hold-up man used a gun, and the Warlock Shop had no defense."

People laughed. It was engaging. And funny. *I* was engaging and funny. And I was on television.

At first I didn't believe I was on television. Even in LA we knew CBS headquarters was at an architectural treasure called Black Rock on Fifty-second and Sixth. These studios were on Fifty-seventh and Eleventh in some converted old dairy. And who was Jim Jensen? And where was Walter Cronkite?

I half believed someone was playing the world's most expensive practical joke on me, Extreme Candid Camera, hiring people to say they'd seen me on TV. It wasn't until I saw myself interviewing Miss Universe on NBC and ABC that I really believed it.

Dylan, one of life's truths is that you don't feel older as you grow older. I've been on TV in New York for thirty years. I had years where I was on at 6:00 and at 11:00 doing different stories. For two years I was on at 11:00 on WABC-TV and *Good Morning America* on the network, which cost me a marriage, to Melissa, and almost killed me besides. But it wasn't until a few years ago, a very few years ago, signing my first contract after my cancer had been diagnosed, that I began to convince myself that this probably is what I'm going to be when I grow up: a movie critic on TV.

The hard part wasn't the "this is what I'm going to be . . ." part. It was the admitting I'd grown up part.

Keep the doors open as long as you can, Dylan; life has a way of closing them shut behind you anyway.

And if you follow your passion, and if we've raised you right so your passions are productive and just, you won't have any regrets. Even when you follow them into places where things don't work.

If I'd been following some kind of career track, I never would have been able to change career goals at twenty-nine, move across the country and give TV a shot. But, other than following my passions, I didn't have any career goals.

And if I'd closed doors behind me, I never would have been free to spend the summer of 1968 writing jokes for Bobby Kennedy, or two years writing a Broadway musical, or the summer of 1965 in Macon, Georgia, working for Martin Luther King. And I would have been the loser.

8

Making a Difference

Dear Dylan,

The first letters you learned were ABC. You learned them from Big Bird on *Sesame Street* and from me and Ena singing you the same ABC song we learned when we were little. But the first letters African-American kids learned who were born in the South before 1965 were C and W, so if they ever needed to use a bathroom in a public place, or wanted to drink from a water fountain, they would know which one to use. Bathrooms and drinking fountains were segregated. Colored Men, White Men on a bathroom door; Colored Only, White Only on a drinking fountain. That's what "Jim Crow" was, and — I don't know if you'll be able to believe this — it lasted a hundred years. In America.

I grew up in a poor neighborhood. City

Terrace in East LA. It's almost all Chicano now, Mexican American, and the last time I drove by my old apartment at 3320 Pomeroy Street, I was surprised that there were no sidewalks. Then I realized that they didn't tear the sidewalks up when we moved out; there had never been any sidewalks.

This was Los Angeles during the war years. There was a population boom, people came to LA from all across the country, attracted by high-paying defense jobs, not to mention the weather. But no new housing could be built to accommodate them because all the resources went into the war effort. That meant you lived where you could, not where you wanted to. Which meant I grew up with Jews and Japanese people and Mexicans and Irish kids and even non-Jewish Russians left over from an earlier migration. Years later, probably thirty years later, I figured out that my friend Edward must have been black. It didn't occur to me then; I remember he was dark complected, had curly hair, and when the first-grade teacher taught us to spell our religions, Edward announced that he was a Methodist. I remember this because anybody could spell "Jew," and there were so many

Catholics, spelling that wasn't a big deal either. But I was the only kid in the first grade who could spell Methodist, and because I was a Jew I never got the chance.

The great thing about growing up in a mixed neighborhood is that nobody looks funny, nobody has a funny name. My grandmother lit candles on Friday night, my friend Manuel's grandmother, up the hill on Pomeroy, lit candles on Sunday. But they lit them for the same reason. His mom always had a pot of beans on her stove that we'd get to dip in with a fresh tortilla; my mom would render chicken fat, *schmaltz* to you, to use instead of butter when she cooked meat dishes. We weren't Orthodox, but she wouldn't consider mixing milk and meat any more than she'd consider bringing home pork chops.

When Manuel was over and she made *schmaltz*, we'd both get to spread some rye bread with the cracklings, the *gribbenes* or *greev'n* in Yiddish. Kirk Douglas once bemoaned the way he raised his children: "I was able to give them everything," he said, "except the privilege of growing up poor."

I vividly remember my first day at school, kindergarten at the Harrison

Street School on City Terrace Drive. The kindergarten had a separate entrance, like it wasn't real school. When my mother picked me up after that first day, she asked if I'd made any new friends. I said yes, a boy named Jose.

My mother had grown up in this neighborhood. So had her brothers. And there was a lot of tension between the Jewish kids and Mexican kids. A Chicano gang once followed her brother, Bebble, home from high school. Bebble was a big kid, played tackle for the Roosevelt High Roughriders, so there must have been a lot of them, because the gang beat him pretty badly. Still, of all the things my mother might have said when I told her my new friend's name, what she did say was, "You know, in Spanish, your name is Jose. And your father's name is Roberto. And your grandpa's name is Francisco but everybody calls him Pancho."

I also remember one day in the first grade we were talking about where we were born. I'd been born in LA, there was a girl named Lucy who was born in New York, someone else was born in Chicago, and a Japanese girl, I think her name was Jeannie, said she was born in a concentration camp. I knew about concentration camps, even at five. I knew I had family who had died in concentration camps. I cried all the way home.

In a book called *Double Victory* about ethnic American experiences during World War II, Ronald Takaki, a Cal-Berkeley historian, tells a story about a City Terrace kid, a Chicano, who grew up next door to a Japanese family. They had two boys about his age, and the three kids were inseparable; growing up with his buddies and his buddies' folks, the Spanish kid learned to speak not-bad Japanese.

He enlisted in the Marine Corps and shipped out to Saipan, where, his first day of combat, he faced waves of attacking Japanese soldiers. He killed sixty Japanese that day and just couldn't handle it. That night he crawled behind enemy lines and, in fluent, idiomatic Japanese, convinced 300 soldiers to surrender. That's what happens when you grow up in a mixed neighborhood.

John Lewis is one of the great people of my generation. He's an average-looking man, he's not a great speaker, but he became a civil rights leader second in stature only to Martin Luther King because of his moral strength. If John Lewis wanted to do it, if John Lewis asked you to do it, it was the right thing to do. He's a congressman from Atlanta now. If anyone had said in 1965 that John Lewis would represent Atlanta in Congress — and that summer, Pascal's Carousel, owned by a black man, was the only restaurant in Atlanta where whites and blacks could eat together — they would've been locked up for insanity. John Lewis himself would have told you you were insane. But he's there, one of the most powerful men in Congress. At the thirty-fifth anniversary of the first Freedom Ride into Montgomery, Alabama, the cop who almost killed him introduced himself and put his hand out for John to take. John embraced him, in tears. He'll end up on a postage stamp. Though, I hope and pray, not soon.

One morning, crossing Broadway, I saw John Lewis crossing the other way.

"Oh, my God," I shouted. "That's John Lewis."

He turned around, and his wife, Lillian, recognized me. And I told him we'd gone to jail together in Americus, Georgia. Which wasn't completely true, because that day they didn't arrest the white guys.

A few years later, over dinner, Lillian

asked me why I'd become a civil rights worker — a question no one had ever asked me before. And the question has haunted me ever since.

John said, "Because he heard the call," but that's not really in my tradition, hearing a call. It presupposes a long list of things I'm not ready to admit to. Not just a belief in God, but a belief in a God who has callings for us, who speaks to us as individuals. I can't go that far.

A few years ago I had a casual dinner with then-Senator Al d'Amato, and in the course of the conversation I mentioned that I'd been a civil rights worker for Martin Luther King.

"What would you want to do that for?" he asked, in a friendly, genuinely curious way. "That was dangerous."

"Senator," I said. "I really believe in that stuff."

It's the way I grew up.

I think the most important advances in the twentieth century weren't the technological advances; they were going to happen, anyway. Witness the fact no one has any idea who invented the computer, because it wasn't invented by one guy in one place but by a lot of people, all over the world, who were able to take someone else's ideas one step farther. The computer, television, instantaneous communication, air travel, even space travel, these things were going to happen anyway.

I think the greatest advance in the twentieth century is in how we treat each other.

It didn't come easy. We had to fight for it. I was part of the fight.

9

I Meet Martin Luther King
and Martin Luther King Remembers

Television had a lot to do with it.

I remember as a ten-year-old boy watching NBC's coverage of the integration of an elementary school in Little Rock, Arkansas. Later I learned, when I went out with film crews myself, how hard it is to pick up any live sound, but there it was. I heard it. Two little black girls, escorted by armed U.S. marshals, walking a gauntlet of screaming adult men and women whose faces were distorted with hate. One little girl said to the other, clear as a bell, "And my mommy says if we're nice to them, they'll be nice to us."

That would've been 1954. Louis Armstrong was disinvited from a State Department tour that year for being too "controversial" when he told a reporter that President Eisenhower should send soldiers in "so the little girls can go to school."

Ten years before, during World War II, Lena Horne was on a USO tour in the South. She was in a theater at an army base in Arkansas, and she looked out into the orchestra and saw that the audience was all white, which she expected, since this was Arkansas and the theaters were segregated even on army bases, but these guys didn't look like GIs. They weren't.

"Who are these guys?" she asked.

"Nazi prisoners of war," she was told.

"Where are my guys?" she shouted. There was a roar from up in the balcony, the Jim Crow section, where the Colored troops had to sit.

Lena Horne walked up the stairs, did her entire show from the first row of the balcony, got a reputation as a "trouble-maker," and the USO never asked her back.

Somewhere there is a picture of me playing my guitar, in a park, singing with a bunch of kids. No mustache, I hadn't grown it yet. It was July 4, 1965, and we were integrating the public park in Macon, Georgia. A man named Baconsfield had deeded the park to the city with the restrictive covenant that blacks not be allowed in.

In 1965 it was against the law for blacks and whites to play ball together in Atlanta, Georgia.

In 1965 segregation was the law in the South. Very few blacks in the South were registered to vote; virtually no blacks were registered voters in the black-belt rural South (called the black belt for the color of the rich earth), where blacks were usually in the majority.

In the spring of 1965 Martin Luther King's Southern Christian Leadership Conference (SCLC) staged a protest march across the state of Alabama. Priests, nuns, and rabbis joined the phalanx of Protestant ministers, black and white, to lead the thousands of marchers from all around the country. When the march tried to cross the Pettis Bridge in a town called Selma, Alabama, the state police tried to turn them back with fire hoses and police dogs and cattle prods. It was horrible. If you were Jewish, the parallel with Nazi Germany was unmistakable, especially the newsreel shots of police dogs, snarling, teeth exposed, straining at their leashes, held back by angry men in black uniforms.

My mother was a very nice lady who liked all kinds of people but who, as far as I could tell, never committed a serious political action in her life other than to vote for Franklin Roosevelt. Which she continued to do till the day she died even though he had been dead for thirty-five years. But two days after the march, I found a copy of a letter she had sent to President Johnson.

"Dear Mr. President," it began. "I was born in Poland and *came* to America. And yesterday, for the first time, watching the police attack the marchers in Selma, Alabama, I thought maybe I'd made the wrong choice."

There were some UCLA history professors on that march. The history department had passed the hat and sent them. When that fact made the *LA Times*, the chairman of the department, an excruciatingly boring professor named Theodore Saloutos, answered the angry phone calls he'd receive: "Sometimes we teach history and sometimes we make it!"

I was a senior at UCLA, majoring in history. After the march, the history department invited Dr. King to speak on the UCLA campus and, in part because of our support in Alabama, he said yes. I don't know how it happened that I became the department's undergraduate spokesperson, but I did.

King spoke at the foot of Janss steps, one of the rare pieces of UCLA that, even today, looks like a college campus and not

Brasilia. It was a great speech (I don't think he ever gave any other kind) filled with visual metaphors — *I have seen the mountain* — and historical inevitability — *not even a thousand armies have the strength of an idea whose time has come.* He'd quote the New Testament for the Christians, the Old Testament prophet, Amos, for the Jews: *And justice shall flow like rivers and righteousness as a mighty stream.* And while he was speaking — it's an old Lenny Bruce line about a plane crash, "Somebody said 'do something religious,' so I took up a collection" — I took up a collection.

When King accepted the invitation to speak at UCLA, his first major speech on the left coast, everybody invited him over for lunch: the governor, the mayor, the county board of supervisors, the president of the university, the chancellor, the publishers of the *LA Times.* King was way too deft a politician to alienate any of them. His excuse was that he was first and foremost a man of the cloth and had accepted the invitation of the University Religious Conference to have lunch that afternoon with the campus ministers in a church basement just off the campus. That's where I met Martin Luther King.

I had taken the money we'd collected to

the campus student store, where the coins were rolled and the bills were counted: $800. That was not an insignificant sum — 800 of those dollars would probably buy $5,000 worth of stuff today. Not a bad haul from kids at a state school. I'd kept the money in cash (just in case Dr. King didn't want to declare the donation), put it in a paper bag, and rode to the luncheon site on the back of the campus Presbyterian minister, the Reverend Don Hartsock's motor scooter. We got there just after the meal ended.

"Dr. King," I said. "I've come with dessert." Big laughs, big applause, Dr. King shook my hand.

As a result of the speech, when King's Southern Christian Leadership Conference announced a summer voter registration drive in the Deep South, called SCOPE, a group of UCLA kids volunteered, and I was part of that as well.

There was a weeklong orientation in Atlanta. We slept in dorms at a black school, Morris Brown College, one of the colleges in the Atlanta University complex. My roommate was a young Jesuit priest whom I was able to convince that abortion should be legal because even if it did mean that I'd go to hell, well, wasn't that my business and not yours? Most of our meetings were at Reverend King's Church. We learned to address blacks as Mr. and Mrs., something whites in the South almost never did. "Uncle," "Auntie," "Doc," "Professor," even "Reverend" were titles white southerners would use so they wouldn't have to address blacks with respect.

We learned that whichever were fewer in a car, whites or blacks, would have to lie on the floor so oncoming traffic would see a car full of whites or blacks, which was OK. A car in which oncoming traffic could see whites *and* blacks meant trouble. It had been less than a year since the three civil rights workers, two whites, one black, Michael Schwerner, James Cheney, and Andrew Goodman, were pulled out of their car on a rural Mississippi road and murdered by the Ku Klux Klan.

(I was one of the first critics to see *Monster's Ball*, and I'm pretty sure I was the first person who wasn't involved in making the film to tell Halle Berry she had a chance at an Oscar. The film is set in Georgia, and I asked if it had been shot there. She told me it was shot near New Orleans, and when she asked why I wanted to know, I told her about my Georgia connection.

"We had to do things you just wouldn't believe," I said, and told her about whoever was fewer, whites or blacks, having to lie down in the car.

"No," she said. "I believe that. My mother is white and my father is black and when we used to visit my white grandmother in Cleveland, my sister and I had to hide in the car so the neighbors wouldn't see us.")

We also learned that the best way to keep tabs on the Klan, or their white-collar collaborators, the White Citizens' Councils, was through the black maids and nannies who worked for them. This turned out to be true. In Macon we learned the White Citizens' Council's every move because they'd talk about their plans over dinner, which was, of course, cooked and served by black folks. Yes, they were that dumb.

There were twenty of us who drove down to Macon from Atlanta that June. God, it was hot. I remember sitting up nights watching my knees sweat. I stayed with the Andersons, Willie and Lula Mae, two ordinary people who were called upon to do extraordinary things. He owned a Sinclair gas station just outside downtown Macon. Their house was right next to the station; their back door opened ten feet away from the gas pumps. It didn't occur to me until I sat down to write this that putting up civil rights workers in a house next to a gas station in 1965 probably wasn't the wisest choice.

Macon was a pleasant place with an old downtown that still looked like a Walker Evans Depression-era photograph, just with slightly newer cars. There was a Woolworth's, a monument to the town's Civil War dead in front of the massive, red-brick Bibb County Courthouse, and, just inside the courthouse, a new refrigerated water fountain with a "White Only" sign on it and a small, ironically white porcelain fountain attached to it as kind of an after-thought with a sign reading "Colored." Of course, I'd seen pictures and news film of Jim Crow signs and had expected to see them in person, but actually seeing it was a visceral thing, like seeing swastikas. And my reaction was visceral, too, like being kicked in the stomach.

For me this wasn't a political choice, it was a moral choice. Prejudice is wrong, racism is wrong. It's as simple as that. And I was lucky enough to have been given the opportunity to do something about it.

I'd done a lot of voter registration and political organizing in LA, and the major difference was that in Macon the food was better. And the music. The best music I have ever heard was in the Andersons' church. They were Church of God people, serious testifying, speaking in tongues, the women in the congregation were either too fat or too skinny — there didn't seem to be any women in between — and they all fanned themselves with a cardboard paddle with a picture of a very white, blue-eyed Jesus on one side and an ad for the local black undertaker on the other. The harmonies soared, the rhythms, well, you know the rhythms, they've been making the pop music charts for as long as there's been pop music. They sang with passion and purpose, and with a little desperation, too. These were people whose lives weren't easy and who, at least on Sunday mornings, thought about what they'd done during the past week to make their lives even harder. They had one road left, and they were singing their way into heaven. *"Get on board, get on board. People get ready there's a train a-comin', it's got a list of passengers a mile long."* If God doesn't let them in, I don't want to go.

The local undertaker who gave out the fans was also the local black political leader and the publisher of the local black paper. He was a big man who looked like two chocolate bubbles atop one another. A cautious man with a deceptively quiet voice, he'd been a very successful contractor and builder until his civil rights activities cost him his contracts with whites, which happened in 1961 when Bill Randall put it all on the line when he refused to move to the back of the bus.

Randall was arrested, his name and his picture and his address were broadcast on the local TV news, and that night his house was firebombed.

The next day Randall was on TV, telling Macon, "I own that house, but I don't live in it." He gave the street address of the house he did live in, all but daring the White Citizen's Council to try again. They didn't.

Ten years later I read about his son, Billy, in *Newsweek*. He'd become the first black from Macon to serve in Georgia's State Assembly since Reconstruction. Macon, like many places, was turning its old train station into an upscale downtown shopping mall. The problem was what to do with the letters carved into the granite over the station's two separate entrances: the one on the left that read WHITE EN-TRANCE, the one on the right that read

COLORED ENTRANCE. Billy Randall didn't want the words sandblasted out. "We have to remember," *Newsweek* quoted him, "and you have to remember."

Billy worked with us registering voters in 1965, and every trip into the Bibb County Courthouse, he'd walk by that drinking fountain labeled "White" and "Colored." Today he's a judge. His office is in that courthouse.

Bibb County named a building in downtown Macon after his daddy.

Macon, the market town for middle Georgia, was peaceful and relatively prosperous with a very paternalistic white community that "took care" of its blacks.

Before we showed up, the whites and blacks were all Democrats together. The white power structure paid election-day homage to the black community with turkeys for the poor, bribes for the ministers, the occasional street light and fire hydrant, that kind of thing. Some blacks — less than 10 percent of the black population — had always been registered to vote, but because the elections had been safely Democratic for almost 100 years, most whites hadn't bothered to register. We did such a good job registering black voters — 4,000 in a town with a total population of about

50,000 — that, in the immediate short run, things backfired completely. I don't know why we weren't smart enough to see it, but we didn't. The whites left the Democratic Party and became Republicans. The white power structure no longer needed the black community, and the net effect of our voter registration drive was a total loss. But that was just in the short run.

I also went to a Ku Klux Klan meeting that summer. We'd befriended two white couples — Sid and Judy Moore and Tommy and Kay Darby. College kids, true southern intellectuals; Sid's now an Atlanta lawyer, Judy died of breast cancer about ten years ago. Tommy couldn't hack the war in Vietnam and split to Canada. He and Kay live in Ottawa, where Tommy, a Ph.D., teaches philosophy.

The Klan had a rally outside Macon, and Tommy and Sid convinced me to go. I joked that I walked in eating a pastrami sandwich on white bread with mayo so no one would even think I was Jewish, but the Moores and the Darbys coached me on how to say "Thank ye" with a southern accent and told me when they passed the hat to put in a half a buck. Hoods were illegal in Georgia, but there were a few dozen people dressed in white robes, even a few very small kids in white robes. Cross burnings were illegal in Georgia, too, so the Klan had a twenty-foot high cross studded with electric lightbulbs. The B-movie version of the Klan. It looked as stupid as it sounds.

They'd found an American Indian who was their featured speaker that night. Racist, anti-Semitic, he talked about how all these outside agitators and foreigners were ruining his country. Where did they find *this* guy, I thought to myself.

Sidney remembers standing next to a Klansman, listening to a speaker orate against these "nigra-loving outside agitators."

"Here's what I'd do if I ran into one of those nigger-lovers," the Klansman told tall, skinny, blue-eyed, blonde-haired Sidney. He twisted something or pressed something and the cane he'd been leaning on became a three-foot sword.

"I'll never forget the look on your face," Sidney told me almost forty years later. "Tommy and I were southerners, we could blend in, but you looked just like a scared Jewish kid from UCLA."

He was right. I felt like I was watching an ancient ritual through a very long lens, watching it through binoculars I was holding backwards, it seemed so far away. Not in far away space, maybe, but in time. This was an antique, a piece of the world that had lived too long and lost its meaning. And we were here to put it out of its misery.

The tone surprised me. The racism was muted, much softer than I expected, the speakers obviously trained to say "nigra," maybe trying to improve the Klan's image. There's a meeting I'd love to have been a fly on the wall for: a bunch of Madison Avenue guys, some polling people, a couple of Ph.D.'s in marketing, and six guys with no teeth and Confederate flags tattooed on their forearms, meeting on how to improve the image of the KKK.

Our headquarters were in Atlanta in Martin Luther King's house. One day, with business to take care of, guaranteeing bail for some of our kids who'd been arrested in Americus, I rode the Southern Railroad's Nancy Hanks from Macon to Atlanta and was waiting in his library when Martin Luther King himself walked in. I could sense him looking at me but I had no idea what to say to Martin Luther King, so I pretended to be very interested in whatever book was at hand. Still, I could sense King's stare. He was trying to figure out who I was, why I was there, where he knew me from. Finally he said, "You wouldn't happen to have any more paper bags with you, would you?"

Martin Luther King knew who I was.

We organized our voter registration drive in Macon with some SCLC help: Andrew Young, Willie Bolden, Julian Bond; I don't remember Jesse Jackson at all. We worked the churches. We'd go to services on Sunday, and the preacher would call one of us to the pulpit. We were like a novelty act, and we sensed it: What are these white boys and white girls doing in this church? But once they realized we knew we were white and we knew they were black, the novelty passed and we talked about the serious business of registering to vote, the possibility of reprisals, the hard work ahead we'd all have to do to make America a better place.

The next day the church ladies would fix a lunch for us and we'd start canvassing. I remember the lunches more than the work. Fried chicken. Southern-style potato salad made with mustard and relish and a dash of hot sauce to give it a little kick. Peach pie for dessert. This was Georgia. It was also the American South in 1965. Because we were there, we were family. No questions asked. Just like family. The instant embrace you'd give a cousin or an uncle you hadn't seen in years. What a great feeling that was.

That summer Lyndon Johnson signed the Voting Rights Act, which did away with poll taxes and literacy tests. The first time I met an adult who admitted he couldn't read was on the steps of the Bibb County Courthouse. I tried to convince him — this was the SCLC line — that it wasn't his fault, that the schools didn't care about black kids, that we'd be glad to teach him to read but, in the meantime, why not go inside and register — "reddish" in American Southern, "reddish" to vote. He'd been a farmer, a sharecropper. He looked up at the sky and said, "Gonna rain about 2:30." I saw a clear sky, maybe the hint of a cloud. It was hot, humid, no breeze, no wind at all. It rained about 2:30. And I didn't get him to register to vote.

We organized carpools to the courthouse. One of our guys, Joe, who's now an economist with the World Bank, drove to Macon from California in his giant '55 Oldsmobile. He carried so many very large women to "reddish" to vote that summer, one of Bruin SCOPE's major expenses was a new back seat for Joe's car.

One day Pat Kennedy, the guy I was rooming with at the Andersons, drove the white Chevy he'd driven from LA out to a town called Dublin, Georgia, where we met with some preachers and a guy who owned a dry cleaners to see about doing some organizing. They told us no. They were afraid, it was as simple as that. And no wonder. We'd traded our California license plates in for Georgia plates as soon as we got into Macon, as a matter of self-preservation. On this particular trip there were two black guys in the car, one lying on the floor in the back, one crouched down in the front. Pat had red hair and freckles and wore a green sportshirt and a pork-pie hat. He drove, I was in the passenger seat, and from the moment we hit town until we drove out of sight, it was *Twilight Zone*. People stopped talking, we could see them stop talking, as the car hit their line of sight; they'd stare at us, and turn their heads, still staring, as we drove by. We figured it out when we got back. The first number on a Georgia license plate referred to the county in order of population. A 1 meant Fulton County, the car was registered in Atlanta. Macon, Bibb County, was 5. That's what everybody was staring at. They couldn't see the black guys, didn't get enough of a look at my *ponim* to know I was Jewish and didn't belong. What didn't belong was this car from Macon in the town of Dublin, thirty miles away.

If we had been stopped, we knew exactly what to do. Nothing. We'd taken nonviolence courses in our orientation. Be polite, don't show fear, and if the beating starts, do your best to roll into a ball, protecting your vital organs with your arms and your hands. The commitment was a real one. We had to believe that what we were doing was more important than pain or even our own lives. I'd like to think I did. I'm very glad I wasn't tested.

One day a huge white guy stopped me downtown, and I figured it was over for me, he was going to lift me up over his head and snap me in two, and he looked big enough to be able to do it. He was a boilermaker, a steelworker, and what he wanted to know was how to contact the union. "I hear guys up north are makin' ten bucks an hour. I'm making four. I don't give a shit who I work next to, not if I can make ten bucks an hour." There's the secret of America in three sentences.

One day an equally large black guy stopped me. He was about my age, at most a few years older. He had a four-year-old boy who kept seeing these commercials on television for this amusement park. But blacks could only go on Wednesdays, and he only had weekends off. "I can take care of myself," he said — and he sure looked like he could — "but what can I tell my kid?"

Martin Luther King III told me that he first found out about racism when he and his mom would drive his dad to the airport. They'd pass an amusement park and he'd want to go and he couldn't.

"That's why daddy is working so hard," he told me his mother had told him. "So one day we'll all be able to go there."

Billy Randall told me about the time he sat down at the counter of the ice cream store in downtown Macon. He was four or five, and his daddy had to pick him up and take him outside.

"That's the only time I ever saw my daddy cry," he told me.

While doing a story on Spike Lee's powerful documentary *Four Little Girls*, about the little girls who were murdered on a Sunday morning in a Birmingham church bombing, I interviewed the father of one of the girls who had been killed. "The hardest thing," he told me, "even harder than hearing about her dying, was having to tell her why we couldn't stop for a hamburger at the Woolworth's when we were doing our Christmas shopping. We'd always say, 'Oh, we'll eat when we get home,' or 'Your momma is a better cook than that.' But this time she really wanted a hamburger. Like the one on the sign. And I had to tell her why we couldn't get one.' "

I saw that Birmingham church that summer. The SCLC convention was in Birmingham in 1965, and I represented Macon, Georgia. In the movement Birmingham was known as "Bombingham," a Klan town. Only Mississippi and the Florida panhandle were tougher. The chimes on the clocktower on Birmingham's City Hall rang the first twelve notes of "Dixie" before they rang the hour. One of the SCLC folks who walked me past the church kept saying, more to himself than to me, "They were little girls. They were little girls."

It's haunted me ever since. I couldn't say what I knew: that to whoever did this they weren't little girls. They were less than human. And believing that is the real crime.

At the convention Dr. King spoke out for the first time in a public forum against the war in Vietnam. This was very controversial in the black community. They thought Lyndon Johnson was good for the blacks, so was the military, and that domestic problems needed to be solved before we should take on foreign policy. This reminds me of the old Jewish joke about two Jews facing a firing squad. When an officer offers them cigarettes, one spits and says, "Feh on your cigarette."

And when they're offered blindfolds, the same Jew says, "Feh on your blindfold."

And the other Jew nudges him and says, "Why do you want to make trouble?"

To King it was a moral issue, and he approached it as a moral issue. When he read his conclusion, that we had no reason to be in Vietnam, I leaped to my feet and gave him a standing ovation. I was the only person standing in the entire hall.

The Beatles' second movie, *Help!* opened that summer. There was a poster for it close to the courthouse, and I asked some of the black kids if they'd heard of the Beatles. Almost all of them had heard of the group, but not one of them had heard any of their songs. Music was segregated. Black radio stations played R&B, almost exclusively by black artists. White radio stations played white artists, and a few what they called "crossover acts."

I didn't know till I got back home that Otis Redding was from Macon. He was on the road that summer, and it never occurred to the kids we worked with that white boys might know who Otis Redding was. But more than once someone pointed out the Greyhound Bus Station where another Macon boy, Little Richard, wrote "Tutti Frutti" while he was washing dishes in the diner. We didn't go to the diner at the Greyhound Station, because they wouldn't let us eat together. Billy Randall, as a young assemblyman, did try to get "Tutti Frutti" declared the official Georgia state rock-and-roll song. He couldn't get it through the assembly, although he did get the state to finance the Georgia Music Hall of Fame in Macon. There's also a statue of Otis Redding, near the dock of the bay, in a beautiful piece of parkland overlooking a bend in the wide, Ocmulgee River. Times have changed.

Back in 1965, UCLA had won their second in a row of NCAA basketball championships that winter. Kenny Washington, the team's sixth man, came off the bench and scored more than 20 points to help win it. I knew Kenny, and I knew he was a Marine brat, spending the summer with his family in Beaufort, South

Carolina. I called him and asked him to come to Macon. We'd get him a car, get him a ride, whatever he needed. The game had been on TV, he was a celebrity here, and he'd be a great role model for these kids — a boy from South Carolina grown up and going to college in California.

He turned me down. And as soon as he started to explain I knew he was right. He was born and raised in Beaufort, and there, he knew everybody. But he was a stranger in Macon, and he was afraid he'd look at someone the wrong way or say the wrong thing. He was six-foot-two, a world-class athlete, earning a college degree, and afraid to visit a town a hundred miles from where he grew up.

We spent Labor Day weekend back in Atlanta, a few hundred of us who'd worked the South for SCOPE. We decompressed, we were debriefed, and we celebrated, too, at the Auburn Avenue Baptist Church. Ralph Abernathy, King's second in command, ran our meetings and, one afternoon, spotted me, third or fourth row, center pew, carrying my guitar.

"I've been in the movement my whole life," Reverend Abernathy said. "But the one thing I ain't never seen is a white boy leadin' freedom songs."

I got up on the pulpit and sang "Walkin' and Talkin' with My Mind Stayed On Freedom" and about a hundred choruses of "Which Side Are You On?" The Albany Freedom Singers, who'd sung their way into a hundred jails in the old South, sang backup behind me. It was one of the great moments of my life.

And I know if I'd just sung a little better, if I'd practiced a little more, today it would be "Joel Siegel and the Pips."

Two years ago I went back to Birmingham, to do a story we called "Driving *Mister* Daisy." I asked the cabdriver, a friendly, overweight white guy who looked like he knew where to eat, where to get the best ribs in Birmingham. He recommended a place in a mall we'd just driven by.

"Looks too fancy, if you know what I mean. I mean real ribs."

"Gotta be Dreamland," he says.

Dreamland it was.

He drove me into the ghetto, but this was a nice place, stand-alone, lots of parking places filled with lots of cars, well lit. There'd been a Dreamland in Tuscaloosa, started in the guy's yard. He sold ribs, sauce, beer, and bread to sop up the sauce with. That's the entire menu. The mayor of Birmingham asked him to open a rib joint in his town to anchor the ghetto, bring in nighttime traffic, make the neighborhood safer. In his Birmingham store (and there's one in Mobile now too) he expanded the menu: cole slaw.

The owner is a black guy. There were white and black waiters and waitresses, integrated tables, integrated couples at the tables, I saw a black guy holding a white woman's hand in Birmingham, Alabama. I saw a man who danced with his wife. Also the ribs are the best I've ever tasted. I order 'em online and you can too: www.dreamland.com.

The next day, we taped the story at a very nice old-age home in Birmingham, which, because it receives federal funds, is integrated. One Sunday night, a very elegant, still strapping-looking black man who'd just turned ninety, was given a list and asked to choose the hymn they'd sing after supper. He confessed, after much hemming and hawing, that he'd never learned how to read.

A wonderful, tiny, sparrowlike white woman, well into her seventies, told him that she'd learned how to teach literacy in her church and she'd be happy to teach him to read. He said yes, he wasn't sure, but he was willing to work at it, and she taught him to read.

Once a week they go to the grocery together. That was the story we covered. She makes out the shopping list, he wheels the shopping cart through the supermarket, reads the list, and buys the groceries. Because he is ninety and doesn't see that well, she drives him to the supermarket. So . . . Driving Mister Daisy. And they've become best friends.

Oh, Dylan, look what your daddy did.

10

Bobby Kennedy's
Joke Writer

Dear Dylan,
It's a story I must've heard a hundred times. My mother knew exactly where she was when she heard that Franklin Roosevelt died. She was on the phone with Sears, Roebuck, ordering me a little red wagon for my second birthday from their catalogue when the radio broke in with a bulletin.

"Oh, my God," my mother said. "The president is dead." She started to cry.

The Sears operator started to cry, too. She told the other operators, and they started to cry. Instead of the small wagon she'd ordered, Sears sent my mother their biggest, a huge Radio Flyer, with real rubber tires, big enough to carry every kid on Pomeroy Street. She thought Sears had made a mistake, but as I grew older (and heard the story more and more times) I became convinced the operator had sent the biggest and most expensive wagon Sears made to cement the bond: two ordinary Americans who would never meet but who'd been together when FDR died.

I was at UCLA when John F. Kennedy died. I was in a poli sci class taught by a good-looking guy with an Irish name in his early forties, about the same age Kennedy was.

A kid named Howard Price and I must have been the first kids to walk past the flagpole that stands in the center of the quad between the library and the humanities buildings. We, the two of us, lowered the flag to half-mast.

On September 11, 2001, we were home. You and Ena and me. We used to have a view of the World Trade Center towers out our bedroom windows. We watched them burn. You and Ena watched them fall. I'd gone to work just in case they'd need some extra hands. I didn't see the towers fall; I watched the people watch them fall. I've never seen anything like it.

A few days later, we learned that one of the kids in your preschool class asked his mommy why she was crying.

"Building fall down?" he told his mommy. "Building need a kiss."

These tragedies are life markers. I'll never forget where I was when Bobby Kennedy was shot. I was there. I heard the shots.

I knew Frank Mankiewicz, who was Bobby Kennedy's press secretary. His father, Herman, who wrote *Citizen Kane*, was before my time, but I'd met Herman's wife and knew Frank and his brother, Don, through mutual friends.

In 1968 I was working as a freelance writer and was living on unemployment insurance, $75 a week. Nothing to be ashamed of. One morning Paul Newman showed up at our Santa Monica State Employment Office to collect the check he was entitled to between movie jobs. No, nothing to be ashamed of, but I don't think Paul Newman does that anymore.

When Bobby announced that he was running for president, I called Frank and volunteered to help in any way I could. I also told him, "By the way, I've got a joke for Bobby."

Frank, a very funny guy who loved a punch line, asked what it was. This was

1968, remember. George Hamilton was this minor league Hollywood movie star who'd been deferred from military service in Vietnam because he was the sole support of his mom. Even though his dad had left them both millions. Hamilton was dating LBJ's daughter, Lynda Bird, at the time.

The joke: Bobby says, "I know my campaign is starting to pick up steam. Last night George Hamilton called for my daughter's phone number."

"You've got a job," Frank said. I became Bobby's jokewriter.

Frank would call and let me know where Bobby would be speaking or who he would be speaking to and I'd send some jokes. Bobby, to be fair, was funny without me. He'd give his canned campaign speech, which he'd always end with a quote from George Bernard Shaw. A quote he'd more often than not make up on the spot. The press who followed Bobby knew that when Bobby said, "And as the great Irish playwright George Bernard Shaw once said, . . ." the speech was over and they'd have to run for the campaign bus if they wanted to get a seat.

One day, I think it was in Indiana, Bobby ended his speech, "And as the great Irish playwright George Bernard Shaw once said: Run for the bus!"

My favorite joke that I wrote for Bobby was a complaint about high prices and inflation. He'd change the street name to localize it, but if he was speaking in Manhattan, for example, the joke would go, "I don't want to say prices are high, but there's a butcher shop on Lexington Avenue that rents meat."

I love that joke.

When he spoke at Cal-Berkeley — this was the '60s — I wrote a joke for him: "They found a great quarterback for the football team. All they have to do is figure out a way to put cleats on sandals."

Four years later, I read the same joke in the *San Diego Union*, attributed to Ronald Reagan.

Thirty years later, I was giving a speech at the University of Nebraska, Omaha, and the introduction mentioned that I'd written jokes for Bobby Kennedy.

"Which jokes?" someone in the audience asked.

I told the George Hamilton story, and the guy whooped. He'd worked for Bobby in Indiana and was in the room in Indianapolis when Bobby came in laughing. "I've got this great joke we're going to use tomorrow," Bobby had said. Yeah, it was my joke.

The job I was unemployed from was in advertising, so I wrote some radio commercials for Bobby's first campaign trip to LA. He landed at the private airport at LAX, and in order to draw a crowd I had to convince Pierre Salinger, Jack Kennedy's old press secretary, who was working for Bobby, that we had to advertise. It had to be radio, because it was cheap and we could pick our audiences: Spanish-language radio for the Mexican Americans, R&B stations for the blacks, the classical station for the Jews. I wrote the spots, Salinger wrote the check. I think you could buy a minute on these stations for under a hundred bucks back then. Bobby got off the plane, stood on the baggage carousel, and spoke to a very diverse crowd of about 500 people. It looked great on the news. Salinger gave me an almost imperceptible nod. "Frank's kid," is how Salinger referred to me. As in "Frank's kid did some commercials."

Years later, when we were both at ABC, I interviewed Salinger about November 22, 1963. He said:

"The next morning the phone rang, woke me up, and the voice on the other end said, 'Mr. Salinger, the president would like to speak with you.' And I thought to myself, thank God, it was all a nightmare." There was a pause, a very pregnant pause, before Salinger continued. "And Lyndon Johnson got on the phone."

The crowd at the airport was loud and happy. So was Bobby. And that was just the beginning. I have met every one of the Beatles, I covered rock and roll for half a dozen years and was backstage with the Stones and Springsteen and Madonna and Kiss. I've interviewed just about every Oscar winner, covered every Oscar night since 1978, but I have never seen crowds react to anyone the way crowds cheered for Bobby.

There's a great Gay Talese line from his *Esquire* piece on Joe DiMaggio, "I Saw the Figure Five in Gold," that every writer of my generation knows. One day at the regular Wednesday lunch I have with my friends, somebody started the quote and we all finished it, in unison, a capella. Marilyn Monroe comes back from entertaining the troops in Korea and tells her husband, "Joe, you never heard cheering like that."

And Joe DiMaggio says, "Yes, I have."

I'm not sure even the great DiMag heard cheering like I heard in Watts and East LA for Bobby Kennedy. Maybe, *maybe* Muhammad Ali has. Maybe.

And it worried the campaign. Every time he went out, his people feared for his life, that he'd literally be loved to death. The closest I came to Bobby was after his motorcade down First Street in East LA. He walked off the bus and passed about a foot in front of me. He was sweating all over, his shirt was torn, they'd grabbed at his arms, shaken his hands, ripped his cuffs and stolen his cufflinks. One of his campaign staff was a designated cufflink guy who'd make sure Bobby got a fresh pair at every stop.

I spent election day at Bobby's headquarters on Wilshire Boulevard. There's a picture of me in front of the headquarters that was taken for *Life* magazine that never saw ink; it was scheduled to run the week that Martin Luther King was assassinated. That was some year, 1968. The headquarters, last time I drove by, were still boarded up, ten years after they'd been burned down in the post–Rodney King riot that I don't think would have happened had Martin Luther King and Bobby Kennedy not been killed.

About ten in the morning, a couple of the campaign guys I recognized walked into the back room I'd commandeered as an office. Among my other duties was procuring marijuana for members of the national staff, which put me on the "people to be trusted" list when a couple of staffers walked into the room with a local black politician whose name I swear I can't remember but I know I could still pick out in a lineup. After assuring him that I was OK, the Kennedy guy pulled a wad of $50 bills out of his pocket — I mean a wad that must have been three inches thick — and started snapping 'em off. I pretended not to notice anything out of the ordinary and, though I'd never been an eyewitness, I knew enough to know that this wasn't out of the ordinary, not on election day. "Walking around money," we called it during the campaign. That guy's walking around money was about two inches of $50 bills.

I'd also known about Bobby and Marilyn Monroe. A high school friend, Chuck Pick, got a college job parking cars at Hollywood parties. Chuck is one of those guys who has never been unhappy. Perhaps because he was the guy who figured out how to handle parking at Hollywood stars' parties: a college kid opens your door, hands you a receipt, parks the car for you on a Beverly

Hills or Bel Air or Brentwood street a block or two away and runs back to the star's house to pick up another car. It's kind of a relay with Mercedes and Beemers instead of batons. Chuck turned this into a million-dollar business, Chuck's Parking. One day I had a lunch meeting with Jesse Unruh, who was, by title, the speaker of the state assembly and, by job description, the Democratic party boss of California. The car pulled up at the restaurant parking lot, and there was Chuck.

"Mr. Speaker, good afternoon," he said as he helped Unruh out of the back seat. Followed immediately by, "Siegel, what the fuck are you doing here?"

It was Chuck who told us about Bobby and Marilyn Monroe. He was parking cars at Peter Lawford's beach house and caught the two of them *in flagrante* in the back seat of somebody's Bentley. In 1963, especially among male college sophomores, this was not a political liability.

Bobby's California primary election night party was at the ballroom of the old Ambassador Hotel on Wilshire, halfway to downtown and across the street from the original Brown Derby, a Hollywood classic where the Cobb salad was invented (by the owner, a guy who, in a remarkable coincidence, was named Cobb. The Brown Derby itself is a prime example of what I call LA's onomatopoeic architecture — it was built to look like a huge hat). That night started as a celebration.

Bobby's competition for the Democratic nomination came from Gene McCarthy, another antiwar Democrat. McCarthy had been the stalking horse; he didn't have much support in the minority communities and, more professor than performer, certainly lacked Bobby's charisma. Bobby drubbed him, won the California primary, and early that night looked like a sure thing to make history: replace an incumbent president on his party's ticket, something that had never been done before.

I remember the excitement. It was baseball season, and I remember Milton Berle getting up on-stage and announcing that Don Drysdale had just set a record for scoreless innings pitched. And I remember Bobby being subdued in his acceptance. I wasn't sure if it was good politics — not wanting to rub things into Gene McCarthy's face because he needed the McCarthy delegates — or if it was genuine humility at realizing he, yes, was allowing himself to think that he would be president of the United States. I had a camera with me and took a few pictures of Bobby at the podium. My Congressman, Tom Rees, was standing near him, and so was Paul Schrader of the United Auto Workers; I remember their names because they were both wounded when Bobby was killed.

I heard the shots. I was standing outside one of the entrances to the kitchen, and I heard this popping sound. Three, four pops. And they sounded like pops. My first thought wasn't "Bobby's been shot!" It was "The press has gotten so far out of hand that Rosey Grier — the all-pro football player who was one of Bobby's bodyguards — picked up one of the photographers, held him upside-down and shook him." I thought the sound we heard was flashbulbs popping. The year before, I'd been in the army and had heard more than my share of gunshots, and a .22 pistol sounds more like a toy than a gun.

When we found out it was a gun and that Bobby had been shot, I was standing next to the wife of Tony Beilenson — a Senate candidate I'd worked for. I'd written a position paper urging him to take a stand against forced integration through busing: the white middle class will leave the public school system, I predicted, and despite the intention to integrate, the reality would be to segregate. I'd be proven right, but he fired me anyway.

His wife was pale, shaking, crying. "Don't worry," I told her. "He won't die. Doctors can do anything. It's 1968."

Thirty years later, in 1998, I went back to the Ambassador, stood outside a locked gate in front of the abandoned hotel, and tried to recreate what I'd seen. I interviewed George Plimpton in New York, who'd been standing next to Bobby when he was shot. And in LA I interviewed Rosey Grier. They told the same story. Plimpton had grabbed Sirhan Sirhan. Grier heard the shots and ran, broken-field, through the crowd. He vaulted over a body he found out later was Bobby. He saw Plimpton holding his forefinger into the barrel of Sirhan Sirhan's pistol. Yes, he told me, he was aware he was risking his life to save Bobby's. Then Grier lifted Sirhan Sirhan off the ground, Plimpton's finger still in the pistol's barrel. Somehow Plimpton ended up with the gun. He still has no idea how.

Thirty years later, they still cried when they talked about it. So did I.

If Bobby hadn't been killed he would've been president. Hubert Humphrey almost beat Nixon. The war in Vietnam would have ended long before Nixon and Kissinger's endgame, which ended up costing a few hundred thousand lives, ours and theirs, that there was no reason to have lost. If you add Cambodia, and you probably should, because American policy created the instability that made Pol Pot possible, Sirhan Sirhan's bullet may have cost the world a few million lives.

At home we've done well, America, we've come to an amazing place: civil rights, women's rights, gay rights, amazing changes since 1968. But if Bobby hadn't been murdered, I think we would have been where we are today ten years ago.

11

Damn Critics, What Do They Know Anyway?

Dear Dylan,
Sometimes in real life, just like in baseball, it's the bottom of the ninth, it's your turn up at bat, your team's behind, and you make an out. Nothing dramatic, not even a great out. A slow grounder to second, a can of corn to right.

For a while I held the record: most money ever lost by a Broadway musical. It cost the cast, the stagehands, the orchestra, and the understudies their jobs; and it cost the dozen nice ladies at the Martin Beck who'd hand out Playbills and show you to your seat their jobs, too, not to mention the guys who printed the Playbills. A couple of hundred jobs that wouldn't have been lost if I'd been able to do mine a little better.

Two years after we closed, I woke up in the middle of the night, sat bolt upright and almost called my collaborator Marty Charnin. I'd figured out the opening. Just a little bit late.

But I worked as hard as I could, I did my best, I followed my passion and almost saw it through. Today I have only one regret, and I've been carrying it with me for twenty years.

Sometimes an idea can be too good.

I had this idea for a Broadway musical, a story I'd carried with me almost my whole life. I knew Marty Charnin, who'd just had *Annie* on Broadway.

"I've got an idea for a musical," I told him.

The entire pitch ran two words.

"Jackie Robinson," I said.

"Great," he said. "Let's do it."

I was a kid when I saw *The Jackie Robinson Story*. In that movie Jackie played himself and Ruby Dee played Rachel; them, I took for granted. To me, an LA kid in those pioneering days of live TV, the real star was a guy named Dick Lane, who played one of Jackie's managers and whom I recognized from Channel 5, where in the very early 1950s he kicked tires and banged fenders and shouted, "Whoah, Nellie!" when he called the wrestling matches. I saw the film on one of those *A double-feature, a Rocket-Man serial, and Ten Cartoons for a quarter, Park Your Kids at the Movies All Day* matinees at the Meralta on City Terrace Drive, where I first fell in love with the movies. And, to me at seven, the movie wasn't a story about not letting someone play baseball because of his race; I don't think I knew anything about race. It was a story about not letting a kid play baseball. Period. And that was something I could identify with, because I knew what it felt like when the other kids didn't let you play. I stunk. I was fat, I was slow, I couldn't catch a pop fly. I was almost always the last kid chosen; if there was an odd number of kids, I didn't get to play at all.

One day over Wednesday lunch with my friends, we were resurrecting our childhood dreams, and I confessed to having dreamed that I'd played right field for the Yankees.

Greenfield pointed out, "In your dreams, you play *center* field for the Yankees."

And I said, "Not even in my dreams was I good enough to play center field for the Yankees."

We didn't have a car, we couldn't afford one, so my daddy drove us in his half-ton Chevy pickup. This was before freeways and seatbelts, and sometimes I'd get to ride in the back of the truck, a '49 Chevy, bright red, with a big, smiling, solid chrome grill.

There was an old billboard painted on the side of a building we'd drive by for a football team call the LA Bulldogs. It was the heraldry as much as anything else that hooked me on sports as a kid. Pirates. Giants. Lions and Tigers and Bears, oh my!

I knew about the LA Rams, gold *shofars* painted on their blue helmets. I even knew about the Los Angeles Dons, a team that disappeared when the Rams came west from Cleveland. But what were the LA Bulldogs?

"That was the league they made Jackie Robinson play in," my dad told me.

The Bulldogs were the LA entry in a West Coast semipro football league. Robinson, I learned later, played for Honolulu. The Honolulu Bears. He would've been All-American at UCLA, but too many sportswriters who picked the All-America teams wouldn't vote for a black ballplayer. And the NFL was whites only until 1946.

Of course I didn't know any of that then.

What I did know was there was this guy with a magic name, Quick as Jack Robinson, they wouldn't *let* play baseball, and then, my father tells me, they *made* him play football for a team I'd never heard of that didn't exist anymore. Wow, was I pissed. I was an even worse football player than I was a baseball player; I could only imagine the team they'd make *me* play on.

The Pittsburgh Pishers. The Detroit Toilets.

Well, I was seven or so.

When I found out why they really wouldn't let Jackie play, I couldn't believe it. My incredulity was one of the benefits of growing up poor in a mixed neighborhood. When they'd show westerns at the Meralta, we'd wear our cap guns and outdraw the heroes, one of whom was Herbert Jeffries, who starred in such features as *Harlem on the Range* and *The Bronze Buckaroo*, riding his horse, Dusky. The casts were all black; white folks weren't supposed to see these movies, but I didn't know that. Black cowboys were no more foreign to me than WASP cowboys named Rogers or Autry or Irish Catholic cowboys named Hopalong Cassidy.

LA was a minor league town when I was a kid. It was a big deal when the Giants

(New York Giants then) and the Indians, who did their spring training in Arizona, would barnstorm through town on their way back east.

I saw my first major leaguers at Gilmore Field, the Hollywood Stars home field, where CBS Television City is today. (I was a Dodger fan so I rooted for the Indians.) Luke Easter was the first major leaguer I saw up close. We'd snuck into box seats on the first-base line, and I almost ended up wearing Luke Easter when he leaned in for a foul ball. He was the largest human being I had ever seen, bar none.

Larry Doby was my favorite Indian. I don't know why. Maybe because I'd somehow glommed on to one of his baseball cards. Doby was fast, and he was a home-run hitter. He was also kind and quite soft-spoken, as I learned twenty years later when I interviewed him for a series of stories I did on the 1940s.

Doby was the first black in the American League. He joined the team on the Fourth of July, 1947. Jackie Robinson had joined the Dodgers, in the National League, at the start of that season, three months before.

Doby lived in New Jersey. We interviewed him in his den, which was filled with trophies. A blow-up of the '53 Topps baseball card that had made me a fan was hung on his wall.

"I joined the Indians in Chicago for a double-header," he told me.

"Lou Boudreau, the manager, walked me into the locker room, and the locker room at Comiskey (where the White Sox played) was long and narrow. The guys lined up in front of their lockers and Lou introduced me to each one. 'Joe Gordon, this is Larry Doby. Bob Feller, Larry Doby.' "

And Larry Doby, a childhood hero, a huge, muscular man not even into his fifties when we did the interview, started to cry. He caught himself. Brushed a tear away with the back of his fist. Looked at it and told me, "And half of the guys wouldn't even shake my hand."

When I mentioned I'd seen him play the Giants in LA, he remembered spring training with the Indians, going through the South, through Texas and Oklahoma.

"Bobby Avila was a Mexican," he said. "He could eat with the team. They'd let him in the restaurants. I don't have anything against him, but he wasn't even an American."

I'd read that he and Jackie Robinson had

each other's phone numbers that season. There really wasn't anybody else they could talk to. Had it been a print interview, I might have asked Doby what they said, what they talked about, if he remembered where he called from, where he had to stay. But it was television, and I could sense he didn't want to remember.

The idea haunted me. And the drama. Marty came up with the title: *The First.* I wrote the book — the libretto to be precise, becoming one of a long line of New York Jew librettists that stretches back to Lorenzo da Ponte, who'd written the libretti for Mozart's *Don Giovanni* and *Cosi Fan Tutte* and retired to New York, where he owned a grocery store after Mozart died.

Marty's office was upstairs from the Carnegie deli where Bob Fosse and Paddy Chayefsky would have breakfast and lunch. Paddy liked me and would ask me to join them.

"Careful," Fosse warned me. "All your best jokes are going to end up as lyrics."

Act 1, Scene 1, which never ended up even close to getting on stage, set up the problem from the point of view of a group of fanatical Dodger fans, a kind of Brooklyn chorus: a Jewish guy, an Irish woman in a green and white uniform who worked at Ebbinger's Bakery (which had gone out of business by 1981) and who'd generate waves of nostalgic applause when she'd mention blackout cake, a Brooklyn delicacy that had gone extinct when Ebbinger's did, and a pint-sized Italian guy who really could sing opera who'd belt out the name of an old-time Dodger outfielder, *Cookie Lavagetto*, to the opening notes of the aria from *Pagliacci*. People laughed so hard they cried.

In 1946 the Dodgers lost the pennant to St. Louis in the last game of the season. We had a guy climbing out of a sewer with a portable radio. The Dodger's first baseman, whom Robinson would replace the next year, was a kid named Howie Schultz. That's who Durocher brought in to pinch-hit.

"Schultz? Schultz? Last year in the army I was killing guys named Schultz!"

"Joe, you were a cook," his buddy nudged him. "You were killing our guys named Schultz!"

I liked that joke. It didn't get used as a lyric. It also never got performed on a stage. We never could figure out how to let the audience know that 1947 would bust baseball wide open when Jackie Robinson joined the Dodgers. How do you have characters let the audience in on things they couldn't possibly know about because they haven't happened yet?

Another joke: "You know that sign in right field? The Dodgers all use Lifebuoy soap? Well, they still stink!" That made one of Marty's lyrics. Rhymed it with . . . kitchen sink.

Something else we could never figure out, one of the real dramaturgical problems that plagued us from the first pitch: how to mix the hard reality and immense heroism of Jackie and Rachel Robinson with what they really do call on Broadway the "happy native" numbers. In this case the happy natives were the Brooklyn fans and Jackie's Negro League teammates, Bingo Long and the traveling Bowery Boys.

The toughest problem wasn't even finding a solution. We were writing, rehearsing, arranging the music, learning the songs, fitting the costumes, and directing the performances all at the same time. That's the way it is with a musical. That's why Larry Gelbart, who wrote *A Funny Thing Happened on the Way to the Forum*, once said, "If Hitler is alive, I hope he's out of town with a musical." The problem isn't solving the problems. You are so overwhelmed, the problem is recognizing what the real problems are. Which I didn't do until years after the show had closed.

We had another problem, too. We needed an audience that brought something to the theater. People who knew the history; people who knew baseball. Frank Rich, the influential *New York Times* critic, who'd grown up in Washington — first in war, first in peace, and last in the American League — didn't know from either one. Our first act curtain was Jackie signing his contract with the Brooklyn Dodgers. There was underscoring. There was a song. Half the audience was in tears. I'd distilled the dialogue from Jackie Robinson's autobiography and a first-person piece Branch Rickey had written for the old *Look* — primary sources, we called them in the UCLA history department — and two secondary sources: as-told-to bios of Clyde Sukeforth, the coach who scouted Robinson and escorted him to Brooklyn, and one of Rickey's assistants, Fresco Thompson, who was there then too.

In Frank's review, the sarcasm bled through the newsprint. "Never has so much been invested in the simple act of signing a piece of paper."

The *Times*'s second-string critic, Mel Gussow, was a Brooklyn guy who reviewed the play on their radio station, WQXR. He said almost exactly the same words. "Never have I cried so much at the simple act of signing a piece of paper." Or something close. If Frank Rich had been murdered walking out of the theater that night, Gussow would have reviewed it in print and we'd still be running. And the *Daily News* would've headlined:

Frank Rich Murdered!
NYPD Arrests 7,000 Suspects!

The *Times* brought Walter Kerr, the great critic of the old *Herald Tribune*, out of retirement to do reviews for the Sunday paper. Kerr loved the show and wrote me a rave — words like "A book so strong this is one of the rare musicals that doesn't need music to hit its emotional highs." Kerr's review ran the day the show closed.

Working with Marty was a thrill. First of all, I liked him. And I could not believe how much stuff he knew. He'd directed Jack Lemmon, and written two musicals with Richard Rodgers. His first job on Broadway was as one of the Jets in the original cast of *West Side Story*. He's the one who answered, "Gee, Officer Krupke," with a loud, gesture-enhanced, "KRUP YOU!"

He was wonderful during auditions, always courteous, never curt. When one young woman tried to sing "I Wish I Were In Love Again," Marty laughed.

"That was my audition song," he said. Her face fell.

"Because," he barely whispered, "it has a range of five notes."

Elston Howard's daughter auditioned for us. Howard had been the first black to play for the Yankees — much to Casey Stengel's consternation. Not because of his race: "I finally get one," Stengel said, "and he can't run."

This is a close cousin to one of my favorite sound bites. Johnny Roseboro played catcher for the LA Dodgers. He replaced Roy Campanella. I did a half hour called "The Duke of Flatbush and Other Bums," when they retired Duke Snider's number. Roseboro told me, "I can't say it any other way. He's the fastest white guy I ever saw play center field."

Roy Campanella's son, Roy Jr., is a friend. Roy Sr., the Brooklyn Dodgers Hall of Fame catcher, was paralyzed from the waist down in a traffic accident that happened the winter before the Dodgers moved to LA. He never played in Los Angeles. He was celebrated with a Roy

Campanella Night at the LA Coliseum, the biggest crowd ever to watch a major league baseball game, and I was in it. People smoked then and, as part of the tribute, 70,000 people all lit matches and held them high as Roy was wheeled in from center field to the pitcher's mound, where the ceremony took place.

Roy Jr. told me the Dodgers had put the family up at the Sheraton Town House on Wilshire Boulevard, and they wouldn't let him use the pool. 1958. Los Angeles. Roy Campanella's son, and they wouldn't let him use the pool.

"We heard the cheers and saw the lights and I was crying, my father was crying, and all I wanted to do was grab the microphone and say, " 'Why won't you let me swim in your fucking pool!' "

Looking back, these things are just impossible to believe. They were even impossible to believe looking back from 1981. And that hurt our show, too.

A few years after *The First*, which opened in 1981 and closed in 1982 — but, let's be fair, it opened in November and closed in January — somebody did a poll and discovered that most major league ballplayers, yes, including black players, did not know Jackie Robinson had broken the color line.

A few years ago *USA Today* did a poll that showed most high school students thought Martin Luther King was a contemporary of Abe Lincoln.

The first time I heard an actor read a line I had written in a different voice than the one I'd heard when I wrote it was like I'd given birth. What an incredible feeling.

The day you hire the cast is a big day for a Broadway show. You find a theater, meet on stage, the cast members meet each other, many for the first time, and the principals sing a song. David Alan Grier played Jackie, his first acting job out of Yale Drama, and he was great. Lonette McKee, almost as beautiful as the real Rachel, played Jackie's wife. Her song that morning was Billie Holiday's "God Bless The Child."

Late the night before, I had a call from my sister in Los Angeles. My father had died during the night. I booked a flight right after the party. I didn't tell anyone in the cast; I didn't want to ruin their celebration. I still can't listen to that song.

And I had another problem. Not long into the writing, Jane's brain tumor was diagnosed. She had the surgery, had the radiation, and went back to work, and so did I. We were in rehearsal when the tumor came back. Most of what happened next is still a blur.

I remember a few of my big laughs.

The Dodgers had an outfielder named Pete Reiser — a Hall of Famer for sure, he hit over .340 as a rookie. But "Pistol" Pete, as they called him, had this noxious habit of running head first into outfield walls. There weren't any warning tracks then. Or MRIs. And they kept playing Reiser before he'd healed, and his career was cut short. You needed to know this to get the joke. You also needed to know the *Brooklyn Eagle* was a daily newspaper in the '40s, and a pretty good one.

Two of our happy natives are expressing concern over the home team's prospects the coming spring.

HAPPY NATIVE ONE:
Did you see the paper? Reiser ran into another wall, he's out for the season.

HAPPY NATIVE TWO:
Ah, that's the *Brooklyn Eagle*'s report. What's in the *Daily News*?

HAPPY NATIVE ONE:
What's in the *Daily News*? I'll tell you what's in the *Daily News*!

Huge laughs from theaters full of New Yorkers.

In the second act Branch Rickey busts up a petition some of the Dodgers had signed, threatening to walk off the field if Robinson played.

That did happen. Kirby Higbe, Bobby Bragan, and "Dixie" Walker were the perpetrators. Leo Durocher got wind of it and, in a fury, told his team, and these are his words: "I don't care if he's black or white or striped like a fucking Zebra, if he's good enough, he's gonna play. And he's just the first, boys. There are more coming. And they're after your jobs."

He said it for real in spring training. Trey Wilson said it in character on the stage of the Martin Beck. Yes, it's a great story; no wonder I wanted to tell it.

For real, the St. Louis Cardinals were ready to walk off the field when Brooklyn came to St. Louis. Stan Musial, not only one of the greatest ballplayers in baseball history but also one of its greatest people, walked into the locker room and told his teammates, "I don't know about you, but I'm playing."

Branch Rickey really did have a meeting with Kirby Higbe, one of the league's hardest-throwing pitchers, and gave him a chance to change his mind. Higbe couldn't, and Rickey traded him to Pittsburgh.

In *The First* I had Rickey lecture him in the formal, nineteenth-century, celluloid-collar English the real Branch Rickey affected.

"I would love to send you to a far-off corner of the Earth. To a place where summer is a blazing inferno and the air itself is unfit to breathe. Unfortunately we don't play major league baseball in Los Angeles."

I not only got laughs, I got applause. I would stand in the wings, in the dark, watching faces watch my play, knowing that in ten seconds, nine, eight, seven, the faces would explode in laughter. Three, two, one, WE DON'T PLAY MAJOR LEAGUE BALL IN LOS ANGELES!

Mass hysteria! People laughed. Whooped and screamed. Punched each other.

There is nothing quite like it. Nothing.

During our first preview you could feel the electricity. It worked. Almost all of it worked. We got a standing ovation. Marty called the cast together.

"We were GR," he said. "That's half of great!"

We then started working twenty-four

hours a day, fixing what wasn't broken.

One morning I woke up itching, stared into the mirror at these blotches all over my face. Hives! I remembered my college abnormal psych course. I was so nervous, so stressed out, so nuts I got hives! As soon as I made the connection, the hives went away.

After the show was frozen, no more changes, no new songs, the only direction Marty would add would be the curtain call, which the cast would take as if they were posed for a team picture, two happy natives up front revealing two signs that read 19 and 47. Jerry Imber and I sat and watched a full performance, start to finish, from the aisle seats in the orchestra we'd give to Frank Rich.

It was *jamais vu*. Three-quarters of the way through the first act, I turned to Imber. "This is pretty good." It was. Imber thought it was even better than that. But he'd grown up in Brooklyn and had gone to games with his dad. If you hadn't gone to Ebbets Field with your dad when you were a kid, it was just pretty good, and pretty good wasn't good enough.

My mom came in for the opening. Jane was beautiful in a gown that was all gauze and gossamer. I wore studs in Dodger blue lapis lazuli that Jane had had made for me on Forty-seventh Street. I still have 'em. This was the night I made the deal with God that God refused.

There was a big opening night party. I missed it. The reviews had come in, all the TV reviews were positive, Clive Barnes in the *Post* was mixed, but Frank wanted the show to close. Marty said I should go with him to the ad agency and help work out some kind of strategy.

I went with him to the ad agency, but there wasn't any strategy to stop the inevitable. We stayed open until the money ran out, about a month. I should have stayed with Jane. She gave me this look that asked: What are you doing? I don't have long. Stay with me.

I could have rewritten the open, given the scenes between Jackie and Rachel more of an edge, made the Kansas City Monarchs more regal and less comic, and I probably should have. But twenty years later, I'm still the only Broadway critic ever nominated for a Tony. And, twenty years later, my real regret is, I should have stayed with Jane.

12

My Wife, Jane

Dear Dylan,

I know you know about Jane, but I don't know how you know. I guess you heard me and Ena talking about her, heard me call her "My wife, Jane," and it confused you. When you were barely three years old, you asked Ena, "Mommy, did you used to be Jane?"

I remember the first time I saw her. I remember our first date. I remember what I was wearing, a white shirt spotted with inch-big red strawberries; the '60s were barely over, and she, I thought, was a bit of a hippie, and I figured the shirt might help. I remember she was wearing an army fatigue jacket and fatigue pants.

We met on the corner of Forty-ninth and Sixth; maybe we were going to the Radio City Music Hall, that I don't remember.

But I do remember she was an hour late. Her cat, Nimbus, had dived out of her window on Eighty-eighth Street. The cat was fine, but it took an hour to find him. And, I remember, I waited.

She was a vegetarian, she loved life, she'd bring bowls of water to the seeing-eye dogs of blind beggars on Fifth Avenue.

Eight years later, Jerry Imber would eulogize Jane, "If she were on the Supreme Court, she'd find for the cat."

We met in 1974. Married in 1976. She died in 1982.

The first time we made love, she got pregnant. She'd been living with someone when we met, and I asked, "Is it mine?" And she vowed never to speak to me again. She eventually changed her mind. I think my begging and crying had something to do with it. I had fallen in love.

It was either a false pregnancy, or it didn't take. Five years later, she decided she wanted to get pregnant. Her gynecologist called me. "Don't tell her, but you can't let her get pregnant. When a woman gets pregnant, hormones cause everything to grow at an accelerated pace, including cancer cells."

Six months before, Jane had been diagnosed with a brain tumor, a grade 3 glioma, growing in her left frontal lobe. She'd had headaches, some pretty debilitating, but she was a film editor at CBS, cutting, matching, viewing the same handful of frames flickering over and over on a Movieola — a loud, clumsy, flickering piece of machinery that videotape would make obsolete. We figured the work caused the headaches.

One very hot summer day, someone found me in an ABC edit room.

"Someone from CBS just called. Does your wife have a history of seizures? She just had one. They're taking her to Roosevelt Hospital."

I don't panic, I'm too much of a control freak. And covering live news events does teach one to prioritize.

I called our friend, Imber, who said he'd be right there. I knew Jane was working with Judy Reemtsma, a *60 Minutes* producer and a good friend, and I knew Judy had epilepsy and was a doctor's wife and would know exactly what to do, so I didn't have to worry about things like Jane choking on her own saliva or swallowing her tongue. And then I ran to the hospital. CBS was at Fifty-seventh and Eleventh. Roosevelt is at Fifty-ninth and Amsterdam (Tenth Avenue), and ABC is at Sixty-sixth and Columbus (Ninth Avenue). I got there before the ambulance.

I had seen, mostly by accident, way more than my share of shivering people wrapped in plastic, gurneyed into emergency rooms, wounded people studying their bleeding as if they're having an out-of-body experience while they wait for the ambulance, even one DOA on the Lower East Side so fresh his car keys were still swaying in the ignition. So Jane wasn't the first person I'd seen lifted out of the back of an ambulance, her eyes showing only whites, her tongue sticking out the right side of her mouth. But she was the first person I knew I'd seen like that. And the first person I loved.

It's the difference between watching a war movie and being in a war.

They were wheeling her into the emergency room entrance when Imber showed up. I don't know how he got there. He identified himself as a doctor and followed her into the hospital.

"I'll come out in a few minutes and let you know what's going on," he told me. This was one of those times when I lost all concept of time; it happened once when I was hit by a car and, it seemed to me, I did an Olympic-qualifying side-horse routine across three lanes of Wilshire Boulevard traffic. It happened again watching Dylan, at two, fall down a flight of stairs. I have no idea how long I waited before Imber came out, forcing a smile, and told me "She'll be fine. They don't know what caused it, but she's fine."

"I want to go see her," I said. They knew me at Roosevelt, the doctors, the nurses, the administrators. At that time I'd been on TV five days a week, five to ten times a week, for six years, and *Eyewitness News*'s demographics skewed so low that not only did the doctors know me but so did the drunks who were waiting in the emergency room with their stained paper bags and the teenage mothers who were waiting with their crying infants. Whatever the protocol was for letting family members into emergency rooms, I knew they'd break it for me. But Imber stopped me.

"You don't want to see her this way, she's just had a seizure. Wait a little bit."

That's what he said. What he meant was "you don't want to remember her this way," and I'm still grateful. Covered in fluids, tubes everywhere, pasty pale, unconscious. He was right. If I had seen her, that would have become the image I'd bring up every time I thought of her.

They kept Jane in the hospital that night, and the next day drove her up to St. Luke's, fifty blocks north, where the two hospitals shared their CAT scan, a new machine in 1978. The next day a resident who couldn't have been more than five-foot-four and didn't look more than sixteen pointed to a gray circle on a milky, thick X-ray.

"Tumor," I heard. "Surgery."

"Brain surgery." Just the words scare the hell out of you. "Open heart surgery?" Piece of cake. "Lung resection?" Hell, I've gone on to have two. But brain surgery plays back images of Boris Karloff or, even scarier, Mel Brooks, Gene Wilder, and Peter Boyle. I told Jane if things didn't go well I could always teach her to sing "Puttin' on the Ritz."

I'm not sure when, but it was around this time Ed Bradley did a classic *60 Minutes* piece with George Burns. He took Burns to the cemetery where Burns's wife and partner, Gracie Allen, is buried. Burns told him he comes here fairly often, maybe once or twice a week, to talk to Gracie.

Bradley, very hesitatingly, obviously fearing the answer might take him to a place he did not want to go, asked, "Does she talk to you?"

Burns answered, "No. I miss her. I'm not crazy."

Burns also told Bradley that when Gracie took a turn for the worse and didn't have long to live, he bought her a new fur coat.

"I must be getting well," Gracie told her friends. "George bought me a new mink."

When Jane went in for her second operation she told me, "Don't buy me a fur coat. I saw the story."

I didn't. I remembered a Broadway opening where she kvelled, "That's the most beautiful Missoni shawl I have ever seen." Then, when the woman turned to face us, Jane said, "No wonder, that's Mrs. Missoni."

I bought Jane a Missoni sweater set. She'd wear it twice.

The truth is, there are reasons brain surgery is so frightening. Actually, *were* reasons. Even with X-rays, which don't do a very good job of photographing tissue, brain surgeons had almost no idea what they were going to find when they opened up your head. It's a lot better now: CAT scans and MRIs provide road maps, so there are fewer surprises, and it's not nearly as dangerous as we believe. No, it's not rocket science. But, then again, it is brain surgery.

One of the things Jane and I did was plunge ourselves into the ritual of learning about the disease, checking out possible therapies, finding the best surgeon. Immersing oneself in the disease has the odd effect of distancing oneself from the terror of confronting the disease. That is how, I would soon learn against my will, the rituals religions have developed to deal with the death of a loved one somehow distance us from the tragedy of their deaths and the inevitability of our own.

Some of the best advice we got: Never let the chairman of the department get near you with a knife. I'm sure there are exceptions, but this passed the common sense test: surgeons become surgeons because they love to cut. But brain surgery isn't a game of inches, it's a game of millimeters; neurosurgeons go in there with microscopes, and when they lose their edge, that's when they become administrators.

Jane understood. Tom Wolfe's *The Right Stuff* was the book we were reading then, and the analogy between brain surgeons and astronauts was made more than once. "We want the guy with the right stuff," Jane decided.

We found him at New York Hospital: Dick Frasier, who was from a small town in Canada and had all the virtues of a fighter pilot and the ultimate movie-quote recommendation from more than one of his peers: "If I had it, I'd want him to operate on me."

The surgery went fine. We checked Jane into New York Hospital, where she spent the night. I was up at 6:00 a.m. to see her before she went in. Something else we learned — you want to be the first operation of the day. The doctor is at his best, and if you're not the first and there are complications with whoever is the first, you might be postponed a day or two.

I remember waiting outside the recovery room, waiting to hear from Frasier, waiting to be able to see Jane. "That's Joel Siegel," I heard people say. "I wonder why he's here?"

Jane told me that while she was in the recovery room she heard nurses saying, "That's Joel Siegel waiting outside, I wonder why he's here?" She wanted to shout, "Me, me, because of me!" But her head was bandaged and she couldn't speak.

When we were told Jane needed radiation we went to Memorial Sloan Kettering to check out their clinic. I heard people say, "That's Joel Siegel, I wonder why he's here. He couldn't be here for *him*."

When a little bald-headed boy walked up and asked me for my autograph, Jane and I started to cry, and we knew we had to find someplace else.

We did. What a town New York is. We found a private clinic in a townhouse on an East Side street where Jane had her radiation.

She was tired. Her hair fell out. That's something doubly insidious about cancer; it not only threatens your life, it seems to attack your vanity. The one thing Jane liked most about herself was her hair. Brown, almost black, she kept it long and wavy. When it fell out, one thing I was able to do was use my show business resources to find the best wig maker in New York. His name was Patrick Moreton. He'd done Liz Taylor on Broadway, and he did the Metropolitan Opera. He made two wigs for Jane, and on her weekly visits to him, which eventually became his weekly visits to her, he would set them and comb them and catch her up on the Broadway gossip.

One night, at a Broadway opening — I know it's a line out of *The Sunshine Boys*, but I can't remember if it was the Morosco or the Belasco — Jane came back after intermission and very proudly announced, "Gilda Radner knows who I am."

"What do you mean?" I asked.

"Well, we were waiting in line for the ladies' room and started to talk. I introduced myself and she said, 'Oh, everybody knows Joel Siegel's wife always wears a headband.'"

Jane told her why. As fine as Patrick Moreton's wigs were, Jane didn't feel comfortable unless she wore a headband to hide the wig line.

(Jane and Gilda became friendly and would seek each other out on line at the ladies' rooms at Broadway openings. When Gilda died, I wrote Gene Wilder a long letter, survivor to survivor, spouse to spouse, and we sought each other out. When someone you love has cancer, I've learned from both sides now, no matter how much you love them, there are doors you can't open for them, rooms you can't enter with them. I'd promised Jane I would find a place where she could be with other people who had cancer, just to be with them and share. I called everyone. That place, then, didn't exist. A few years later, when she got cancer, Gilda had found that kind of place in California. Gene, I learned, had promised he'd find Gilda that kind of place in New York. Together we sent for Gilda's California therapist, Joanna Bull. Today there are Gilda's Clubs in fifteen cities. We've had 40,000 members. There's a tough initiation requirement: you have to have cancer. I became a member when my cancer was diagnosed. There is an oil painting of Jane in one of the meeting rooms in the first Gilda's Club, on Houston Street in New York City.)

Jane recuperated, Jane recovered, she went back to work, she'd win an Emmy for a documentary she cut after she'd had surgery, and I went into denial. Jane didn't, which I learned after she died when I found this in one of her sketchbooks:

Once upon a time there was a boy named Joel and he loved a girl named Jane and they were living happily ever after until this tumor got in the way and all at once things were very different. Joel and Jane were just little people and death didn't belong yet. You can understand their confusion. Jane knew they'd have no after; Joel thought they could still play happy. Every fairy tale will show you that "happilyeverafter" is one gigantic word, but since there's no prince who can battle tumors

She didn't even end it with a period.

At least she knew I loved her.

One of the few things the doctors were right about was when they told us the tumor would probably reoccur in two and a half years. It did. Through it all, Jane was kind and gentle; even her fits of anger about what had happened to her were small in scale, as if she'd bought shoes the wrong size on sale and couldn't return them, or the pasta had accidentally cooked too long.

One day, in Connecticut, a huge, loopy black-and-white dog, a puppy who hadn't grown into his paws yet, showed up. He had no collar. We decided to keep him. Jane named him "Sheridan Woofside, the dog who came to dinner." We took him home and tried to housebreak him. When Jane would come home from radiation Sheridan would be so happy to see her he'd jump up on her, and because he was more than five feet tall on his hind legs and she was so weak, he'd knock her over. We had to give him up. (We found him a home on a farm with a ten-year-old boy as a buddy.) That hurt Jane.

One night she hugged me and, in one of the few times she let me know how frightened she was, said, "Joel, don't let me die."

I promised I wouldn't, but I couldn't

keep the promise. The best I could do was make her want to live.

We went to Italy — our second trip. It was September, and no matter how I manipulated the days we stayed in Rome and Venice and Orvieto and Lake Como, we were going to end up in Florence on Yom Kippur.

"If you think I'm going to fast in Florence," she told me, "you're crazy."

"OK," I told her. "But you'll be seeing God long before I will."

We laughed so hard we cried.

And the tumor came back. For some reason it came as a surprise that she could have more surgery. A reprieve, we thought. Dr. Frasier, angry, told us, "If I have to I'll put a zipper in there so we can keep taking it out."

Jane wrote a note, in grease pencil, on the back of an envelope, in case she went into surgery before I got to the hospital that morning. I still have it, framed, pressed in Plexiglas.

Dear Joel —
I love you, more than anything in the world and my life, I love you.
Thank you for so much happiness and understanding.
All my love forever

Jane

One morning on *GMA*, it must've been after a story about a fire and someone running into their house to save something valuable, Charlie and Joan and I were talking about what we would save. I don't remember what I said, but whatever it was, I lied. The truth then, before Ena and Dylan, was that this note from Jane was the most valuable thing I had.

This time the surgery didn't work.

There was one unforeseen positive side effect. The left frontal lobe controls socialization, and when the tumor did come back, when things got bad, Jane had no idea how bad things were. She didn't know what she couldn't remember, or how hard it was for her to speak. When she would miss a word, I tried to turn it into a game, acting words out like charades.

She would stand in the kitchen, facing the shelves where we kept our bread and coffee and produce. "Are you hungry?" I would ask.

It wasn't until after she died that I understood that no, she wasn't hungry. Those shelves were also where we kept her medicine. She wanted more medicine because she knew it wasn't working and she wanted to be well.

One day I caught her about to stir a pot

of boiling soup with her finger instead of a spoon. She had no idea.

But she did have insights. One morning when I was changing the sheets she asked why, and I told her she'd wet the bed. Her mood changed completely and, very thoughtfully, she said, "Oh, my God, I do that, too." We had talked about going to Paris, she had never seen Paris, and when we mentioned it to Dr. Frasier, he thought for a second and said, to me, "Too much travail," finding a word Jane would no longer be able to understand.

A few visits later, he asked Jane to count to ten. She got to three.

A few months after her second surgery, we were walking into our apartment, there was snow on the ground, she looked at me with the old Jane's eyes and asked, "Joel, am I getting better?"

I told her she was. I thought she was. She knew she wasn't. Another CAT scan showed the worst.

A stray cell, all it takes is one, had formed a *glioblastoma*. The word is almost onomatopoeic. A glioblastoma is a type of tumor that, literally, explodes in your head.

She'd had a scan before her last surgery, and the tumor wasn't there. In two months it had grown to the size of an apricot. Dr.

Frasier gave me a stack of articles from *Lancet* and the *New England Journal of Medicine* on the futility of operating on glioblastomas. I never read them.

Because of the location of the new tumor, I was told, she would eventually become paralyzed on her right side. I assumed it would take months. It took days.

Her family came to visit, to say goodbye. Her older sister and her older brother came, and his three-year-old daughter shouted, "Auntie Jane!" and ran into her lap like nothing was wrong.

The next morning Jane asked, "Where are you going?"

"You always said I should see a shrink. I have an appointment." Her name is Olga Silverstein and, on and off, I've seen her ever since.

I should have started seeing her earlier — I would have been more attuned to things I needed to take with me from those last months.

Jane had started seeing a psychiatrist too. He was a perfect fit for her; he had suffered a severe stroke, and he knew he was terminal. She really looked forward to their time together. He died before Jane did, and that took an awful lot out of her will to go on. I didn't take her to his fu-

:ral, she went alone. I have no idea why I ᵤᵢdn't take her, what I thought was more important. He gave Jane a copy of an article he'd written, "Death Where Is Thy Sting," about living with dying. I still have it, and every time I run across it, I regret not taking Jane to his funeral. Olga would have told me to go with her. It would have been an hour or two more we would have been together. If you're living with someone who is dying, it's not the things you do that cause pain, but the things you don't do. Her dying happened so quickly, it seemed logarithmic, the way the fast forward speeds up on a CD.

The day after her family came, she started to have seizures, and the day nurse I'd hired a few days before, who'd attended Gene Shalit's wife when she was dying of cervical cancer, told me Jane should go into the hospital. It was January, it was cold, and the EMS people carried her to the ambulance on a stretcher through two-foot-high dirty New York slush. Dr. Frasier told me they would load her up with steroids that night. I didn't understand until I saw her the next morning that the steroids had shrunk the tumor — not enough for her to speak, but at least enough for her to regain consciousness. Her mother, Belle, was with me, and I asked Belle if we could be alone.

"Jane," I said. "If you can hear me, blink your eyes twice." She did. Hard, so there would be no mistake.

I told her Dr. Frasier had said that dying was just like going to sleep. I told her that she wouldn't have to fight anymore. I told her that one day I would see her again. But I can't remember if I told her I loved her. How could I forget that? And if I did, did I tell her how much I loved her?

That night at 1:30 in the morning, the hospital called. Jane had died.

We Jews bury our dead in a hurry. The Swedes and the Irish and people from colder climes can have weeklong wakes, but it's hot where we come from, and we've got to get 'em in the ground.

The funeral home asked if I wanted to hire a *shomer*. The word means "watcher." A shomer is an observant Jew who watches the body, praying all night, to keep the soul from escaping. At least that's the reason I heard in the house I grew up in, though to keep the body from being stolen and held for ransom is probably better history. My immediate reaction was, "Absolutely not!"

The funeral director, very young as I remember, explained to me that these were poor, elderly, religious people — who else would do something like this? — and hiring them gave them honest work and meant that they didn't have to accept charity. A lot of the rituals around death are like that; they have other social functions. It's Darwinian. These are some of civilization's oldest rituals and there have to be reasons for those that are still around.

I don't remember much of the funeral. Jane was buried in Pittsburgh, where she grew up, and I don't remember the burial at all. It is when the rituals end that the real sorrow begins. The dangerous time is not when your spouse is dying but a few weeks, a month, a few months later, when you wake up feeling fine and turn around to an empty bed and you, finally, understand it will be empty forever.

A friend's husband died shortly after Jane did, and we helped each other, as best we could. In one phone call, she told me she was very worried about her fourteen-year-old son.

"He used to get A's in English, now he's getting D's. He can't write a book report."

I realized why. I hadn't been able to read a novel since Jane died. My hold on my own life was so tenuous I was afraid to let go enough to let my imagination float into someone else's.

Ninety percent of all pop songs are about losing someone. I couldn't listen. To Gershwin, to Porter, to rock and roll. You never know when Jonathon Schwartz is going to play *She Was Too Good to Me*, or *I Thought About You*, or *Help Me, Rhonda*, or, God, even *These Are a Few of My Favorite Things*.

I needed music so I started listening to opera. In languages I couldn't understand.

I think about Jane every day. She wore a pewter necklace, in an animal shape she called an "arrow bird." Five years after she died, I was in the Tucson airport thumbing through a book on the Southwest and found a picture of one similar to hers; this one was a bear fetish, worn to ward off illness. I said her name and turned to my right to show it to her.

She'd worn out the knees on the fatigue pants she'd worn on our first date, she knew how good she looked in them. She was trying to impress me, too. One day I noticed they were newly and perfectly patched.

Three years after she died I unpacked my own fatigue pants. I'd gotten them the hard way, government issue. They'd been cut off at the knees. Both knees. She'd patched hers with mine and didn't tell me. I'm sure it happened before she got sick, it was meant to be a joke. One day I'd find them, carry them into the living room, give her an accusing stare, unfold the pants and we'd laugh.

I still have the pants.

While this was going on, I was writing *The First*.

A few months ago, Olga, whom I've been seeing again since my diagnoses started turning against me, asked me what the worst thing I ever did was. I answered, "When I tried to make a deal with God."

"If you won't let me have Jane," I asked God, "at least let me have this show."

I don't know why I asked it that way and not the other way. Maybe God knows. Maybe Olga knows. But I lived a moment out of Fitzgerald's *The Diamond as Big as the Ritz*. The Earth grew quiet, I could feel a chill in the air, and God took them both.

I only have one letter from Jane. I was in Israel, working, and we were going to meet in Rome. It was the only time we were apart. If you have a life-threatening illness, write a letter, write some notes, and put them where your spouse or partner or children will find them after you've died.

I still have some of her books. I still

check the margins for notes in her handwriting. I'll wear a tie we picked out together or the watch she gave me as a wedding gift when I'm going someplace where I think her spirit might be. And I don't believe in spirits. Not for a second. But there are times when I need to know Jane was real and that she loved me.

A Lesson for Dylan

"I feel cheated," I told Olga. It could have been a few months, it could have been ten years after Jane died. I still feel cheated today, right now.

"You were cheated," Olga told me. "You were cheated out of growing old together."

It took me a long time to understand what she meant. It took me until I felt myself growing old.

Dylan, it's something I wasn't able to do, maybe something I've never been good at, maybe something I was cheated out of, but it's something I miss: someone to grow old with. Someone you don't have to apologize to when you take your shirt off, when your hips get bigger and your hair gets thin, when you wake up in the morning with bags under your eyes too big for carry-on, United Airlines would make you check 'em at the gate.

Find someone you like, you really like, and stick with it.

I don't think I can find someone I can grow old with because I'm already old. But the luxury of hearing someone you love sigh and knowing exactly what it means and what to do is something I'll never know but it's my deepest wish for you.

Another Lesson I Learned After Jane Died

After Jane died, I know it's a wild generalization, but it was the black kids and the Latinos I worked with who had an easier time of coming up to me and giving me a hug and telling me how sorry they were. Kids from big, sprawling, poor families where you learn to share everything — even sorrow. It was the middle-class kids who were anxious, whose body language let me know how uncomfortable they were, who didn't know what to say.

Dylan, when it's hard to know what to say to someone who is ill or who just lost a loved one, say, "It's hard to know what to say, but I want you to know I'm sorry." It means an awful lot.

PART 4

Who We Are

13

We're Still Here

Dear Dylan,
One day you will ask how the Holocaust happened, and I won't have an answer. I'm not sure anyone does. One reason it's so easy for some people to deny that it even happened is that it's virtually impossible to believe something like that could happen.

But it did. To our family. And if we had been there, it would have happened to you and me.

I was watching *The Joy Luck Club*, a very good movie, and, during one scene, I started to sob so hard I almost doubled over. The occupational hazards of being a movie critic: once more an image on a screen connected with a powerful memory I didn't know I had.

The people on the screen were Chinese immigrants, living in San Francisco. A letter had come from their old country with news of the death in the family of one of the main characters. The character, American raised, didn't speak Chinese, and the aunt who read the letter lied to her and told her everyone was fine.

I remembered almost exactly the same scene from my childhood. It was in my parents' bedroom; it was just after the war; I guess I was three or four. All the women in the family were there, even Mrs. Fink, a very old woman, whose skin was as transparent as tissue paper, and just that fragile. She was my mother's great-aunt; her high-pitched voice and soft Yiddish accent made her one of my favorites. They were reading a letter in Yiddish from our old country, and they were crying.

"What's wrong, mommy?" I asked.

"Nothing," she told me. "This is a letter from Poland that tells us everybody in our family is OK."

The film brought it all back. My mother lied to me. This was the letter that told her that everyone had died: her grandparents, aunts, uncles, cousins.

And it was even worse than the letter explained, even worse than she could imagine.

In *Masters of Death*, Richard Rhodes writes about discovering that it was Pinsk, of all places, that the Nazis chose to be the first city in their occupied eastern territories to be officially declared *Judenrein*, free of Jews. In two murderous sweeps, the SS rounded up and massacred all the Jewish men in Pinsk, but the *Einsatzgruppen* troops, new to the task of shooting civilians at point-blank range, balked when it came to killing women and children. They couldn't do it. It would be another year before better-trained, battle-hardened, more obedient, or more inured SS troops would return to Pinsk to finish the job. Which gave my great-grandmother and great-aunts and their children and their neighbors' children a year in which they could relive their worst nightmare every single day.

But a few months later, another letter came from Germany, from an American GI. He had met my aunt, Dvaireh, and her two children, Sarah and Itzhak, in a displaced persons (DP) camp in the American zone. Their story: When Hitler and Stalin divided Poland in half in 1939, Pinsk ended up as part of Russia. Stalin, paranoid as always, arrested everyone in the Russian half of Poland who had any organizational skills — labor leaders, political organizers, school teachers, priests — and sent them all to Siberia. My great-uncle Zyskind, Dvaireh's husband, was the secretary-general of the Zionist Party. He was convicted of some trumped-up crime and sentenced to twenty years in the gulag. But when you were sent to Siberia, your family was allowed to go with you. Zyskind's did. And Joe Stalin saved their lives.

After the war, Zyskind was still in prison, but Dvaireh and her children were free to leave Siberia, and they did. They made their way to Germany and then to Israel.

Years later, against all odds, Dvaireh wrote a letter to Mrs. Khrushchev, the wife of the Soviet premier: "You have my husband, he's served his sentence, you don't need him but I do. He hasn't seen his children in twenty years, he has grandchildren he's never seen."

Very few Jews were allowed to leave the Soviet Union then, but, for some reason, the letter worked. Mrs. Khrushchev intervened, and Zyskind was allowed to emigrate to Israel.

As for the GI who wrote the letter, my uncle Muttie rounded up a couple of cartons of Lucky Strikes, which were as good as gold in postwar Germany, where cigarettes were used as currency, and sent them to him.

I remembered the detail about the cigarettes, which was fascinating to me as a little kid. They used cigarettes instead of money? And when I recalled that memory to my mother, she started to cry all over again. "And you know," she said, "the soldier who sent the letter wasn't even Jewish."

And something has happened between then and now, Dylan, in the way we see the Holocaust. Then we were *victims,* now we are *survivors,* and that is all the difference in the world.

Hitler is gone. The most powerful military force on Earth had made war against a defenseless people. As the war came to an end, given the choice of using their limited oil reserves to truck bullets to the eastern front or ship Jews to concentration camps, Hitler used the last of his resources to kill Jews. But we survived. The Warsaw ghetto held out longer against the Nazis than whole countries in Europe had. And we're still here.

14

Our Cousin, Dov

"Maybe you wonder why we never fought back," my cousin Dov asked me. I was twenty years old, a junior in college, on my first trip abroad.

Steve White and I went to Europe. We lived on $100 a month, including gas for the new MGB he'd picked up in London. We stayed in youth hostels, ate in student restaurants, followed two girls to Vienna, visited friends on a UCLA exchange program in Bordeaux, and went to Israel on a whim. I wrote my mother to alert the family. We took a boat from Patros, Greece, to Haifa. The food was inedible, the hold was so dark when they turned the lights off, it was like the gag the rangers pull at Carlsbad Caverns; you literally could not see your hand even when it was pressing against your nose less than an inch from your eyes. And there, as we marched off the gangplank, was my *Tante Dvaireh*, my mother's aunt, armed with my high school graduation picture, checking the picture against the face of every passenger until she found me.

"Yossel?" she asked. "Yossele?"

We took the Haifa-Afula bus to the family's kibbutz, Kibbutz Yifat, where Steve and I would milk cows and prune apple trees. One day I collected garbage and rued that there were no pigs to feed it to.

In America we're newcomers — I'm first generation American-born — but our family in Israel are the equivalent of pilgrims who came on the *Mayflower*. Two years after my mother and her parents and her aunt Rutke and her children came to America, her aunts who didn't have children, who were still teenagers, emigrated to Israel: Tziviah, who would remain childless, and Odel, who would one day come to America on a visit; I remember her as quiet, purposeful, and educated. Her daughter, Rina, would marry an Auschwitz survivor, and her son, Ze'ev, would become one of Israel's leading archaeologists. Ze'ev was one of the foremen on the Masada dig, and his crew discovered the bodies of the Jewish zealots who committed suicide rather than surrender to Rome. Ze'ev himself found the lots they drew to decide who would kill whom; his discoveries proved a legend and made history. Dylan, you've met his daughter, Noga.

Dvaireh had been too young to come to Israel in the 1920s. She tried to come to Israel on the *Exodus*, the real *Exodus*, with her son, Itzhak, and her daughter, Sara. Dov was her son-in-law.

The real *Exodus* was an overcrowded, rusting hulk of a ship that never made it past the British blockade of Palestine. No one ever thought it would. A few days out of Italy, one of the decks on the ship collapsed, and Dov landed in Sara's bunk. That's how they met. "I had to marry her," he says. Dov has been laughing at his joke for fifty-five years.

They lived and still live in Ramleh, a town near Ben Gurion airport, in a tiny two-bedroom apartment they and their two daughters gladly shared with me and Steve. We were sitting on my bed — which doubled as the couch when my bedroom became the living room, which it did during daylight hours except during mealtimes when it was also the dining room — when Dov, nodding at the blue numbers tattooed on his forearm, asked that question and, then, surprising me, answered it.

"We did fight back," he said, with more sorrow than pride in his voice. "We did."

I can understand Yiddish, but I don't really speak it. My Hebrew consists of calls to prayer and a few other words I'd picked up when I studied for my Bar Mitzvah: boy (*yeled*), girl (*yaldah*), and shut up (*sheket*). Dov's English was even worse than my Yiddish. But somehow we found enough words in common for him to tell me the story of Sobibor, the Nazi extermination camp where the Jews fought back, where 300,000 Jews were killed and 300 survived — and Dov was one of them.

"I was fourteen when the war broke out," Dov began. He was a poor kid from Lodz, Poland. I never asked about his family, if he'd had brothers or sisters. When the Jews were forced into the ghetto, Dov escaped, then escaped back into Lodz because there was no place to go. When they were sent to Warsaw, he escaped again, then escaped back into the Warsaw ghetto because there was still no place to go. Then he was sent to Sobibor, one of three Nazi extermination camps. Because he was young and healthy, he wasn't killed outright but was chosen as part of the cadre, meaning he stacked suitcases carried by Jews who thought they were going to work camps; he clipped hair and pulled gold teeth from their corpses.

"You know what the most valuable thing in the camps was?" he asked. "Lager," he called them, the German word for camp.

"Diamonds?" I guessed. "Gold?"

He shook his head. "A leffel," he said in Yiddish. A spoon.

If you had a spoon, when they let you eat you could eat like a human being.

In Sobibor there was a place the Jews and their guards called "Canada," a faraway land of riches where clothing, jewelry, even food taken from victims was warehoused. One of the guards there, Dov remembered, wanted to see if Jews could fly. "He had us climb up on the roof then jump off using an umbrella as a parachute. I was a skinny kid, I fell, I didn't get hurt."

He told me about another guard, an officer, Stengel was his name. He would chase Dov through the camp, using a whip and shouting, "Run, run, child of Israel. Maybe you'll run to Palestine." A year after he told me his story I read they'd caught Stengel, working at a Volkswagen plant in Brazil. Dov testified at his trial. Stengel recognized him. "I should have killed you," he said to Dov from the witness stand, "when I had the chance."

Dov testified at the Eichmann trial. After he testified at a war crimes trial in Frankfurt, a group of young Germans followed him back to his hotel and beat him. "I told them," he told me, "I survived worse."

"I had typhus," he told me. "I had a fever, I couldn't work, I hid in the lager. The guard who found me beat me, whipped me. I don't know how, but his beating cured me. I felt better."

The Dutch Jewish community was virtually exterminated at Sobibor. And Russian-Jewish prisoners of war were murdered there. When the Nazis captured American or British soldiers, the Jews among them were almost always treated as POWs, which at least gave them a chance. When the Nazis tried to segregate "Jewish personnel," "all Jews step forward," there are hundreds of stories of whole companies of men risking their own lives, all stepping forward. But the Nazis treated Russian-Jewish prisoners as Jews.

At Sobibor that would be the Nazis' downfall.

"One day a Russian paratrooper came into the camp. A major." Dov pronounced it "Mayger," with a hard g. "An officer, six foot tall, head shaved bald. He looked around, saw what this was and said, 'Tomorrow at four o'clock, we kill Germans.' "

"There were clocks?" I asked.

"They were Germans," Dov answered.

Dov was in the shoe repair shop at 4:00. He picked up one of the steel forms they used to mend boots and smashed the German guard who was with him over the head. It had been twenty years since it had happened, and he winced when he told it to me. "He was not a bad man," Dov said. And Dov ran for the fence.

He became part of a band of men who were looking for the Polish underground. They had rifles they'd taken from the Germans, and ammunition. And they found the Polish underground.

"Hand us your rifles and your bullets," they were told. "We'll give you food." They gave up their weapons, and the Polish underground opened fire on them.

"As soon as I heard bullets, I ran." Dov told me.

There were two Polish undergrounds. The Communist underground, which had Jewish members, and the Royalist underground, which was as anti-Semitic as the Nazis.

Dov's gang dug two hideouts, about a mile apart, so they wouldn't all be found.

"One morning someone from the other group comes shouting, 'The Germans are here. The Germans are here.' They had followed him to our hideout. We had no guns, but someone looked in his pocket and found three bullets. There was a tunnel to get into our hideout, very small, big enough for one man. So, very loud — and in German so they would understand — we shouted 'Pass me the rifle!'

" 'Let me have the pistol!'

" 'Give me the machine gun!' And held the bullets with sticks over a fire.

"It worked. These were soldiers, not SS, and when they heard the bullets they thought we really did have guns, they thought we could shoot them if they tried to come in, and they ran away."

They found two Jews, brothers, farmers who had lived near Sobibor, hiding in the woods. "They couldn't read or write," Dov told me. He mentioned a fourth member of their group, but I don't remember anything about him.

The four went to the brothers' farmhouse and saw smoke coming out of the chimney. Two Polish girls were living there, one had a German soldier's baby, the other was the sister of a leader of the Polish bandits. I didn't ask any more, I had this image in my mind of what Polish bandits would look like, on horseback, knives held between their teeth, kerchiefs wrapped pirate fashion on the heads, that I did not want reality to interfere with.

The three men kept the two women from turning them in, professing love, playing one against the other. Dov made it sound like a Feydeau farce. He, still a teenager and too young for the women, would inherit one of the largest fortunes in Lodz when the war was over, the women were told, and they would all be rich.

When the brother came to visit his sister, Dov joined his band and rode with the Polish bandits until the war was over.

"We drank a fifth of vodka a day to keep from freezing," Dov told me.

After the war he went back to Lodz and didn't find anybody he knew.

There is a documentary on the *Exodus* where you can see Dov on the ship's deck. He's small, with curly hair. Someone is waving the Star of David, which would soon become the Israeli flag.

The *Exodus* was turned back by the British, and Sara and Dov and Dvaireh and Itzhak were interned in a British concentration camp on Cyprus, then sent back to a displaced persons camp in Germany.

When they did get to Israel, Dov told me, "There was a war. I got off the boat and they gave me a gun. Even though I was killing for my country, I wasn't . . ." he searched for the right word and knew he had to settle for one that wasn't a perfect translation. "I wasn't . . . happy," he said. "I don't like killing."

Yom Ha'Shoah is a new Jewish holiday, the day we remember the Holocaust. Each year, Dov, who is something of a hero in Israel, is asked to represent the survivors in a national ceremony. I like to think he has become a hero not because he survived Sobibor, but because he survived Sobibor and never learned to like killing.

15

A History of the Jews in Four Jokes

1. A deep, booming voice awakened Abie in the middle of the night.

"Abie," it boomed, "Sell the business." Abie figured it was a bad dream, turned over, and went back to sleep.

The next night the same thing happened. "Abie," a deep voice boomed. "Sell the business." Abie figured it was the same bad dream, turned over, and went back to sleep.

But the next night he heard the voice boom, "Abie, this is the third and last time I'm going to tell you: sell the business!"

The next day Abie sold the business. For $3 million. And the voice came back.

"Abie, take the money, go to Las Vegas, go to the Bellagio, walk past the reception desk into the casino, go to the first blackjack table you see, and bet it all, the whole three million."

Abie did. The dealer called the pit boss, the pit boss called the manager, the manager called the owner, the owner called the bank. Abie's cashier's check was good. A huge crowd had gathered. The owner nodded his head, the dealer dealt Abie a queen, dealt himself a down card, dealt Abie an eight, and flipped himself a king.

"Take a hit, Abie," the voice boomed.

"But I've got eighteen, I'll bust!" Abie muttered.

"Take a hit," the voice boomed again.

Abie did. It was an ace.

"Take another hit," the deep voice boomed.

"But . . . but . . ." Abie was shaking.

"Take the card, Abie," the voice demanded.

"Hit me," Abie mumbled to the dealer who flipped Abie a second ace.

"One more," the voice boomed.

Abie broke into a cold sweat, his right hand grabbed his left arm to stop the shooting pain.

"Take the card, Abie," the voice boomed.

Abie motioned with his fingers. The dealer snapped a card out of the shoe.

A third ace.

"Twenty-one!" Abie shouted. "I win! I win!"

And the deep voice boomed, "Un-fucking-believable."

In that joke, Dylan, is the entire 4,000-year history of the relationship between God and the Jews. Martin Buber called our unique relationship an I-Thou relationship, more familiar, more *heimish* than the I-You or I-it relationship Catholics and other Christians and Muslims have with God. They communicate with God through an intermediary who might get it wrong. We get it wrong right from the source.

"Follow Me to the promised land," God says. *"Oops, I forgot, I must have promised it to those guys, too."*

"What's that? I didn't tell you to turn right instead of left so you'd get the oil? I must've forgot. Nobody's perfect. Not even Me."

I remember my mother's father, my *zaideh*, who lost half his family in Pinsk, who tried to shoot his trigger finger off to get out of the Czar's army and missed and shot off his ring finger instead — you'd figure they'd let him out because he was such a bad shot, but they took him anyway. I remember him shaking his head when things would go wrong and saying to no one in particular, in Yiddish of course, "Next time, choose somebody else."

2. There is a terrible flood in a midwestern city. A rabbi is standing on the roof of his *shul,* water is lapping at his feet, and a boat rows by.

"Save those who need saving," the rabbi shouts. "God will take care of me."

An hour later, the water up to his waist, a second boat rows by. "Save those who need saving," the rabbi shouts again. "God will take care of me."

One hour more, the water up to his chest, yet another boat comes by.

"Save those who need saving," he shouts. "God will take care of me." And a huge wave knocks him down, and he drowns.

He enters heaven, and at his first meeting with God he asks, "Please, oh, Lord, I don't mean to be presumptuous, but I tried so hard to lead a good life, to follow your commandments, I was so certain you would save me. Why did you let me drown?"

And God says, "Schmuck, I sent three boats."

3. It's a cartoon: An old man with a long white beard, wearing robes and holding a shepherd's crook is standing on top of a mountain looking up into the heavens. The caption? The old man says, "Let me get this straight. You want me to cut off half my *what?!*"

4. Moscow, 1989. At four o'clock in the morning a line begins to form in front of a butcher shop. At seven o'clock there are hundreds of people in line when a butcher in a white blood-stained smock walks out the front door and stands between the two policemen who have been guarding the shop.

"All Jews waiting in line, go home. No meat for Jews."

A few dozen people leave the line to go home.

At nine o'clock the same butcher walks out and shouts, "All Ukrainians, go home. No meat for Ukrainians."

A few dozen people leave the line to go home.

At ten o'clock a different butcher walks out with two additional guards and shouts, "All non–Communist Party members, go home. No meat for non-Communists."

Perhaps a hundred people quietly walk away.

At noon a third butcher walks out and tells the twenty or so people still waiting in line, "There's no meat today. Sorry, we have no meat."

And one Communist turns to another and says, "Fucking Jews, they get all the breaks."

16

Cooking in Self-Defense

My mother was a lot of things. Loyal and loving, she loved her family; my father had more than 100 first cousins, and she was the one who kept them in touch with each other. She read and wrote Yiddish, and her letters to her aunts in Israel kept us in touch with our family there.

She was short, my mother. "Four foot eleven and three-quarters inches," she would proudly announce as if she'd willed herself to stay that short and her success was some kind of triumph. When she learned to drive, on a 1952 Kaiser, the seat had to be pushed all the way to the front so she could reach the pedals, which meant there was no way she could see over the steering wheel. She squinted out the frog-eyed front window through the steering wheel spokes, her hands gripped white-knuckle tight on the top of the steering wheel at an exact ten minutes to two. The Headless Drivers of Fairfax Avenue, director Barry Levinson named the breed.

She was up-front, Old World; she didn't even wear makeup. With Libby, what you saw was what you got. She was also tougher than she led you to believe. After my father died, my sister, Phyllis, and I were worried that she wouldn't be able to take care of herself, that she'd rattle around alone in the three-bedrooms-and-a-den house my dad had built, haunted by memories of him. Phyllis and her family were living in Big Bear, a hundred miles east of LA, and I was in New York. We made a deal with our mom: I found an apartment for her in a high-rise half a block from the Pacific Ocean in Santa Monica. She had a room with an ocean view, they provided the meals, she had her car for shopping and visiting. She agreed to give it sixty days, we agreed we wouldn't sell the house, we wouldn't do anything till the sixty days were up. On the sixtieth day, she called the movers, packed and unpacked, made all the arrangements, and moved back home for good.

While she was in the apartment she met the mother of one of my friends who was on the same floor. When I saw him a few months later he asked if I really called my mother twice a day.

"Of course not," I said.

"Hmm, my mom said your mom told her that you did."

We never did find out whether my mom was lying to his mom or his mom was lying to him.

After she moved back home, my mom did consent to wearing one of those alarms around her neck that would dial 911 in an emergency. It never went off. She died in her sleep half a dozen years after she moved back home.

On Oscar night in 1989, I was directing my limo driver through the back roads of West LA on a shortcut to the Santa Monica Freeway.

"How do you know these streets?" the driver asked me.

"Wait a minute, I'll show you." I called my mom. "Get out on the front porch," I told her. "I have a surprise for you."

"That's how I know these streets," I told the driver. "That's my mom."

The car stopped, I gave her a hug and a kiss, and that was the last time I saw her. She died a few weeks later.

Going through her closets after she died, I found every one of the gifts I'd ever sent her. Cashmere sweaters Melissa and I had sent her from London, cashmere sweater sets Jane and I had sent her from Rome. Wearing the sweaters wasn't important to my mom; having her son, Joel, send them to her was what mattered.

She never threw anything away. In one of my desk drawers, Dylan, you will find my World War II ration book, my name written on it in my mom's beautifully flowing cursive script — *Joel Steven Siegel.* During World War II the government rationed things the war made scarce, like sugar, like butter, like pairs of shoes. Just in case World War II came back, she was ready. "You never know," I can still hear her say.

She was one of the few moms in America who didn't throw away her son's baseball cards, which is why, Dylan, you'll inherit 1954 and 1955 complete sets of Topps cards worth thousands. And, because she didn't throw away my comics, you'll find stacks of *Mad*s and *Superman*s and *Archie*s and *Captain Marvel*s waiting for you in the closet in the country. By the time you're old enough to be trusted with them, the comic books will be over seventy years old and worth even more than the baseball cards.

Yes, I miss her. I would have wanted to see how happy you would have made her, Dylan, how happy she would have been just watching you smile. Protective, smothering, demanding, a quintessential Jewish mother in a hundred different ways. Every way but one, in fact. She was a terrible cook.

Part of the reason was that her mom was a good cook. Her mother ruled her kitchen with an iron hand, not to mention an iron pan. We'd go to Bubbie's for all the holidays, so my mom never cooked or had to learn to cook the big feast meals on Passover, Rosh Hashanah, or, here in America, Thanksgiving.

Something more subtle and more Jewish was at work as well. Judaism doesn't quite know how to deal with eating meat. The *shoykhet,* the ritual slaughterer, has to be an educated man, and his term is proscribed; the guys who made up these rules didn't want anyone to learn to like killing, even killing animals. Meat is to be well cooked, maybe for health reasons when we were wandering around the desert, but, just as likely, for moral reasons, so we don't develop a taste for blood. My mother took no chances. She cooked everything until it was well cooked. Very well cooked.

In those days before microwaves with digital timers and Swift Butterballs with pop-up thermometers, my mom had her own way of knowing when dinner was ready. She cooked by color. When everything was the same color, it was done.

She didn't know the meaning of the word "medium-rare." She also didn't know the meaning of the words "Parsley, sage, rosemary, and thyme." Or cilantro. Or oregano.

"Libby, where's the salt?" my father would ask before dinner every night for forty-two years.

He of course didn't mean *where* is the salt, he meant "why isn't the salt on the table?"

My mother would answer, "In the cupboard," every night for forty-two years. It was her way of being reminded that he needed her and loved her. After my father died, I noticed she kept the salt on the kitchen table.

I learned early on if I wanted to eat good cooking and it wasn't Pesach or Jewish New Year's, I was going to have to learn to cook it myself. So I did.

And it's not hard. It's not magic, it's chemistry. Most of it, anyway. Mix an acid and a base, like buttermilk with baking soda, and the new mixture releases carbon dioxide gas and the pancake batter rises. Or mix egg whites with a dash of cream of tartar, and the egg whites will retain their stiffness.

That's chemistry. The magic happens when the smell of the kitchen, the taste of what you've made creates sense memories more vivid than even words or pictures. There are a zillion cookbooks out there, Dylan, and you won't find these recipes in any of them.

Bubbie's Tsimmes

Bubbie means grandmother, but I had a bubbie, Bayle, my mother's mother, and a Grandma, Lena, my father's mother. I always wondered how kids whose families came from English-speaking countries told their grandparents apart.

(When I interviewed Jay Leno, I asked him about the difference between living in New York and living in LA. Two things, he told me. The beach is in the wrong direction, and here in LA, everybody's grandmother speaks English.)

Bubbie was a good cook, too, though she overdid it on the Crisco or the Nyafat or the chicken schmaltz, depending on whether she was cooking *milchiks*, *fleishiks*, or *pareve*. This dish goes with all three, it's even Kosher for Passover.

Tsimmes means mix or mixture. It also means "mess," making a big *tsimmes* out of something. It's also something I cooked on Pesach, and any other time I made Grandma's brisket.

Six carrots, peeled and sliced (into half-inch rounds. Don't be too neat, don't be too worried about the width. First time I made *osso bucco*, following somebody else's grandmother's recipe, I found myself mincing the garlic, chopping the onions, like a three-star *sous-chef*. Eventually I figured if the food is that beautifully prepared, no one will believe I cooked it. Be a little sloppy, let your guests know it really was homemade.)

Six yams or sweet potatoes. Cut off the end, peel and slice into half-inch rounds.

One pound of pitted prunes. (When you ate my bubbie's cooking, you needed the prunes. They had a hot water bottle hanging on a nail on their bathroom door, with a rubber nozzle attached to it. This wasn't a hot water bottle, I later learned, it was an enema bag. *Conneh* is the Yiddish word for enema. It was my bubbie's cure for just about everything. And it worked. Once I learned what the word meant, all she had to do was mention the word *conneh*. What cough? What fever? Sure, I'm well enough to go to school.

There is a great Yiddish theater joke about the actor who falls down, dead, in the third act of *King Lear*.

"Oh, my God, he's dead!" one of the actors shouts.

From the balcony comes a cry, "Gib him a *conneh!*"

"But he's dead!" the actor shouts back.

"It couldn't hurt!"

Yes, the joke is also told about chicken soup. But, if you've ever had a *conneh*, or ate my bubbie's *tsimmes*, it's much funnier this way.)

So, where were we? Ah . . .

6	carrots, peeled and sliced
6	sweet potatoes, peeled and sliced
1	pound pitted prunes
1	cup brown sugar
1/4	teaspoon salt
1/2	teaspoon cinnamon
6	tablespoons margarine (or butter if you're cooking *milchedik*)

Approximately 1 cup sweet wine, grape juice, or water

Cook the carrots and sweet potatoes in a saucepan in a little bit of margarine, water, or cooking oil until tender but not soft. Grease a casserole dish or Dutch oven, and layer the sweet potatoes, carrots, and prunes, seasoning each layer with some brown sugar, a sprinkle of salt, and, if you like, a dash of cinnamon. This was Jane's addition to the recipe. Pour the wine over the whole *tsimmes,* bake at 350 degrees for about a half an hour. Uncover and bake until the top turns golden brown or looks good enough to serve, at least another half hour. You can also lower the oven and cook it much longer.

Grandma's Brisket

I got this recipe from my father's mother at someone's Bar Mitzvah. It had been a closely held family secret. Boy, was I surprised when I got it out of her.

1 whole brisket
2 white onions
1 package Lipton's Onion Soup Mix
1 bottle Heinz Chili Sauce
4 cloves garlic, chopped
Water

Roasting pan *or*, my preference (because you don't have to wash it you can throw it away), large aluminum foil roaster from the super-market

Take the brisket, please. Make sure it is a whole brisket. NOT first cut or prime cut; you want the whole brisket with the deckel, the fatty piece of meat that sits on top of the first cut. DON'T let the butcher trim off too much fat, either. Your guests can trim all they want when they eat it, but the brisket needs the fat to cook in.

Preheat the oven to 350 degrees.

Slice the two onions into quarter-inch slices.

Shmear the onion soup mix on the brisket. Top and bottom.

Shmear the chili sauce on the brisket. Top and bottom. This will not be neat. (There is no chili in Heinz Chili Sauce; I have no idea why it's called Chili Sauce; it's sold next to the ketchup. Do NOT use anything like Tabasco Sauce. My grandmother was from Romania, not Trinidad.)

Place the brisket in the roaster deckel side up.

Stud the roast with chopped garlic.

Place the onions on the roast.

Add water until the brisket is sitting in water one inch deep.

Cover the roaster with heavy-duty aluminum foil. And here comes the hard part:

Place on a center rack in the oven and DO NOTHING FOR TWO HOURS.

Nothing.

Don't peek.

Nothing.

After two hours, take a peek. Make certain there is still water in the roaster. If there isn't, add some, keeping the level at about an inch.

If you want to add carrots, potatoes, etc., you can do so now.

You can also slice the brisket if you like. Slice against the grain.

Return it to the oven for at least another hour.

I cooked this before Rosh Hashanah on *Good Morning America* about ten years ago. The recipe is still on their Web site. I got a call a few years later from a woman in New Iberia, Louisiana, where Tabasco sauce comes from, where they really know how to eat, asking for the recipe; she'd misplaced her copy and wanted to make it again. "Grandma!" I shouted toward the sky. "We're a hit!"

Jane's Lokshen Kugel

Lokshen Kugel can either be sweet or savory, but it's always a side dish, never a dessert.

Jane's family was Hungarian, and Hungarian Jews were much more assimilated into their country's society and culture than other Eastern European Jews. They were also better cooks. They cooked with spices, and they could afford sugar. Jane's Lokshen Kugel uses both.

½ stick butter, melted
1 pound egg noodles, the inch-wide kind
2 cups cottage cheese
2 cups plain yogurt, NOT nonfat
4 eggs
½ cup sugar
½ cup golden raisins
1 small can crushed pineapple in heavy syrup, *or* 1 apple, peeled and diced, seasoned with 1 teaspoon apple pie spice

3-quart Pyrex baking dish, lightly greased with some of the butter

Preheat oven to 350 degrees. Cook noodles in boiling water until done, following the directions on the package. Combine cottage cheese, yogurt, eggs, sugar, raisins, and pineapple or apple and spice. Drain the noodles in a colander and add to the rest, mixing well. Pour into baking dish, drizzle remaining butter over top, bake for 45 minutes or until the top is browned.

Joel's Blueberry Cobbler

Filling:
2	quarts of blueberries
1	cup light brown sugar
4	tablespoons butter
2	tablespoons tapioca

Juice and zest of ½ lime

Crust:
1	cup sifted flour
1	teaspoon baking powder
1/4	teaspoon baking soda
1/2	teaspoon salt
3	tablespoons butter
3/4	cup buttermilk

Preheat oven to 425 degrees.

Mix blueberries and sugar, add lime juice and lime zest, add tapioca (this keeps the fruit filling from getting too thin). Put in deep dish pan, dot with butter, and bake for 25 minutes. While the filling is baking, sift the dry ingredients into a bowl. Use your hands to cut in the 3 tablespoons of butter. Pick up a handful of flour and butter and run them through your fingers until they are well mixed. The mixture should be lumpy like oatmeal. Add the buttermilk, stir, but keep it lumpy. Spoon large drops of dough onto the blueberries. Cooking the blueberries first will keep the crust and filling separate. Bake 25 minutes or until the biscuit dough has browned. Serve with ice cream.

Plums (use lemon instead of lime), blackberries (use more sugar), and peaches (add a teaspoon of apple pie spice) work well. It's not necessary to peel the plums or the peaches.

Romanian Omelet

First, steal three eggs.

Uncle Shep's Chicken Soup

So here I am in Maui, talk about the promised land, at my old friend Shep Gordon's house, where the front lawn rolls into the Pacific, where two palm trees just happened to grow the perfect distance apart to hold a hammock so comfortable it's impossible to read more than two pages of the national edition of the *New York Times* without falling asleep. And for lunch? The best chicken soup I've ever tasted.

Shep, besides creating and managing a hit parade full of rock-and-roll stars (we met when I was in the army in Fort Huachuca and he and one of his first clients, Alice Cooper, were getting started), spent a few years shlepping for and learning from three-star chef Roger Verget.

No, he's not your real uncle. But once you taste this chicken soup, you'll wish he was.

8   quarts chicken stock
2   large chickens
6   carrots, peeled and cut up
8   celery stalks
3   sweet onions (white onions, preferably Vidalia. Shep lives in Maui, so he uses Maui onions)
Fresh dill
Salt and pepper
Egg noodles

Put the chicken stock in a large stock pot, bring to boil, and turn down to simmer.

Add the other ingredients EXCEPT the dill, salt, pepper, and noodles.

Every twenty minutes or so, add a large pinch of dill and skim the *schum* off the top. *Schum* must be Yiddish for scum, either the real word or a transliteration; either way, you'll know it when you see it.

When the mixture is becoming soup, add salt and pepper to taste. Simmer until the chicken falls off the bone. We're talking hours.

Cook noodles separately.

Shep adds, "In the tradition of all great Jewish chicken soups, find someone to tell you what is wrong with it while you are eating it, preferably an older relative."

Chicken Soup Hints

Chicken stock:

I don't know anyone who makes their own chicken stock. Canned stocks can be salty, so if you do use them, buy the sodium-free kind and add your own salt. A better bet: in New York, Zabar's, EAT, Dean and DeLuca, and other specialty food shops sell frozen stock.

Chickens:

A necessary ingredient. There is a theory that dinosaurs still walk the Earth, they evolved into birds. Looking at a plucked chicken, the theory does make sense. Observe the huge hind legs out of proportion to the rest of their bodies, the tiny little chicken-heads. Imagine them the size of the T-Rex at the Museum of Natural History. It really does seem possible. But when Shep says "large" chickens, he doesn't mean that large. He doesn't even mean roasters. A couple of pounds each is large enough.

Cut them into quarters, plop 'em in — yes, including the skin and the fat, and even, if you're adventuresome, the giblets. The *gorgle* (the throat), the *pupik* (I have no idea what part of the chicken that is — well, I do have an idea, but I don't want to know if I'm right), and even the feet were delicacies when I was a boy. So were the unborn eggs, the *eyelakh;* we come from a protein-deprived culture. Chickens today are mass produced and assembly-line dressed. Ask a kosher butcher, but I don't think they sell *eyelakh* anywhere anymore. Chinatown is the last place in New York where you can still buy chicken feet. Try them. Tastes like chicken.

17

Yiddish, A Brief History

Dear Dylan,
I know you'll never speak Yiddish, but you already know more Yiddish than you think. *Pupik. Tushie. Keppeleh. Kitzel. Shaneh Ponim.* And every Yiddish word you know, every Yiddish shrug or inflection, is a victory for my parents and grandparents, proof that we have survived.

I've put together a list of Yiddish words and phrases and sayings that I know you will hear, because I want you to know where they come from: they come from us.

It's one of those *Believe It Or Not* facts we all collect: Did you know the Eskimos have nineteen words for snow? It makes sense for the Eskimos to have nineteen words for snow. They live in it. They have a life-or-death need to know if it's falling gently or coming down in a blizzard; if it's packed snow, powder, grainy, or icy; if it can support the weight of a seal or a human being or a polar bear. And it makes sense that the Inuit language has created so many ways to describe the different kinds of snow so quickly.

I'm not fluent in Yiddish. I'm nowhere near fluent in Yiddish. I can read and write it because I learned the Hebrew alphabet for my Bar Mitzvah. Then, fresh out of college, I bought myself a copy of Uriel Weinreich's *Yiddish-English Dictionary* at Foreman's Bookstore on Fairfax Avenue, up from Canter's, and a copy of that day's *Jewish Daily Forward* at the newsstand around the block, and forced myself to translate the lead story. I knew, at best, every fourth word. That's how I know I'm not fluent in Yiddish.

The first words I ever heard were probably Yiddish words. Yiddish speakers call it *mame-loshn*, the mother tongue, and it really was my mother's. Yiddish was her first language, and she was always as comfortable speaking and writing Yiddish as she was English. I learned to understand Yiddish because, when I was a little boy, that was the language my folks spoke when they didn't want me to know what they were talking about. But I never learned to speak it. If they'd heard me speak Yiddish, they would have spoken Russian or Polish when they didn't want me to know what they were talking about. To this day part of me associates Yiddish with grown-up secrets, and it's a reflex that dies hard. More than once I've turned to Ena and started to ask her, in Yiddish, if it was time for Dylan to take his bath or go to sleep — questions, when asked in English, that summon up a tearful "No no no, not yet!" from the depths of little Dylan's soul. I find myself starting to ask, *"Du denkst er vil shlufn?"* *"Do you think he wants to go to sleep?"* And break myself up.

Ena is a Quaker from North Carolina; not a lot of Yiddish was spoken at Sunday meeting in Charlotte when she was growing up.

I have a Yiddish vocabulary of maybe a thousand words and have no idea how to conjugate a verb. "I go store. Buy bread." My Yiddish is very much like Tarzan's English. Tarzan's scream, though, is one of territory and triumph. In Yiddish the scream comes from a thousand years of pain.

Even with my limited Yiddish, it took

me less than two hours to come up with twenty-nine words for "schmuck." Not twenty-nine words for the male member; twenty-nine variations on the theme "You stink!" Twenty-nine ways to devalue our self-worth and describe the ironic and the literal joys and sorrows of human failure.

Alter Kocker, Bonditt, Chazer, Farshtunkener, Kalike, Kvetch, Meeskeit, Mishugeh, Momzer, Nar, Nogoodnik, Noodge, Oomglick, Paskudnyak, Pisher, Putz, Schlong, Schmuck, Schnorrer, Schvantz, Shlemiel, Shlemazl, Shmegeggy, Shmendrick, Schmo, Schnook, Schtunk, Trombenik, Zhlob.

Yes, the Eskimos need nineteen words for snow. For all I know, Arabic may have fourteen words for sand, and the French may have forty-two words for body odor, but what kind of people needs twenty-nine words for schmuck? And those are just the words I know, with my thousand-word vocabulary and a preschooler's syntax. Is it any wonder Sigmund Freud was Jewish? Or, as he has been referred to more than once by fellow *landslayt*, "Sigmund Freud, that schmuck."

Problems with self-worth and self-esteem not only permeate the Yiddish vocabulary, they also affect the way we feel about the language itself. Most Jews believe Yiddish is some *shlemiel* of a language, not a real language but some kind of bastardized German in Hebrew letters. My father's mother always called it *Yargon*, jargon, apologizing when she couldn't remember the English word but only the Yiddish, as if Yiddish were the orphaned stepchild of a real language. My grandmother was wrong.

Yiddish is a real language, a thousand years old, that predates modern German. Its roots are less Germanic, in fact, than the old French the great Jewish scholar Rashi wrote his commentaries in. A living language, it grew and changed as the Jews moved from the south of France to Alsace to what is now Germany. As evidence, take the name Dreyfuss, as in Captain and Richard and Julia Louis. *Dray* is Yiddish for three and *fus* is Yiddish for foot and I always thought the name meant "three-foot" and referred to an ancestor who was either very short or very well endowed. But Trier, a medieval capital of culture and learning in what is now Germany, was spelled *Treve* in Medieval French, and pronounced something close to *Dreyfuss* in Yiddish.

As the Jews traveled, we picked up words and phrases and cultural prejudices and left some behind. *Smok* is a Slavic word for guess what? Apparently, in the Balkans, since the Jews moved out, they only need one word.

As a kid growing up in a house where English wasn't always the first language, there were times I wasn't sure what language I was hearing. Or speaking. This is an American thing, not a Jewish thing. An ABC videotape editor, David Chan, born and raised in New York's Chinatown, came back crestfallen from his first trip to mainland China. "I speak a dialect of Cantonese known only on Elizabeth Street," he told me. Lee Tierce, an art director I worked with in advertising, had to go to the bathroom in the Uffizi in Florence and remembered his Sicilian-born grandmother always called it *"baccuse."*

"Dove il *baccuse?*" he asked a guard, who stared at Lee as if he were crazy. Lee, of course, asked again, louder. Still nothing. He finally drew a toilet on the back of his guidebook and the guard pointed him down the hall. When he came back to LA and told his folks, they were hysterical. *"Baccuse"* was the way his grandmother pronounced "back-house."

In Israel, saying no to the pickled herring breakfast at my family's kibbutz, Kibbutz

Yifat in the Jezreel, I was trying to explain that I didn't like fish. *"Ich glach nit . . ."* "I don't like. . . ." That I knew. I couldn't think of the word for fish, I couldn't think of anything my grandparents had called fish *except* "fish." So I sucked my lips together and did seal flippers with my hands and my *Tante* Dveyre laughed and said, "Ah, *feeish!*" That's why my grandparents never called it anything but fish. They *were* talking Yiddish.

Easy words my grandparents used, I was sure were English. Polysyllabic words, I was sure were Yiddish. This rule did hold true most of the time. When we moved to West LA, my first best friend was a Mormon kid named Jimmy Christiansen. One morning I was at his house for breakfast, watching his mom make us pancakes. When she asked Jimmy to hand her the "spatula," I couldn't believe it. My grandmother pronounced it *spehtchuleh,* but it was the same word. I ran all the way home, shouting, "Mommy, Mommy, Jimmy Christiansen is Jewish."

According to *Yiddish: A Nation of Words,* a new book by Miriam Weinstein, there are 144 words in the *Oxford English Dictionary* with Yiddish roots, including the word "Yiddish," which is Yiddish for "Jewish," and "Yid," which is Yiddish for "Jew." ("Yid" is our match for the N-word. It's OK when we call each other "Yid." *Vos makht a Yid?* is a typical greeting between close friends. But when gentiles call us "Yid," our hackles rise. There's an old saying: "The worst name you can call a Jew is 'Jew.'")

For each Yiddish word that gets into the *OED*, there must be twice that many in common usage in American English, especially in towns like New York and Hollywood, which have large and vocal Jewish populations. Yiddish may be a dying language, but Yiddish words will live on. As will Yiddish inflections, sayings, even attitudes that have become part of the American mosaic.

From your mouth to God's ear.

Lie down with dogs, wake up with fleas.

If my grandmother had wheels she'd be a bicycle. (A Bowdlerized version of the original: If my grandmother had balls she'd be my grandfather.)

Fancy-shmancy. And every other phrase that mocks the meaning of the first word by creating a rhyme beginning with "shm . . ." for the second word.

Go know (*gey veys*)

Don't ask (*freg nisht*)

Enough already (*genug shoyn*)

Be well (*zay gezunt*)

Enjoy!

I should care? (I should go around weeping? I should care? I should go without sleeping?)

God only knows. (No, Brian Wilson of the Beach Boys isn't Jewish. But Tony Asher, who wrote the song, is. And so are Brian Wilson's kids.)

The bottom line is, according to Sol Steinmetz's *Yiddish and English*, even the bottom line is from Yiddish: *di untershte shure.*

There are many reasons for this explosion of Yiddish words, ideas, and culture in the twentieth century. Some were the revolutions in technology that made everyone's world simultaneously smaller and larger: the car, the airplane, the telephone, the electric light, movies, the phonograph, radio. These coincided with an internal revolution in the Jewish fifty-eighth century. We had begun to discover the secular world, and, grudgingly, painfully, the secular world would finally begin to let us in. Though usually on the quota system.

Napoleon made the Jews of France citizens and placed them under secular law, but in most of Eastern Europe the Jews didn't come under secular law until the late 1800s. When Galicia, in what had been southern Poland, became part of Austria-Hungary, not much more than a century ago, the emperor's apparatchiks would come into a *shtetl,* take a census, repair the tax rolls (they always let us pay taxes), and give the Jews secular names. They'd line us up into four columns: Big, Small, Black, White. *Gross, Klein, Schwartz, Weiss.* That's where those names came from and why they're so common. *Siegel* is a religious name, it was my name before. So are *Cohen, Levi, Katz* (a contraction of *Cohen-Tzaddik,* wise priest), *Kaplan* (the same root as Chaplain, a Latinized version of *Cohen,* which means priest).

There'd be a butcher, *Fleischman,* a merchant, *Kaufman,* the guy who owned the tavern, *Kretschmer,* the man who made the whisky, *Bronfman.* Rich Jews, Jews with an air, Jews with an eye to Western, Victorian culture, would *shmear* the census taker so they could be given an elaborate Victorian name like *Rosenblumen,* which, when they came to America, their kids would shorten to Ross. But, then, we Jews have thousands of years of experience when it comes to making things shorter.

Yanked from the fourteenth century into

the twentieth, we suddenly found ourselves involved in European politics. We were poor, so we were on the left. I was shocked, I mean shocked, when I bought my copy of the *Forward* and there in the upper right-hand corner was the motto right out of Marx, *Arbeter fun alle lander, fareynikt zikh!* "Workers of the World, Unite!" Eugene V. Debs Socialism was the far right wing of the American Jewish community, except for the Orthodox, who eschewed politics. The Yiddish radio station in New York, WEVD, "the station that speaks your language," was named for Debs.

Show business, that most democratic of vocations, opened up to Jews. The Yiddish theater was started in Jassy, in Romania, in the 1890s. There was an international Yiddish theater circuit before World War II. A year or two on the road would include stops in Warsaw, Berlin, Paris, London, Montreal, New York, Philadelphia, Mexico City, and Buenos Aires. On one tour, in one town, a young woman held her year-old son up to Boris Thomaschevsky, a dashing star of the Yiddish theater.

"Mr. Thomaschevsky," she shouted. "Remember when you played here two years ago? This is your son."

"My son?" he said and gave the little boy

a couple of *kitzels* under his chin.

"Here are two tickets for tonight's performance!"

"I don't need tickets," the woman pleaded. "I need bread!"

"Bread?" Thomaschevsky said. "Next time fuck a baker."

Much of the Yiddish theater was, like much of any culture's theater, sap and pap. Melodrama, cheap tears. Slapstick, cheap laughs. But there was serious theater as well. King Lear, a father betrayed by his daughters, a Yiddish theme, translated into a Yiddish classic. Another story: A Jewish cabbie picked up the great Shakespearean actor Louis Calhern at Penn Station.

"What brings you into town?" the cabbie asked.

"I'm doing Lear on Broadway," Calhern answered.

The cabbie thought for a minute and asked, "You think it'll play in English?"

The Adlers and Lee Strasberg, who would revolutionize American theater with their un-theatrical, natural approach to acting, had their roots in Yiddish theater. So did Sidney Lumet, Joe Papp, even Marlon Brando.

Tony Curtis's first job was on Second Avenue in a Yiddish play. He told me the story. He played a spoiled rotten kid who never worked, whose parents worked their fingers to the bone so he wouldn't have to work. But the Depression came, and his father lost his job. "Our son will have to get a job," his father declaimed. Curtis, whose real name is Bernie Schwartz, proudly remembered his first line on any stage: *"Ich vil besser shtarbn!"* I'd rather die!

Brando isn't Jewish, but he studied with Stella Adler and, in 1947, costarred with Paul Muni in an Adler-directed pageant about the birth of the state of Israel. In the closing tableau, Muni, who is playing the Zionist leader Theodore Herzl, dies in Brando's arms as Brando, muscles rippling, sunburnt and stone gorgeous, covers Muni with the Israeli flag and reads a powerful eulogy. Brando tells the story in his autobiography: On opening night, he covered Muni's face with the flag, started to deliver his lines, and noticed something odd out of the corner of his eye. Centimeter by centimeter, Muni, who's supposed to be dead, was slowly pulling the flag off of his face.

Gershwin, Harold Arlen, Rodgers and Hammerstein, Rodgers and Hart, barely a generation away from Europe, created American musical theater.

Jascha Heifetz was one of dozens who played his way out of Russia. Irving Berlin, whose only memory of Russia was of his *shtetl* burning during a pogrom, would write "Easter Parade" and "White Christmas" and "God Bless America."

At Yehudi Menuhin's Carnegie Hall debut, violinist Fritz Kreisler turned to pianist Artur Rubinstein and asked, "Artur, isn't it hot in here?"

Rubinstein replied, "Not for piano players."

Almost 100 years later, Alan King, celebrating Carnegie Hall's centennial, looked around the hall and said, "Tchaikovsky, Mahler, Koussevitsky, Toscanini, if only these walls could talk . . . they'd have some accent."

Yiddish-speaking intellectuals codified the first Yiddish dictionary ever at the end of the nineteenth century. We had begun to take ourselves seriously. There had always been Yiddish writing, mostly women's novels and religious tracts for women, who were rarely taught Hebrew, but now there was Yiddish literature. We'd always been "people of the book." Armed with that tradition and the writer's best friend, an outsider's eye, we made our mark in American literature and its derivatives: film, radio, and TV. And these were brand-new businesses, start-ups that required more chutzpah than capital, where Jewish entrepreneurs could make their mark.

My friend, Jeff Greenfield, once introduced a panel of speakers at a media conference, "Our guests today are Steven Spielberg, David Geffen, and Jeffrey Katzenberg. I'm Jeff Greenfield. Our topic is, 'The Myth of Jewish Control of the Media.' "

"Free thinkers," not just nonreligious but anti-orthodox Jews, would hold fancy dress balls on Yom Kippur on the Lower East Side. My *zaideh* and his brother-in-law, Uncle Falk, would head into the gentile part of Pinsk on Yom Kippur and eat *chazer.* Pork. They didn't like it, he told his son *Mottke,* my uncle Muttie, who was the one who later told me, but they ate ham on Yom Kippur every year anyway. *Aftselokhes.* One of my favorite Yiddish words, accent on the first and third syllables: *AF-tze-LOKH-ess:* For spite.

That was the social, intellectual, economic, and religious foment we brought with us when one-third of the Jews in Eastern Europe came to America, our first good choice in looking for a place to live since Moses crossed the Red Sea.

What happened in America is that we didn't have to hide. We didn't have to keep secrets. We didn't need Yiddish. Or Ladino — the Sephardic equivalent of Yiddish written with the Hebrew alphabet. Or Tat — the Persian equivalent of Yiddish written with the Hebrew alphabet. Yiddish is studied in dozens of colleges, but always as a second or third or fourth language, never as a first.

There is a National Yiddish Book Center in Amherst, Massachusetts. YIVO, the Yiddish Folk Institute, is in New York City on West Sixteenth Street. There is one surviving Yiddish press in Buenos Aires. But it's just a matter of time.

Today Yiddish is on a United Nations watch list along with 2,000 other endangered languages and dialects. Of those 2,000, only Yiddish had ten million speakers just 100 years ago. And among those endangered languages, only Yiddish has a Nobel prize in literature.

Putting together the glossary in the next chapter, I was struck by the fact that not only does Yiddish have at least twenty-nine words for "schmuck," it has no word for trouble in the singular. The Yiddish word is *tsoris*, troubles. Plural. Yiddish grammarians may know of a singular form of *tsoris,* but I don't. I never heard it. Never heard anyone use it.

Yiddish for snow is *shney.* One word for snow. But with so many troubles, who cares about a little snow?

18

A Glossary of Yiddish Words
in Common American English Usage
Including 29 Words for Schmuck

A.K.
Alter Kocker
Literally "old shitter." An old Jew.

Three old Jews are sitting on the porch at their old-age home, complaining.

The first says, "I haven't had a good bowel movement in three days, I'm lucky to have one a week."

The second says, "What are you complaining about? I'm lucky to have one a month."

The third shakes his head, "I don't know. I move my bowels every morning at 7:30, like clockwork."

"Nu?" said the other two. "What are you complaining about?"

"I don't wake up till 8:15."

Amen
It's Hebrew, among other biblical words

that have entered our language, probably through Latin or Greek, like Jubilee and hallelujah. And Leviathan and Behemoth, biblical words that probably have Egyptian roots.

In Yiddish, amen is pronounced "Aw-mane," and in *shul*, it's almost always sung.

Apikoyresher

I had an uncle who called me an "Apikoyresher Yid." It's a Yiddish pronunciation of the Greek philosopher Epicurus, and it means someone who's way too assimilated.

Aroysgevorfn

Thrown out, thrown away, wasted. *Varf* (vawrf) is Yiddish for "throw." Which has to be where "barf" comes from (college slang for "throw up" when I was in college). I once sent a photographer into a Hasidic neighborhood to get some B-roll for a story. I can't remember the story, but I remember the photographer, Hal Seiden, coming back with a huge smile on his face. He'd shot some Hasidic kids playing stickball, waving a broomstick and wearing *payess* (earlocks), and the kid at bat was yelling, "Varf the ball! Varf the ball! Varf the fuckin' ball!"

Bagel

Of course the word is Yiddish, though bagels, these days, are as all-American as chop suey and pizza pie. McDonald's sells a "McBagel" with ham and melted cheese. Every time I see an ad for it, I want to scream: Don't they know you're not supposed to mix milk and meat on a bagel?

Lox, by the way, is Yiddish. Also Swedish. And American. Which is fitting, because we learned about it here. If our families had been able to afford a delicacy like smoked salmon, living hundreds of miles from the sea in the middle of Poland, they never would have left.

Bubbe, Bubbele, Bubbie, Bubby

Grandma and its diminutives, or so I thought. Also used as a gender-free term of endearment, as in darling or sweetheart. As in "my *bubbie* used to call me *bubbele*." "Philologos," who writes an excellent column on Yiddish in the English-language *Forward* (at www.Forward.com), traces the same word to two roots: Grandmother *bubbie* comes from the Polish and the Slavic "grandmother," but *bubbele*, as in sweetheart or good little boy, comes from the German *Bub* or *Bube*, which goes "back to Middle High German *Buobe*, meaning a young man, squire, or knave, and deriving from Old High German *Buoba,* which was a man's name . . . which has been proposed by etymologists as the source of our English word 'boy.' "

"Given the Germanic origin of most Yiddish words," Philologos concludes, "it strikes me as implausible that German *Bubi* and Yiddish *bubele,* both with very similar meanings, should be unrelated."

You know what that means, Dylan? It means *bubba,* which is southern for "good old boy," and *bubbele,* which is Yiddish for "good old boychik," come from the same word. Grits meets *marmeligeh.* North Carolina meets Pinsk.

Bubbemayse
Literally, "grandmother's story," as in old wives' tale. But this *bubbe* comes to Yiddish from old English via Italy. The medieval Bevis of Hampton tales were very popular in Renaissance Italy, where Bevis became *Buovo.* The soap opera tales were translated from Italian into Yiddish and read by women who rarely learned to read Hebrew. In Yiddish, they were *Buovo-mayses.*

Bupkes
Beans. But it's come to mean, "It's worth

about as much as goat droppings," because goat droppings look a lot like beans.

Chazer
Chazerai

Pig, from the Hebrew. *Chazerai* is pig stuff. Garbage.

Chotchke
Tchotchke
Tsatske
Tzatzke

A plaything, in Yinglish — something cheap and easily breakable. My grandmother always pronounced it *tchotchke*. In Yiddish it's written with the letter "tsaddik" and properly pronounced *tsatske*. The diminutive is *tzatzkele*, which, much to my amazement as I grew older, also referred to that other kind of plaything: a female, a mistress, a girlfriend on the side. As my grandmother also used to say: You could have knocked me over with a fender.

Chutzpah

Yiddish hubris. You know the definition: someone who's murdered his mother and father and asks for the mercy of the court because he's an orphan. Here's an example of a Yiddish word becoming an English word because there isn't any English word that says so much so well.

Cockamamie

It's English, it means stupid, impossible, a "cockamamie" dream. It allegedly comes to American English from a Yiddish mispronunciation of "decalcomania," phony tattoos you'd lick and press on that were faddish in the 1930s. The new *Joys Of Yiddish* cites a George Harrison lyric from 1989, "Didn't want to be a star — wanted just to play guitar / In this cockamamie business."

Friends in the music business had George over for dinner one night. Their kids ended up playing guitar with George, who, it turned out, knew "Hava Negilah."

Pre-Beatles, he explained, he was a working musician and, of course, he'd played Bar Mitzvahs in Liverpool.

Davn
Dav'n

The act of saying your prayers.

Drek

It means "shit," the noun, but, in usage, it's not nearly as vulgar or as angry; in a hierarchy of words that mean "waste," "drek" is closer to "crap."

I heard a story when I worked in advertising that ad people swear is true. In the late '40s, just after the war, advertising was a gentiles-only business and, most often, it was Protestant gentiles at that.

Detergents were replacing old-fashioned laundry soap in the marketplace, and Proctor and Gamble had spent millions creating and test-marketing a new detergent they wanted to call "Drek."

The problem was, no one at their ad agency could say, "Hey, you can't call it 'Drek,' schmuck. 'Drek' is Jewish for 'shit'" — for fear that someone higher up in the agency would say, "How do you know that, Schuyler Greene? What was your name before?"

Finally someone at P&G headquarters in Cincinnati 'fessed up, and they changed the name to "Dreft."

Emess
From Hebrew, the truth.

Farbisn
Farbissiner
Bitter. As in "a *farbissiner* Yid." As in *Frau Farbissiner*, one of Mike Meyers's creations in his Austin Powers films.

Farblondzhet

Lost. Really lost. It was one of Danny Thomas's favorite words — and, talk about lost, he was Lebanese.

Farshtunkener

Stinking. Noun and adjective.

Feh!

It means "feh."

Feigeleh

Literally, little bird, from the German. But it's also the Yiddish name of my sister Phyllis. In usage, it means "gay." And it's used less and less.

Finf
Finif

It's the number five, and it's where the slang-for-five-dollar-bill "fin" comes from. There's a lot of Yiddish and Yinglish in film-noir dialogue and pulp fiction. See *Ganef*, *Shamus*, and *Smack*.

Fonfeh
Fonfer
Funfer

In contemporary TV talk, it means to stumble in your speech, to get tongue-tied, as in "Let's try that again, I funfered those last two words." In Yiddish, *fonfeh* means "to talk through one's nose."

Fress (verb)
Fresser (noun)
To eat, but "ess" is to eat like a person; "fress" is to eat like an animal.

Ganef
It's Hebrew for thief. The plural is pronounced "ganOVim." English citations go back to Dickens.

Gefilte Fish
One of the few Yiddish dishes that can qualify as a gourmet dish, especially when my cousin Naomi makes it. Similar to the French *"quenelle."*

Gevalt!
Always followed by an exclamation point. A sharp, loud, piercing cry for help, for mercy, for compassion. If it's not followed by an exclamation point, it's not a real *"Gevalt!"*

Glitsh
Literally a slip. In English, "glitch" is universally used as a computer term, as

in a software slip-up.

Gottenyu!

One plea short of a *Gevalt!* Literally, "Dear God!"

Goy

Goy is the singular, *goyim* is the plural, *goyish* is the adjective.

Every group has a word that means the other guy, and goy means someone who isn't a Jew. It's sometimes pejorative; a *goyisher kop* means "gentile head" — someone who may be a Jew but who is particularly thickheaded. But it's also sometimes purely descriptive.

The Italian word for non-Italians is "straniero" as in "stranger," or foreigner. In Mexican Spanish it's "gringo," in Armenian you're an "odar," and to a Mormon a non-Mormon is a "gentile." Even me.

Gribbenes
Greevn

Cracklings. The crisp and incredibly delicious shards of skin left in the pan after you render chicken schmaltz. Old Yiddish proverb: "Never buy *gribbenes* from a *moyel.*"

Hak Mir Nisht Keyn Tshaynik

"Don't bang my teapot." A polite and colorful way grandmothers had of telling their *eyniklakh* (grandchildren) to shut the fuck up.

Tshaynik means teapot, from the same linguistic travels from the Far East that have made china a synonym for dishware.

Heymish

Homey. Home-like. Comfortable.

Hoo-hah!

Accent on the hah. It's Yiddish.

In Mitn Drinen

In the middle of everything. Usually refers to a surprise; used as in "when all of a sudden, ..."

Kaddish

In Aramaic, it means "holy." Didn't know you knew any Aramaic, did you? The *kaddish* is the Hebrew prayer for the dead that begins, "Yisgadal, v'yiskadash. . . ." Besides being a sacred prayer of remembrance, it is often invoked ironically, as when someone is asked to accomplish an impossible, though not a life-threatening task. A Catholic ballplayer would cross himself when he would come up to bat against Sandy Koufax. A Jewish ballplayer would shout at Sandy in a mocking way, "Yisgadal, v'yiskadash!"

The prayer does not mention dying or grief but is a glorification of God, His name, and His work. Aw-mane.

Kalike
A cripple.

Kaporeh
It means "sacrifice." On Yom Kippur, very Orthodox Jews "shlug kapores," something not-so-Orthodox Jews don't like to talk about. You symbolically transfer your sins to a chicken which is swung over your head.

When I was a little boy in East LA, there was a live Kosher chicken place at Pomeroy Street and City Terrace Drive, where my mother would point at a chicken, say "that one," and then I'd hear a squawk and some thumping coming from a fifty-five-gallon drum. What I remember most is the gas flame shooting from an open jet — it seemed to me to shoot ten feet in the air. They'd use it to singe the feathers before they'd pluck the chicken. I also remember the chicken feet floating in the soup pot and the unborn eggs (*eyelakh*), a profound chicken-soup delicacy. Unlike beef, the whole chicken is kosher, and we ate the whole chicken. We were that poor — not in East LA but in Eastern Europe, where the traditions began. There was a Yiddish saying, "When a Jew eats a chicken, one of 'em is sick." I also remember watching an old man swinging a chicken over another man's head. In perfect Yinglish, my mother said, "He's schlugging kaporres."

Kashe

Barley groats, from the Slavic. Its homonym means "question," from the Hebrew. "The feir kashes," are the four questions asked by the youngest during Passover. They begin, "Why is this night different from all other nights?" This is the punch line to a thousand jokes. The Hebrew is *"Mah nishtanah halilah hazeh . . ."*

Keyn Eynhoreh
Kinnehoreh

Keyn is Yiddish for "without," and *eynhoreh* is from the Hebrew for "evil eye." The Jewish philosophy is simple enough: the evil eye is everywhere, and just when things start to go well — it zaps you.

Saying "keyn eynhoreh," contracted to "kinnehoreh," and sometimes holding your first and second fingers up to your lips and spitting or mock-spitting through them three times with a loud "Ptu" for each spit may or may not ward it off. If it doesn't, it means you didn't do it right.

Kholeryeh
Choleryeh

A plague. Used as a curse, "a kholeryeh," a plague on your house. From "cholera."

Kibitz

To provide color commentary. A *kibitzer* is the commentator.

Every Monday and Thursday, every *Montik* and *Donershtik,* we read a portion of the Torah, the first five books of the Bible. They have to be read perfectly, there is no room for error. If the reader mispronounces a word, a syllable, even fonfers a single letter, it is a mitzvah, a commandment, for a member of the congregation to correct him. Out loud. When I read this in *Life Is With People,* I had an epiphany (a Greek word) and understood why a Jew will interrupt someone telling a story or a joke and correct him. Out loud. It's not impolite, it's a commandment of the Lord.

Kishke

It's from the Slavic, it means "guts," "chitterlings," "intestines." My cousin, Ronnie the Doctor, a gastroenterologist, uses Kishke on his California license plate and as his e-mail address. I have memories of my mother's father scraping *kishkes* clean, stuffing them with flour, potato, carrots, and spices, and making "kishke." Also called "derma," from the German word for "guts." Through the 1960s the highway from New York to the resorts in the Catskills was called "the Derma Road," a pun on "Burma Road," a crucial and headline-grabbing route to India during World War II.

Kitzel

Verb. To tickle. The old Jack Benny radio show had a running character named "Mr. Kitzel," who spoke with a very thick Yiddish accent.

Mrs. Nussbaum was the name of the Yiddish resident of Allen's Alley on Fred Allen's radio show.

"Oh, Mrs. Nussbaum!" Allen would introduce her (this was radio, characters had to be introduced by name so the listening audience would know who they were).

And she would reply in her thick Yiddish accent, "You were expecting, maybe,

Weinstein Churchill?"

Ethnic accents were OK in that pre-PC America. The best place to hear what an American Yiddish accent sounded like is probably on audio copies of these old radio shows.

Kop

Pronounced "kawp." Head. *Keppeleh* is diminutive and endearing.

Kosher

In common, nonreligious, non-Jewish usage, it means "OK."

Kreplach

When I was a kid, the menu at Wan Q on Pico Boulevard described won-tons as "Chinese *kreplach*." Today more Jews know what won-tons are than know what *kreplach* are. America *ganef*, as my *zaideh* used to say.

Kreplach may have come to Yiddish from the French; it would mean "little crepe" and would refer to the dough that covers the meat or cheese filling. Or it might come from the German *Krapfen*, which means fritter.

Kurveh

Prostitute. I had no idea there was a Yiddish word for such a thing.

Kvetch

It means "to squeeze or press." It's come to mean "complain." And, used as a noun, a complainer.

Kvell

To swell with pride. I really did think this was an English word. It's not. But it should be.

Landsman

It's always transliterated "landsman," although in Yiddish it's pronounced "LANTSmen." It means countryman, *paisan*. And the plural is *landslayt*.

The Letters to the Editor column in the *Yiddish Forward*, the *Bintele Brief* (literally, "bundle of letters"), ran a famous complaint from a Russian Jewish mother whose daughter had married a Hungarian Jew. His demands for special foods, the way he wanted his house cleaned, the way he demanded that his children be raised were driving her daughter around the bend. "So you see, dear editor," *di shvigger* (the mother-in-law) concluded, "mixed marriages never work."

Latke

A pancake. We make potato pancakes on

Chanukah because we celebrate the miracle of one day's worth of sanctified oil burning for eight days by eating fried foods. Not bad for a religion. OK, you can't eat anything on Yom Kippur, but come Chanukah you have to eat fried food. In Israel, instead of potato latkes, they eat jelly donuts on Chanukah.

Lokh in Kop
A hole in the head. "I need this like I need a hole in my head." ". . . *azay vi a lokh in kop.*"

Lokshn Kugl
Noodle pudding. And I make a mean one.

Mah Nishtanah
See *Kashe.*

Mame-loshn
Yiddish. Literally "the mother tongue."

Mamzer
A bastard. Plural: mamZEYrim.

Marmeligeh
Mamaliga
Cornmeal mush, a Romanian staple. I was speaking to a Jewish group out on

Long Island. Someone asked what my favorite food was when I was a kid. The answer was, "Marmeligeh with lox wings and lox tails." As I said the words, I asked myself, "What kind of people eat lox wings and lox tails?" and said aloud, "Oh, my God, we must've been poor." It hadn't occurred to me until that moment.

Maven
Meyvn
(Swallow the last syllable and pronounce it MAV'n, like the mavens do.)
An expert.

Mazl
Hebrew for luck. *Tov* is Hebrew for "good" so *"Mazl Tov"* literally means "Good luck." See *Shlemazl*.

Mazuma
Money. Sol Steinmetz suggests that it's "the earliest Yiddish loan to American English," and cites usage by O. Henry, Jack London, Sinclair Lewis, and Carl Sandburg. *The Joys of Yiddish* quotes *American Speech*, 1926, which says that the word "may come from the Chaldean *m'zumon*." And I *know* you didn't know you knew any Chaldean.

Mechayeh

A pleasure, always preceded — at least by my dad when he'd come home from work, unlace his work shoes, and sit down in his oversized leather chair — by a huge, heartfelt sigh. As in "Ahhhhhhhhh . . . A *mechayeh*."

Meeskeit

Ugly. Not a sight for sore eyes, a sight that will make your eyes sore.

Megillah

From the Hebrew: The story of Queen Esther, in the Bible. The holiday of Purim celebrates one of the biblical Jews' rare victories with noisemakers, costumes, pageants, and three-cornered cookies called *homintashn*.

Another tradition is to get roaring drunk on Purim. But you have to read through the entire story of Esther, "the whole *Megillah*," before the party starts.

Mentsh
Mensch

In German it means "human," but in Yiddish it's often bestowed as a title, and it has everything to do with honor, trust, and character. And, yes, a woman can be a *mentsh*.

Mishugeh

"Mishuggy" is an American mispronunciation. *Mishugeh* is the adjective for "crazy." *Mishugenah* is the noun. *Mishegass* means craziness. As in, "He is *meshuge*." "He is a *mishuginah*." "It's all *mishegass*."

Mish-mosh

A mess, a mix-up.

Mishpokheh

Family. It's from Hebrew. *Gantse mishpokheh* means the whole family.

Moyel
Mohel
Moyl

The person, usually a rabbi, who performs circumcisions.

A tourist in a small town needs a watchmaker. He walks by a small shop with a display of watches in the window, walks in, and asks the man behind the counter if he can fix his watch.

"Sorry, I'm not a watchmaker. I'm a *moyel*."

"Why do you have watches in your window?"

"What would you put in the window?"

On the *Rugrats Celebrate Chanukah* video, when they travel back into biblical Jerusalem,

334

a sign in a shop window reads "MOHEL" in Hebrew letters. A sign hanging from the door says, "Cut rate." I like the watch joke better, but I wanted whoever animated the Rugrats to know that somebody got that joke.

Naches
Nakhes

Use a guttural *ch*.

The special kind of pride and joy that comes from your pride and joy.

Henny Youngman would ask if you'd want to see a picture of his pride and joy and he'd pull out a wallet-sized photo of a bottle of furniture polish next to a bottle of dishwashing soap.

I heard Milton Berle tell this joke in Atlantic City, where I traveled just because I wanted to see Milton Berle play a nightclub.

Three Jewish women are sitting on a porch in Miami Beach. One says, "My son, a doctor. And not just a doctor, he owns his own hospital, that's how successful my son the doctor is."

The second says, "Hah, my son is a lawyer. But not just a lawyer. He owns 200 apartment buildings, that's how successful my son the lawyer is."

The third doesn't say anything. Until the other two demand "What about your son? What does he do?"

"My son," she shakes her head, "doesn't do anything."

"He doesn't do anything?"

"No," she shakes her head again. "He's a homosexual."

"A homosexual?" The other two are aghast.

"And he doesn't do anything?" one asks.

"How does he live?" asks the second.

"He has two very good friends," the third woman answers. "One is a doctor, owns his own hospital, the other is a lawyer who owns 200 apartment buildings."

OK, Milton Berle told it better.

Nafkeh
Prostitute. There are two Yiddish words for such things.

Nar; Narishkeit
Fool; foolishness. But almost always the childlike, innocent, harmless kind of foolishness.

Nogoodnik
Yinglish, the *nik* suffix is Slavic, and a word radio comedians loved (words with a K sound in them are funny, one of the first rules of comedy). Because the suffix had

become familiar, "Beatnik" and "Sputnik" were easily absorbed into English.

Noodge

It doesn't come from "nudge"; it's from the Slavic, but that's what it means: someone who tries to "nudge" his way in, like the midget member of Borrah Minovich's Harmonica Rascals.

Nosh

A snack, noun, or to snack, verb. In Jackie Mason's painfully funny one-man Broadway show, I honestly thought I was going to hurt myself I laughed so hard listening to his shpritz about how "Jews eat, gentiles drink. I'm not making this up. Listen for yourself during intermission. The gentiles will meet in the lobby, 'After the show, let's go meet for a drink.' The Jews'll say, 'D'jeat yet?' It's true. The good thing for the gentiles, though, they don't have cockroaches. No," he tucked his head into his neck like a Jewish turtle. "How much can a cockroach drink?"

Nu

So.

Nu?

So?

Nudnik
Another -nik word. A pest.

Ongepatshket
A *patsh* is a slap, here as in something slapped together. *Onge* (or *ange*) is a prefix that means "over." So, overdone. Too much. Her makeup looks *ongepatshket*. Her carrot *tsimmes* tastes *ongepotchked*. Two more examples and this definition would be *ongepotchked*.

Oomglick
Unlucky. See *Shlemazl*.

Oy!
Oh!

Oy, Vey!
Oh, woe!

Oy Vey Iz Mir!
Oh, woe is me!
"When the bomb was dropped on Hiroshima, Einstein's immediate response was, '*Vey iz mir*.'" *The New Yorker*, November 25, 2002.

Paskudnyak
My father's father's favorite curse. He'd

pronounce it with four syllables, PA-SCOOD-NEE-ACK! This was one of the first words I looked up when I found a copy of Weinreich's *Yiddish-English Dictionary*. The definition, "foul fellow," somehow softens my grandfather's intent.

Pisher
It must be onomatopoeic, no?

Pupik
Navel.

Putz
Schmuck. Once obscene, now in general usage; once a pejorative, now, often, a term of endearment. And, I'm told, it's not related to the German *putz*, which means "to polish."

Rachmones
It means "compassion." It's a mitzvah. Your Hebrew name (and your grandfather's Hebrew name) Rachmiel comes from the same root word, which is Hebrew for womb.

Schlong
Obscene. *Schmuck*. It's Yiddish for "snake."

Schmo

A euphemism for *schmuck*.

Schmuck

In German it means "men's jewels." I have a picture of me standing underneath a sign over a jewelry store in Vienna that specialized in antique cuff links, studs, and stickpins. "Antik Schmucken," it reads, as good a caption for a picture of me as any I can think of. But that may be an etymological accident.

Dictionaries will tell you it comes from the Slavic, *smok,* which means "oaf." And Yiddish experts agree, though it makes more sense to me that it found its way into Slavic, where it may or may not mean "oaf," from the Yiddish, where it definitely means "dick." Not "penis," it's not clinical, and not "phallus," it's not technical. It means "dick," it's obscene. Although it does sneak into polite usage; the *New York Times* crossword puzzle once used it as a seven-letter word for "oaf." And *schmuck* is in such common usage in New York, one very Waspish young woman from Westport, Connecticut, who worked at *Good Morning America* swore to me that her father told her it was the Jewish word for truck driver. Which is why cabbies would shout *"Schmuck!"* at drivers who cut them off.

One night, about 11:30, in a cab going west on East Eighty-fifth Street, suddenly there was a traffic jam. Cars were honking, traffic was backed up. Our cabbie, a Haitian, to judge from his name, opened the door, stood on the running board, and peered down the block, where, I could see from the passenger side, someone was trying to back into a too-small parking space. "Ah," the Haitian cabdriver gritted his teeth. He smacked his forehead with his right palm and shouted, "C'est schmuck, ça!"

Schneider

A tailor. To *"schneid"* is to cut. In New York *schneided* is what you've been when you get zero, nothing, *gornisht* in a game of gin rummy; in the rest of America you've been "blitzed."

Schnook

Euphemism for *schmuck;* a big radio word on the Jack Benny show in the '40s.

Schnorrer

Beggar. Also a verb: *"schnoren"* is "to beg."

Schvantz

Obscene: *Schmuck.*

Seykhl

Sense. The opposite of a *goyisher kop.*

Shabbos

From the Hebrew, *Shabat.* We Jews invented the day off. The other days of the week in Yiddish are taken from German: *Montik, Dinstik, Midvokh, Donershtik, Fraytik, und Zuntik,* which can come in quite handy when you're in Vienna and want to buy a ticket for the opera for Tuesday night. Going through my choices, staring at the concierge at the Sacher, I realized I had no idea how to say "Saturday" in German. I still don't. Saturday night I stayed in.

Shabbos Goy

"Sabbath gentile." Because Orthodox Jews are forbidden to work on the Sabbath, and the making of a fire is considered work, and turning on a gas stove or making the electric contact necessary to turn the lights on or start an elevator are considered modern variations on the same theme, Orthodox Jews in mixed neighborhoods would ask gentiles, usually young boys, to help with the forbidden chores.

The great New York writer Pete Hamill was a shabbos goy. So was Mario Cuomo. So was Colin Powell. (In Brooklyn, Queens, and the Bronx, respectively). So was Sir Michael Caine (in the East End of London; he still speaks Yiddish). And so was a young Elvis Presley. When he lived in a public housing project in Memphis, a young Orthodox rabbi lived in an apartment nearby, and Elvis, of a Saturday, would turn on his lights and light the stove.

Shammes

The caretaker of a synagogue, from the Hebrew *shomer*, "to watch."

Because the name Seamus is similarly pronounced and because there were so many Irish cops, the Gaelic name is also given as the root for the pulp-fiction, film-noir, '40s slang for cop. Both roots helped the word move into common usage.

Sheyn
Sheyneh

Pretty. Beautiful. *Sheyn ponim*, beautiful face.

Shiva

From Hebrew *shiveh*, "seven." We sit *shiva* for seven days, the seven days of mourning after the death of an immediate family member. Mirrors are covered, garments are rent, and in Orthodox families a *minyan* comes to the home each day to say *kaddish*. We wait for a year to unveil a gravestone. The Orthodox will picnic on the grass, because to grieve for more than one year is to doubt the will of God.

Shlemiel
Shlemazl

You know the difference. A *shlemiel* is someone who will be fooling around on the observation tower of the Empire State Building and fall off. A *shlemazl* is the guy he lands on.

It actually happened, in Tel Aviv. Someone was trying to commit suicide, jumped out of a window, landed on a passerby which broke the jumper's fall, he was fine. The passerby died. The poor *shlemazl*. An *oomglick* is even unluckier than a *shlemazl*. If the guy lands on you, you're a *shlemazl*. If the building lands on you, you're an *oomglick*.

In the twelfth century, the Spanish rabbi Abraham ben Ezra defined *shlemazl* this way: If I sold lamps, the sun, in spite, would shine at night. If I made shrouds, men would live forever.

Shmaltz

Fat, especially chicken fat. Used in place of butter in kosher homes when a meat meal is served. The cracklings left after chicken fat is rendered are *gribbenes* or *greevn*. My mother made her own chicken fat and kept it in the refrigerator in a Skippy's Peanut Butter jar.

There's a Romanian-Jewish restaurant on the old Lower East Side, Sammy the Waiter's, that has one of those glass pitchers other restaurants use for cream or maple syrup, filled with schmaltz on every table. Marvin Hamlisch's dad used to play accordion at this restaurant. It was during one of his breaks that Zero Mostel stood up and shouted at the top of his lungs, "This food killed more Jews than Hitler!"

My theory is that although Jews in Eastern Europe were poor, we were fairly certain of two good meals a year: for the new year in the fall and for Passover in the spring. So we invented a cuisine we could taste for six months just to remember.

Shmaltz and its Americanized adjective, *shmaltzy* (in Yiddish it would be *shmaltzik*), also refer to high-cholesterol styles of music and tear-jerking drama.

Shmear

A verb, to smear, to spread. A noun, the stuff you smear or spread. It's New York deli talk. "A bagel with a shmear" means with cream cheese, *Schmierkase* in German.

Shmear's secondary meaning has become more popular than the original: the verb "grease" as in "bribe." *Shmear* the head-waiter. I need $5 to *shmear* the super, the messenger, the mover. I was watching *The Great McGinty* the other night and was surprised to hear Akim Tamiroff, playing a cartoon-corrupt politician in the 1940s Preston Sturges classic, say "Don't worry, we'll shmear him."

Shmek

A sniff or a taste. *Shmek-tabak* is Yiddish (and also German) for snuff. Yiddish gangsters knew enough to take a taste of uncut heroin to see if they were buying the *emess*, the real thing; which is why "heroin" is called "smack."

Shmatteh

Rag. The *shmatteh* business is the "rag trade," women's ready-to-wear. The *shmatteh* district is New York's Seventh Avenue.

Shofar

The ram's horn that's blown during the Rosh Hashanah and Yom Kippur services (unless the holiday falls on *Shabbos*).

Sholom Aleichem

Yiddish for Aloha, hello and good-bye. *Sholom Aleichem* means "Peace be unto you." The response, in Yiddish, is *"Aleichem Sholom,"* "Unto you be peace."

The great Yiddish writer took his pen name from the greeting.

And yes, it means exactly the same thing and is pronounced almost exactly the same way as the Arabic.

Shpritz

Spray. In comedy a *shpritz* is a rant and it's used as a verb and a noun. Chris Rock shpritzes on racism.

Shtetl

It means small town, the diminutive of the German *Stadt,* which doesn't mean "state" but "town." Read *Life Is With People*, a serious study of *shtetl* life, with a foreword by Margaret Mead, undertaken by a team of sociologists in the 1930s. They didn't foresee the Holocaust, but they understood that even without outside help, this kind of village life would never survive the twentieth century.

Shtick

It comes from the German, it means "piece." *"Nokh a shtick oogah, Yossel,"* my *Tante* Odel would coo as she pushed another piece of honeycake onto my plate. *Oogah* is Hebrew for cake. I'm Yossel.

In show business, a *shtick* is a piece of business. The spit-take was a famous Danny Thomas *shtick*. The great Flydini is a hysterical Steve Martin *shtick*. Writing theme songs for Oscar-nominated movies is a great Billy Crystal *shtick*.

Shtunk

From the German, stink. See *farsh-tunkener*.

Shvartz (noun)
Shvartzer (masculine)
Shvartzeh (feminine)

Black. From the German. It is used to mean "African-American," sometimes descriptively but, more often, negatively.

Shvitz

Sweat.

Tisha B'Av

The ninth day of the Hebrew month of Av and, after Yom Kippur, the second most important fast day on the Jewish calendar. The first temple was destroyed by Babylonia on Tisha B'Av. The Romans, coincidentally, destroyed the second temple on Tisha B'Av. The Nazis began implementing their "final solution" on Tisha B'Av, but that was no coincidence — Goebbels was a student of such things.

Tokhis
Tukhis
Tushie

Ass. Once obscene as *"tukhis,"* now in common usage, even baby-talk as *"tushie."* Pronounced with a guttural *ch*, it's often a sign as to who is and who is just trying to pass. In *The Tale of the Allergist's Wife* on Broadway, Valerie Harper pronounced it "tukus." This was a dead giveaway that, although she played Mary's Jewish neighbor Rhoda Morgenstern on the famous sitcom *The Mary Tyler Moore Show*, and she had her nose done, to boot, she was raised a *shikseh* named Valerie Harper.

"Tuchis Af'n Tish" is Yiddish for "ass on the table," meaning completely vulnerable, "let it all hang out."

Trombenik
A bum, a loudmouth, a *blufferkeh* in Yinglish.

Tsimmis
Tzimmes
It's a baked dish, often made with sweet potatoes, carrots, potatoes, prunes (in my family, anyway), sometimes with meat, and always sweet.
It also means something complicated. "Don't make such a *tsimmis* out of it."

Tsedaka
Tzedaka
Tzedawke
From the Hebrew for "charity." But because charity is a *mitzvah* and because *mitzvah* means both a blessing and an obligation, *tsedaka* also means "justice" and "righteousness." I always liked that about being Jewish. It's also Neil Sedaka's last name (a Turkish Jew).

Tsoris
Tzuris
Troubles.

Yenta
A gossip. Overbearing. Shrewish.

350

Yeshiva Bocher

A Yeshiva student.

After a year away studying, a Yeshiva bocher comes home. His mother answers the door, and there he is, with his long beard and *payess*, a black wide-brimmed fur hat, a long black frock coat.

"Oy," his mother shouts. "Joe College!"

Zaftig

Rubenesque. It's become an American word, used in the *New York Times* sans quotation marks or italics.

Zhlob

Does "slob" come from "zhlob" which comes from the Slavic, or is it the other way around?

PART 5

People I Met Along the Way

19

I Don't Care If You Want To, I'm Paying, You'll Listen

Dear Dylan,
If all goes well, real well, you'll be eighteen when you start college, and I'll be seventy-three.

OK, let's assume I'm somewhat mobile at seventy-three, and vaguely coherent — here's what's going to happen: You're in Boston or Connecticut or maybe Palo Alto or even UCLA. I'm in town, I've probably come into town just to see you, but make up some kind of business excuse because I don't want you to know how much I miss you, and we make a date and I take you and a friend to dinner. A good restaurant. A very good restaurant. Because I miss you and I love you and because I want to make sure you have at least one meal every six months you don't have to brush green stuff off of after you find it plopped face down in the back of your refrigerator. Remember, Dylan, I went to college too.

Over dinner we do the famous father-son college dance. You pretend to listen politely to the windy stories I tell, and I pick up the check. Just because the people in the stories I tell were once-upon-a-time world famous won't make listening to 'em any less painful. It's kind of like sitting through the commercials when you watch TV. Yes, they're a bother, but somebody's got to pay for the good stuff.

Just in case I won't be around to visit you when you're away at college (but because I'll be picking up the check anyway), I've written down the stories.

In a way it's easier on your old dad. Easier than hearing you ask, in all sincerity, who was this Paul Newman guy? Or, with a dose of sarcasm, come on dad, Robert Kennedy? That old president's brother? He died fifty years ago!

(Dylan will be a college junior in 2018. It will have been fifty years since the assassinations of Bobby Kennedy and Martin Luther King. He was born in 1998. I've done the math.)

Most of these stories come from interviews I did and people I met while I was working. If you want to watch the actual stories, I'm afraid I'm not going to be much help. I saved a few stories on videotape, you'll find them in my office, and a few more are on file at the Museum of Broadcasting. For all the stuff I saved, I saved very little of me.

I hated to watch myself. Along with Paul Newman and Mel Gibson and Clint Eastwood and Gene Kelly and Julia Roberts, who all told me they hate to watch me, too.

Easy joke. Sorry, guy.

One of the questions I'd ask the actors I interview is, "If one of your old movies shows up on television, do you watch it?" Most actors — including all of the above — say "No," and, when they show up at a compulsory world premiere of one of their films, they tend to enter grandly, pose for pictures, acknowledge the applause, and sneak out of the theater during the opening credits.

Gene Kelly told me he'd never watch one of his films on television. He said, "All I can see are the mistakes." He was the only one who could see the mistakes he made. Mine are a bit more obvious, even to the layman.

I'd run out of rooms when one of my pieces was airing on a time delay. I never watched any of the syndicated specials I did. I never watched when I filled in for Siskel with Roger Ebert. I was afraid I might see something I didn't like, change it, and get fired. I don't know why what I do works, but, God, I'm grateful it does.

I also think live television is supposed to be ephemeral. Watching it as it happens, we forgive the rough edges. Looking at something done five or ten years before, we expect the polish and perfection of a film or a TV commercial. The proof of this is that an hour of live TV broadcast takes exactly an hour, whereas I have never taped an hour show that took less than three hours to finish. Somebody always says, "We can do that a little better."

Most of the things I saved, I saved for future use: interviews with Jack Lemmon and Walter Matthau, Milton Berle and George Burns, I'd use for obituaries; a tour of the naval base at Lakehurst, New Jersey, with the guy who covered the explosion of the Hindenburg ("Oh, the humanity!"), rehearsal footage of Madonna and Al Pacino and Denzel Washington on Broadway (different plays). I also saved interviews with all four Beatles, which were used and reused, and a couple of audio-only remnants: that transcription of me on the old Art Linkletter radio show and a three-inch reel of audio tape labeled "John Lennon."

If you can find a reel-to-reel tape deck to listen to the Lennon tape, you'll hear a lot of mumbling and someone with a very pronounced Liverpool accent, Lennon, laugh and say, "Joel, get out of the way. Out of the way, Joel. Get out of the way."

20

I Meet the Beatles

John

The Immigration and Naturalization Service, those same folks who would one day do such a good job on September 11, 2001, were trying to deport John Lennon back in 1974 in a case that dripped of Nixonian meddling because Lennon had been convicted of marijuana possession in England.

"It was planted by a headhunting English cop who's now in jail for planting dope on people," Lennon told me. He plea-bargained guilty because Yoko was pregnant with Sean, "and I thought they'd get deported and they said they'd let her off if I . . . made a deal."

I covered the story for WCBS-TV and, because one of the editors figured having a TV crew gave me better access, for *Rolling Stone*, which titled the piece "Lennon: Back in the U.S.S.A."

That day there was a hearing at Federal Court in New York City, downtown on Foley Square. No cameras were allowed in, but I was, with what we redundantly referred to as "print press." Lennon's lawyer recognized me from TV and I watched him whisper to John and John looked over, and he recognized me, too. I was floored but, I think, I was also too nervous to show it. The lawyer sent someone over to me and asked if I wanted to interview John after the hearing.

He was as straight, as normal, as unaffected as he could be. He knew he was John Lennon, but, other than understanding that he had to comport himself in public as if everyone was watching — which everyone was, so no nose-picking, no public displays of anger or impatience, no behind-the-back yanking out a wedgie — he was a regular guy. A little smarter, a little funnier, but with the same kind of easygoing, supreme confidence that I'd noticed in the world-class jocks I knew at UCLA, like Walt Hazzard and Rafer Johnson.

His lawyer gave me a list of 118 emigrants who were allowed to stay even though they had prior arrests or convictions far more serious than Lennon's, including one convicted murderer.

"There are narcotics dealers that've been allowed to stay," Lennon said.

"Murderers, rapists, multiple convictions for dope, heroin, cocaine. What the hell. I'll fit right in." He really said it.

Someone named Paul had something to do with Lennon's defense. "Make sure you talk to Paul," he told his lawyer — then, turning to me, added "Not *that* Paul."

The Beatles had broken up not long before, and the question on everyone's mind was "When will they get back together?" There was a constant stream of rumors. World tours, simultaneous around-the-world satellite pay-per-view broadcasts. After David Geffen signed Bob Dylan, the word, from a reliable source, was that Geffen would bring them together because he'd done everything else and that was the ultimate challenge.

I don't think it's possible to overestimate the impact of pop music on American culture in the 1960s and 1970s. Which, of course, was why Richard Nixon's INS was after John Lennon in the first place.

When we walked out of the hearing room, John and I were together, talking. Small talk. Music stuff. I think we were talking about Randy Newman. This is the courthouse you've seen in a thousand movies, the Foley Square, *Twelve Angry Men* courthouse with the forty-foot-tall Ionic columns crowning an acre of marble steps. We walked outside into a phalanx of TV reporters who didn't want someone from another network in their shot.

"Joel," crew guys shouted at me. "Get out of the way."

Lennon loved it.

"Joel, get out of the way," he clucked in Liverpuddlian. Everybody's shotgun mike picked him up, and I had the Channel 2 crew transfer the track to audiotape for me.

Lennon liked the piece. He sent me a card, which I framed: "Thanks for the Immigration piece in *R. Stone*," he wrote and added a "Kilroy was here" kind of caricature of himself.

What he didn't see, because *R. Stone* cut it, was the sidebar I'd put together on folks the INS didn't seem to care if they stayed in the country. They were Nazi war criminals mostly, including a guy who lived a very public life in San Diego who'd been the minister of defense in the puppet government Hitler had set up in Croatia. There was corroborating testimony that he'd not only sent thousands of Jews and Gypsies to concentration camps, but that on his desk he kept a small wicker basket filled with eyeballs of his victims. He could stay.

But John Lennon was too dangerous to stay in America.

Not too long after that, I was covering the opening of the Ringling Bros. Circus at Madison Square Garden. It was a spring ritual for feature reporters in New York, and in past years I'd ridden an elephant (cars are more comfortable, and having ridden my elephant directly behind some-one else's elephant I can safely report that automobiles also pollute a lot less), and done what circus folk call a "walk through" the audience dressed as a clown (little kids, all awe and innocence, approached me like they were walking up to Santa Claus. "Hello, Mr. Clown," they'd say. What a wonderful feeling!). One year I'd actually performed as a clown, wearing a fireman's cap and ready to toss a bucket full of crepe paper streamers at the unsuspecting midget who dove off the top of the ladder into a trampoline. Edward R. Murrow never did that.

By this time I'd convinced the assignment desk I really was capable of covering the circus as me. In civilian clothes. We stood in the first row shooting Gunther

Gable Williams, who, when his animal act was finished, walked right up to our camera, a black panther on his back. He maneuvered the panther's head no more than four inches from the camera lens, smiled and asked, "Is this close enough for you?"

Three hours later I thought of what I *should* have said. There is a word for this, coming up with things you should have said three hours late. It'll come to me in a little while. I should have said: "Any closer we'd be breakfast."

What I did say was "Yes."

I looked past Williams into the audience and saw a familiar face point and laugh. It was John with Yoko and their son Sean, who was then about three years old.

We circled the Garden and I did a quick interview: What's your favorite thing about the circus?

"The little doggies," Lennon answered. Surprised the heck out of me. I always hated the little doggies.

Would you give it all up to run off and join the circus?

"I've already given it all up," he answered. "Maybe I'll join the circus next."

The video of that very happy family enjoying the circus and enjoying each other is very moving; it would become even more powerful in a year or so.

We were shooting wide shots of John and Sean and Yoko from about twenty yards away when Mick Jagger showed up, stopped to say hello to Sean and gave John a piece of paper. John waved the paper at our camera and shouted, "Anyone want Mick's phone number?"

About a year later, I was at a Broadway opening of something called "Sergeant Pepper's Lonely Hearts Club Band," a musical of other people doing Beatles songs. John Lennon was there, not with Yoko but with May Pang, Yoko's either present or former assistant, with whom he was supposedly having an affair, supposedly with Yoko's consent, or at least that was the rumor. Someone in the play's PR office figured it'd be safe for me to sit next to John.

So there I was. God knows I start to itch and squirm when people try to be hyperclever about my stories or my on-camera persona, and that happens to me maybe once a month. It must happen to Lennon a thousand times a day, I thought, so I didn't try to say anything clever, I didn't try to be funny, I didn't try to say anything other than "hello." And, May Pang to his right, I certainly didn't ask him how Yoko was. Which, I imagine, is why the play's PR people sat me there.

Before the show started, someone thrust their Playbill at Lennon and asked for his autograph. In very broad pantomime he made sure everyone who was watching understood that if he gave this guy an autograph, he'd have to give everybody his autograph. He waved an X with the guy's pen about six inches above the Playbill and showed the audience he hadn't written anything, shrugged his shoulders, and motioned to the hall. Everyone seemed to understand, and no one else asked for his autograph that night. But at least 500 people came by with their cameras and flashed a bulb in my eyes as Lennon waved. After about 450, I said to him, "I never thought I'd feel sorry for John Lennon," and he said, "Nah, it's OK. That's why I live in New York. People here leave me alone."

A few months later someone didn't.

If anyone knows Alaina Reed (she'd later play Olivia on *Sesame Street*), please tell her that when she started to sing "Yesterday," John turned to me and said, "She is great. She sings it better than Paul."

"I'll never tell," I said. I hope the statute of limitations is up on promises made to geniuses. John Lennon was one of the handful of people in the second half of the twentieth century who helped create what's best about the twenty-first.

Get hold of the Beatles' first press conference when they landed at JFK. If you can believe it, those four kids, and they were kids, in their early twenties, were feared and reviled. "When are you going to get a haircut?" a reporter asked George.

"I just had a haircut," he answers, smiling.

"What do you call that haircut?"

George answered, "Arthur."

A Hard Day's Night is one of the great movie musicals ever. It really is. My second favorite Beatles movie is *I Wanna Hold Your Hand,* and the Beatles aren't even in it, that's how strong the memories are.

And besides that, in a very few years, they wrote a hundred great songs. I was driving my mom's '65 Chevelle, four doors, white with blue vinyl upholstery, up the San Diego Freeway, with Terry Gilliam, when one of the rock stations played an advance copy of "Penny Lane." We got so excited when the baroque horns came in that I had to pull off onto the service lane or we would've died, that's how much the music meant.

John got into a lot of trouble when he said the Beatles were more popular than Jesus. He didn't say the Beatles *should* be more popular than Jesus; he was stating a fact. My favorite Lennon quote was his answer to a snooty question about Beethoven.

"Ah," Lennon kind of sneered, "he was lucky, too."

If you've ever done anything creative — and it worked — you know exactly what he was talking about. Where does it come from? Lennon didn't know. He was willing to bet Beethoven didn't know either. Nobody knows.

That's why performers are so superstitious. They have no idea where it comes from, how they turn it on, why it doesn't stop.

Paul McCartney swears that he dreamt "Yesterday," which has since become the most recorded song in history. He actually went around humming it and playing it for people for a few weeks, asking them if they'd heard it before. When enough people convinced him they hadn't, he wrote it down.

Paul

Here's a little-known fact: Paul McCartney and I had the same girlfriend. Francie.

Francie Schwartz from New Jersey. And she wrote a book about it.

Well, she wrote a book about her relationship with Paul called *Body Count.* It's a very good book about a talented and intelligent woman's coming of age in the '60s when women were still called girls and weren't supposed to come of age.

I'm not in the book and I've never been sure whether to be relieved or insulted.

Francie was a writer who was hired on at the same advertising agency I worked at, Carson/Roberts. Advertising is a lot of fun, because, I learned, you work with a building full of people who all want to be doing something else: writing novels, making movies, getting drunk, getting laid. Ralph Carson invented the "Have a nice day" greeting; Jack Roberts invented the smiley face to go along with it. Other than that, and the work they made us do every once in a while, it was terrific fun. Even watching Ernest Gallo actually spit on a storyboard for a TV commercial he didn't like. It was fun because we kept convincing each other we really were writers and artists and movie directors, not advertising people, so our egos weren't on the line. For a bra account, Hollywood Vassarette, I put a bra on the Statue of Liberty. The headline: "Free at last, Free at last, Thank God, Almighty, I'm free at last."

The first draft was Martin Luther King wearing a bra.

Francie was Paul's girlfriend after Jane Asher and before Linda Eastman. She was there when the group broke up, for which she blamed Linda and her lawyer father, never Yoko or John, and, frankly, I wasn't sure she was really there at all until five years later, covering the first Beatles' fan convention for *Rolling Stone*, I bought a photograph of Francie and Paul together for five bucks.

I do know things about Paul McCartney that few if any other males know, and I'm not going to tell you those things.

OK, I'll tell you a few.

"Why Don't We Do It in The Road?" was a question Paul asked more than once while he was driving his Aston Martin.

(A '60s TV actress told a much better story to her publisher about the kind of story she would not put into her autobiography.

"Once I gave Frank Sinatra a blowjob while we were driving in from Malibu," she said.

"Come on," the publisher scoffed. "That's not news."

"I was driving."

"Oh.")

"She Came in Through The Bathroom Window"?

She did. A groupie. One of John's groupies.

The first time I interviewed Paul, once the interview was over and the camera had clearly stopped running, I told him, "We shared a girlfriend."

He asked who, I answered "Francie Schwartz."

He laughed and said, "Let's change the subject."

Paul is not only very accessible and very nice, he wants us to know it. There's a piece of advice the queen mum gave to the future Queen Elizabeth when she was still a princess and England was at war. "You will never remember the people you meet today," her mum told her. "But the people you meet will never forget you."

Each time I interviewed Paul I watched while he introduced himself to each member of my film crew at the start of the interview, then, when he left, shook the hand of each crew member and thanked them by name. "Thank you, Frank," to the cameraman. "Thank you, Carol," to the gaffer. It was a trick, of course. But it was something he made himself do because the impression he left on perfect strangers was important to him.

I interviewed him in London in the early '90s about his foray into classical music: he'd composed a symphony that would make its American debut at Carnegie Hall. Paul's offices were on Oxford Street, and I needed a tie and stopped in at the cricket outfitters, Kent and Curwin, on the corner of St. James. (I only know four or five blocks of London, but I know them real well.)

The salesman was an American who recognized me from TV.

"What are you doing in London?"

"I'm on my way to interview Paul McCartney. That's why I'm buying a tie."

"You know," the salesman told me. "When I was at Harrods I sold him a few shirts, and the next time he came in he remembered my name."

What a good guy.

On that trip to England, we did a series on the Beatles that I'd win an Emmy for. We did some shooting in Liverpool and watched the Beatles' songs come to life. "Number 9" had been Ringo's address. George's father was a bus driver whose bus route passed Penny Lane; we found the bank, we found the fast-food shop (shoppe?), though fish and finger pie is no longer on the menu. Strawberry Fields was an orphanage behind the house where

John grew up; there is graffiti on the concrete fence posts, not just in a few dozen languages but in three or four different alphabets. The most powerful moment was in the Liverpool churchyard where Paul had met John when they were little kids. There's a gravestone in the churchyard. *Here lies . . . Eleanor Rigby.*

The last time I spoke with Paul was at an Italian restaurant on the East Side, *Sette Mezzo.* He was with Linda; they might have just come from cancer treatment. I said hello, she remembered me from New York TV and started quizzing me about restaurants in Chinatown. She looked terrible. She looked like she was going to die. I couldn't think about anything but the way Jane looked, puffed with cortisone, just before she died. I wanted to tell Paul how sorry I was, how I had been there, but, of course, I couldn't.

At the Oscars in 2002, I saw Paul on the red carpet with Heather Mills. Yes, I looked at her legs. I couldn't tell. I truly hope he's happy.

George

I can tell you exactly when I interviewed George. Jane and I were either about to be married or had just been married. I'd put together a tape for our party, and while I was schmoozing George while the crew was setting up, I told him that the first song on my wedding tape was "Here Comes the Sun." That makes the date sometime in late fall or early winter of 1976. What I remember about George is that he didn't seem to care, wasn't impressed, made me feel like he wished I hadn't bothered; or at least hadn't bothered him.

Twenty-five years later, watching a videotape of that filmed interview, putting together his obituary, I understood. He was shy. So shy he was embarrassed by the attention. He was uncomfortable inside his image.

He had a solo album coming out, he was being sued for stealing someone else's song (as common in the music business as whiplash is in car wrecks).

We talked about the possibility of the group getting back together. Not bloody likely, he said. "That's where we learned," he told me. "Getting back together would be like you going back to school."

"You know," I said. "I don't know if you do it in England but we look forward to school reunions here."

"Give us a bit of time," George said. Not

smiling. There was a pause before each answer, every word chosen with care.

When I asked if his public image got in the way of "work you try to do, of living the kind of life you want to live?" he sighed.

"That was part of the reason we all packed it in . . . I'm just a human. It just happens I've got a white suit on."

I flashed on a memory I had of the great basketball player Kareem Abdul-Jabbar, who was then Lew Alcindor, seven feet tall and a freshman at UCLA. We passed each other in a hallway on the first day of classes. Everybody was looking up at him, of course, and the look on his face said, "All I want to do is be anonymous, be like everybody else." I got the same feeling from George.

He'd ridden the bus to school with Paul, who was two years older and had a pre-John band called the Quarrymen. George would fill in when they needed an extra guitar. He was good. He'd be the reason Paul would play bass.

Twenty-five years later, George had made his peace with us and we with him. Though it wasn't any shorter, he no longer had long hair. He didn't stand out so much in a crowd, though, come to think of it, he was wearing a white suit. He looked like an old guy who looked like George Harrison.

It was November 2000. I was in London for Terry Gilliam's sixtieth birthday party. He'd bought out a neighborhood restaurant, nothing very fancy, which made the evening even more special, to serve dinner for about a hundred people. The Pythons were there, and Jonathan Pryce, who starred in *Brazil*, and a doctor friend of his, and friends of his kids. Besides his very elegant-looking mom and his younger brother, an LA cop who looks nothing like him, I think I'd known Terry longer than anyone else in the room. The first time either one of us had sold something to a magazine it was something we did together. It was a cartoon of Sonny Liston leaning out of the frame holding a razor blade. "Use Gillette Blue Blades or I'll Kick Your Ass," was the caption. He drew it, I wrote it, and we sold it to something called *The Outsider's Newsletter* and split ten bucks.

I argued and pleaded with him not to leave his house, which was dug into a Laurel Canyon hillside so steep there was a funicular to take you from the garage to the front door. He was leaving the country for London, following a Brit reporter named Glenys, who was very striking, very glamorous, very out of our class (or at least the class we were in then), and very much Danny Kaye's mistress.

He didn't listen. In England he met up with the Pythons, did the animated intros and outros for their revolutionary TV series, appeared in the occasional sketch — who knew he was a genius? — and would go on to direct *Time Bandits*, which, for a time, held the record as America's biggest grossing foreign-made film and which was produced by George Harrison. Who, that night, was my dinner partner.

One of the choices on the menu was "Cured Salmon." George called our waiter over and, in his most charming Liverpool accent, asked, "Excuse me, but of what disease was this salmon cured?" He really did. Walter Shenson, who'd produced *Hard Day's Night*, told me they beefed up George's part when they discovered how funny he was.

As a birthday gift, George gave Terry a banjo once owned by a British vaudeville star named George Formby, whose half-camp, completely infectious music George Harrison loved to play. George strummed "Happy Birthday" and George and Terry sang half a dozen hysterically hideous vaudeville tunes I'd never heard before, George Formby tunes that never made it across the Atlantic. A good thing. Had they, we might have canceled Lend-Lease.

Yes, Terry sings. Maybe not better than George, but louder. In the '60s we came up with camp too soon to do anything about it. "No matter how young a prune may be, his face is full of wrinkles," went one of the tunes Terry actually learned. "We get wrinkles on our face, prunes get wrinkles everyplace!"

We also took a meeting with Lenny Bruce's mom, Sally Mars, and a goodfella buddy of Lenny's named Frankie Ray. We had an idea for a movie: *Lenny Bruce Lives!* We opened in a men's toilet. The camera holds steady as someone, back to camera, walks into frame, and stops at a urinal. We hear a zipper unzipping, a rush of urine, a flush of water, the zipper being zipped. The person, still with his back to the camera, leaves the frame. We zoom in, tight, to the graffiti he left behind.

LENNY BRUCE LIVES!

I learned two things at that meeting. It was two years after Lenny OD'd in the toilet and his mother was still blaming herself. "When I used to MC at strip joints I'd take Lenny with me. I had a filthy mouth and kept apologizing to him. And he told me, 'Don't worry, Mom, what are they going to do, arrest you?' "

And she told me that a few days before he died, Lenny was hitchhiking in the Hollywood Hills — he'd sold his car to pay for drugs — and Mort Sahl drove by and didn't pick him up.

But I wasn't Joel Siegel yet, and he wasn't Terry Gilliam, yet, and nothing came of the meeting.

Terry was raised a serious Christian but dropped out as a teenager. The issue, as he explains it, was whether God has a sense of humor. Terry voted yes. His church voted no. Terry went out on his own.

When he came in from London and stayed with us in New York, Jane moved the good China and the crystal to the front of the kitchen cabinet just in case Terry looked in. He's one of maybe half a dozen people who've known all of my wives. When Jane died he sent a telegram: "I would do anything to ease your pain."

George didn't want to talk about music that night. He wanted to talk about movies. Hand-Made Films, his company, financed *The Life of Brian* and Terry's *Time Bandits*. We talked about *Mona Lisa* with Bob Hoskins and how that created a straight line of great Brit films noirs through *Lock, Stock, and Two Smoking Barrels, Croupier* and *Sexy Beast,* and how these are great films that might never have happened had it not been for *Mona Lisa,* which wouldn't have happened without George. He liked hearing that, and it's also true. He seemed to be much prouder of his films than of his music. The subtext of our conversation was that he didn't want the movie part of his life to be forgotten. George knew that he was dying. I made sure, in his obit, that we found a clip of him as an extra in *Life of Brian* and talked about Hand-Made Films.

"What's the major difference between making a record and producing a film?" I asked.

"When you record you know the song and you know how it should sound. When you make a movie you have no idea what the finished product is going to be."

"I have to ask," I said after an hour or so, "how are you feeling?" I knew he'd had throat cancer. I'd read that it had spread to his lungs. I didn't know if it had already metastasized to his brain, and I don't know if he knew it that night. I'd had half my left lung taken out the previous June, and the spot on my right lung they hadn't yet diagised had been there, ticking, for a slow and long six months.

He told me how healthy I looked.

"Fat," I told him. The secret of eternal youth.

Catherine Deneuve said about women aging, "Over fifty, it's either your ass or your face." Diet and exercise, and your ass might look like it did when you were seventeen, but your face sags. Put on some weight, and you won't need cortisone or Botox, but you might have to buy two tickets if you fly Southwest Airlines.

"The cancer doesn't bother me," he told me. "But I'm still haunted by the stabbing."

Someone had broken into his country house, a huge country house, two years before. George had been stabbed a dozen times. His wife, Olivia, saved his life, beating the guy off her husband. "That," he told me, "is real fear. I still have nightmares. That will be with me the rest of my life."

I was in Disney World when George died, taping some interviews with kids about Walt's 100th birthday for a piece that would air the following week. Early that morning we drove out to Orlando's ABC affiliate, where they set me up with a local crew and a monitor, outside next to a patio table, a couple of palm trees behind me. Maybe it was the surreal setting, maybe it was hearing Diane and Charlie through a headphone so the Q and A felt like a phone conversation, or maybe it was because I was truly shocked, but my guard was down, and I said things I otherwise never would have said.

George was a Beatle. The Beatles were supposed to live forever. John was shot dead, assassinated, but George died of natural causes, the way most of us will die. He died of cancer. I have cancer. We'd had dinner, I'd sat and talked and joked with him a few months before.

"We talked about our cancer," I told Diane and Charlie, staring into a camera lens.

"He had just been diagnosed with lung cancer, I'd had surgery six months before on my left lung. People who have cancer are very matter-of-fact about it and that's the way we were. We agreed we didn't know whether this was going to kill us, but we also agreed that we weren't going to let it make us stop living. He was in the middle of recording an album. We were at a mutual friend's birthday party. He picked up a banjo, picked up a guitar and entertained. He was George. He was wonderful. And I never thought, not for a moment, that I would outlive him."

Ringo

This will be short.

I always thought Ringo was a schmuck.

I interviewed him at the Guggenheim, where he was fronting an ad campaign for Visa or Mastercard, which lets you know right there how successful the ads were.

This was well into the '90s, and I was told he didn't want to talk about the Beatles. Which is kind of like getting an interview with a guy with a foot growing out of his forehead and you can't ask about the foot.

My last question was, "You know, we share a birthday."

"Ah," he said. "July 9th!"

We were born on July 7th. So were Marc Chagall and Gustav Mahler and Satchel Paige. That was Ringo's idea of a joke.

What a schmuck.

21

Never Ask a Question Unless You Really Want to Know the Answer

Robert de Niro is such a great actor that the first time I saw him, alive and in person, I wasn't sure it was Robert de Niro.

I was in London. Terry Gilliam was showing an early cut of *Brazil* to people who'd worked on the film, and because he couldn't make the screening, he asked me to seek out de Niro and let him know the print wasn't color corrected, the opticals weren't ready, and most of it had a temp score.

"Bob worries about things like that," Terry told me.

The screening was in a very private London screening room. There were at most two dozen people waiting in the lobby, and I had to figure out which one was de Niro by process of elimination. He's shorter than he should be. And shlumpier. In person he looks more like a cabbie or a butcher whose buddies are always telling him he looks like de Niro and who's wife always knows better. Maybe that's why he's such a great actor. He really does become the parts he plays.

When I figured out nobody in the room but this guy could possibly be de Niro, I walked up to him, introduced myself, and gave him Gilliam's message.

He nodded and looked like he didn't want to be bothered, so I didn't ask him about the line from *Taxi Driver*. Then. I waited a few years and asked him during an interview.

You know the line, one of the great lines in movies: de Niro staring himself down at the mirror in his rathole of an apartment and shouting, "You talkin' to me? You talkin' to *me?*"

The story I'd heard is that Marty Scorsese, the director, was in the building across the street so he could shoot the scene through the window, and de Niro was wearing some kind of wireless receiver in his ear so he could hear Scorsese set up the shot, move him left or right if he had to, and feed him his lines. The problem was, back in the day, wireless technology wasn't quite what it is today, and even normal New York traffic caused a lot of interference, so de

Niro wasn't sure what Scorsese was saying or even who he was talking to. Hence:

"You talkin' to me?" And, again, louder, more forceful, "YOU TALKIN' TO ME?!"

Isn't that a great story? Then I made the mistake, during an interview, of asking de Niro if it was true. He looked at me like I was nuts.

"Nah!" he said. "It was in the script."

Another great movie story is about the time Paul Newman, a kid fresh from Cleveland, auditioned for Sam Spiegel, who was then producing films under the name S. P. Eagle.

Newman didn't get the part, but Spiegel was taken with him anyway and called Newman aside to give him some advice.

"Have you ever thought your name was too . . . too . . . too . . ." Spiegel funfered.

"Too Jewish?" Newman asked.

"Yeah. Have you thought about changing it?"

And Newman answered, "Yes. I have. To S. P. Newman."

I asked Joanne Woodward. She told me it was true.

Doing interviews, especially for TV, you have to ask obvious questions. There is a line between an obvious question and a stupid question, and I have, more than once, crossed that line.

When Paul Newman won his Oscar for *Color of Money*, I asked him if he thought he'd been able to play the part so well because he'd already played the same character, Fast Eddie Felsen, in *The Hustler*. I thought it was a good question until the words came out of my mouth and I realized I was asking an actor if he thought he could act.

The correct answer was, "No, you dumb schmuck."

Newman actually answered, "No, I don't think that was necessary."

He was more polite to me than he was to Sam Spiegel.

Gene Kelly gave me one of his last interviews. I'd been told he was a tough interview, but he was just terrific. We did it poolside at his Beverly Hills home. I had a lot of questions, technical questions that he loved answering.

On The Town was the first real Hollywood musical shot on location. I knew that when they shot in the studio back then — it's still true today — the actors recorded their songs first and lip-synched to the playback. But how, I asked, could you do that in Chinatown and Central Park and in front of Grant's Tomb for God's sake, in *On The Town*?

The way Kelly smiled at the question, I understood he was the guy (he codirected the movie with Stanley Donen) who figured out the answer.

"I had a metronome in my pocket," he said. "We set it to the tempo we'd already recorded. And we didn't have a lot of takes," he went on. "Sinatra was a huge star with the bobby-soxers. We'd drive up to a location in two cabs, the crew would pile out of one and set up, we'd jump out of the other. We had maybe two takes before somebody would see us and shout 'Frankie' and we'd have to get out of there."

"Turned out Sinatra was a pretty good dancer, too," I said. And I shouldn't have.

Gene Kelly gave me the withering look he either learned from or taught to Paul Newman and said, "Of course he was. I taught him."

Kelly, of course, taught us all to love dance as an art form. When he died, Peter Jennings ran "Singin' in the Rain" as Kelly's obit, no voiceover, no narration. "That says it all," Peter said. But it doesn't.

In the '30s and '40s, the big MGM musicals that featured black stars like Lena Horne would set up their songs as what they called "specialty numbers," songs that weren't part of the story line on purpose, so theaters in the South could just cut them out of the films. When Kelly hired the fabulous Nicholas Brothers to costar with him in *Pirate* and they were scripted to be an integral part of the story, and they danced with Kelly so their numbers couldn't be cut, MGM said he'd have to do the film without them. Kelly told MGM, "If I have to do it without them, you have to do it without me." Kelly was one of the top three stars in the world then, and although MGM might have preferred white over black, their very favorite color was green, hands down.

I was telling that story to one of our ABC cameramen, who happens to be named Gene Kelly. He met that other Gene Kelly once, when he was shooting a ball game at Yankee Stadium and backed into the other Kelly's box. This Kelly is African-American, and when he showed the other Kelly his driver's license, the dancer hugged the cameraman, dragged him through the crowds asking very surprised New Yorkers, "You know who this guy is? He's Gene Kelly!"

One of the sound guys overheard *that* and told us a Gene Kelly story he'd heard from his dad, who was one of the New York crew on *On The Town.*

The opening shot: a whistle blows, a hundred sailors get off a boat and the camera finds Sinatra and Kelly and Jules Munshin. There was supposed to be play-back, but the whistle was quiet and the music never started. Kelly walked up to the young kid who was supposed to have clicked on the audio. The kid was very young. Baby-faced. He was obviously just out of the army and more scared of Gene Kelly than he'd been of the entire Japanese fleet.

"Your first day on the job?" Kelly asked.

The kid nodded.

"Don't worry," Kelly said. "You'll get it right the next time."

What a great man. He could also dance a little.

I knew one of the Nicholas Brothers, Harold, fairly well. He told me that the movie star who was nicest to him and his brother was Tallulah Bankhead, which sur-prised me, because her father was a fire-breathing congressman from Birmingham, Alabama. She saw the two when they really were kids, dancing in a Cotton Club review uptown in Harlem. She invited them to join her table, asked if there was anything she could do for them, and before older brother Fayard could stop him, Nicholas, who remembered being six or seven at the time, asked her for a bicycle. Everyone at the table laughed. And the next morning two bikes were delivered to the Nicholas' household.

I worked with a Broadway producer who had worked with Tallulah. Taloo, he would call her. "Young man," she once told him. "I've been down on everything but the *Titanic*."

I never met Alfred Hitchcock; no, even I'm not that old. I did see Fred Astaire once, walking in front of the Beverly Hills Hotel, wearing a tie, green I think it was, as a belt. I saw Cary Grant once, at LAX, wearing a tan suit with a dark blue shirt and rep stripe tie, an almost tactile aura about him. And one day, driving up Beverly Drive, I pulled alongside a Rolls Royce, and you know how you always look inside a Rolls Royce to see if you know who's inside? Jack Benny and George Burns in the front seat, Gracie Allen and Mary Livingston in the back seat. But I never even saw Hitchcock.

It's not that Hitchcock didn't like actors, he just didn't like to talk to them. He and his wife would storyboard his movies. He knew where he needed the actors to stand, what emotions he needed their faces to convey, and he directed them to be there, do that, that's it; like they were props.

He got into trouble doing *Lifeboat* because one of his stars, Taloo, never wore underwear. The lifeboat itself was in a huge tank in Fox's biggest sound stage. The actors had to climb down a ladder into the water to get into the boat and, to make sure she didn't get her costume wet, Taloo would pull her dress over her head.

One morning some close friends of Darryl Zanuck came onto the set with their two young children who were exposed to Taloo exposing herself. Zanuck was livid. He called Hitchcock in and demanded he reprimand her, penalize her, dock her salary, something.

Hitchcock didn't like saying "Good morning" to his actors, let alone reprimanding them. He told Zanuck, "It seems to me that is a problem either for wardrobe, makeup, or hairdressing."

Which brings me to Michael Caine. A great actor, one of the nicest people you will ever meet; even Hitchcock wouldn't have minded talking to him. We had been invited (separately, to be sure) to the Marvin Davises for dinner the night before the Golden Globes in 2002. Marvin Davis is the Denver oil zillionaire who owned Twentieth Century Fox for a small part of the twentieth century and retired to ten acres at the pinnacle of the Beverly Hills. It's one of those houses where, when you stand in the living room, you want to ask someone where the newsstand is so you can buy a postcard to send back home.

Chasen's had been Hollywood's family restaurant for almost forty years. Ronnie proposed to Nancy in one of the booths there. When she was shooting *Cleopatra*, Liz Taylor would be sent Chasen's famous chili once a week. When the restaurant closed, the Davises hired the chef, who, that night, prepared every one of the Chasen specialties for the thirty-eight guests. And, of course, he prepared thirty-eight portions of each of the Chasen specialties, just in case everyone wanted the same thing.

We started with the seafood salad. Next came thirty-eight steaks, thirty-eight portions of prime rib, thirty-eight hobo steaks (a Chasen's specialty), thirty-eight bowls of chili (very rich tasting, spicy but mild, not hot, and very, very good). For the fish course, there was salmon and something called Sole Hitchcock that Michael Caine had been raving about.

"Save some room for Sole Hitchcock," he told the table. "Hitch had it for dinner at Chasen's every Friday night."

I saved some room. Sole Hitchcock was exactly the kind of dish a fat old Englishman would have for dinner every Friday night. The fish was overcooked. There was more breading than fish. And there was no seasoning in the breading. Not even salt.

Michael Caine is a great actor. He also likes me because when he won his second Oscar, for *Cider House Rules*, I said, live on the air, "Oscar, shmoscar, this man is a great actor. When is the Queen going to Knight him?" Now there's a good review. The queen knighted him the following year. Do you suppose she watches *Good Morning America*?

Caine is also a great storyteller. He was going on that night about ginkgo biloba, which allegedly increases memory function because it increases blood flow to the brain. Caine said he'd walked into his drugstore and asked the pharmacist where the ginkgo biloba was, and the pharmacist said, "It's not working, is it?"

"You moved it," Caine said. The druggist confessed he had. And Caine told this terrific joke, Gentile version. First time I'd ever heard a Jewish version and a Gentile version of the same joke.

Gentile version:

Two guys are talking. One guy says, "I've just tried this amazing drug to improve my memory. It's unbelievable."

"What's it called?" the other guy asks.

And Caine begins to gesticulate with his hands and shrug his shoulders and shake his head and finally he asks, "What's the name of that flower? It has white petals all around and a big yellow center."

"Daisy," the other guy says.

And Caine turns his head as if he's shouting into the next room.

"Daisy!" he shouts. "What's the name of that drug I'm taking to improve my memory?"

Jewish version. Same joke. Same setup. Except the guy asks his friend, "What's the name of that flower? A long stem, it has thorns, it's pink, it smells good?"

"Rose," the other guy says.

"Rose!" the Jewish punch line. "What's the name of that drug I'm taking to improve my memory?"

Something Nice About Marlene Dietrich

I was flying from New York to LA, sitting next to a guy in his sixties who knew me more as a theater critic and a Broadway playwright than a movie guy, so it must've been in the 1980s. He worked on Broadway, as a theater manager I think, I have no idea what he told me his name was. He said that he'd been stationed in North Africa during World War II and assigned to Special Services, where he stage-managed USO shows, among other duties.

Marlene Dietrich was incredibly popular with the soldiers during World War II, on both sides it turned out. And she used her popularity to pass messages to resistance fighters, hidden in the lyrics or the arrangements to "Lili Marlene." The French and German resistance would listen to her sing "Lili Marlene" live to the troops and, right out of a spy thriller, she'd alter a word or change the arrangement, and that was the message. Hitler did his best to entice her into coming back to Germany. He would have given her almost anything; she refused, nailing the Nazis with a four-word indictment that deserves to be in stone: *They are murdering children.*

She came to North Africa to meet and

entertain the GIs and probably bed a few as well, though not, I'm certain, our stage manager — though, backstage, she did strike up a conversation with him.

He was from Brooklyn. He hadn't been home in three years, hadn't seen his mother in three years, hadn't spoken to her in two. Dietrich took his mother's phone number and promised to call.

A few months later he received a letter from home filled with exclamation points.

A Mrs. Riva had phoned his mother, told her she had spent some time with her son in North Africa while she was on a USO tour and he had given her a gift to give to her. Could they meet the next afternoon at the Tea Room at the Plaza?

The date was set, the little Jewish lady from Brooklyn showed up at the Plaza Hotel, asked the maître d' for a Mrs. Riva, and was kowtowed toward Marlene Dietrich. Riva was Dietrich's married name.

Her son was well, healthy, out of harm's way, Dietrich told her. And, because they met on Mother's Day, he had given her this for his mother. Dietrich handed her a new but unwrapped Chanel bag. It was obvious even to a Jewish mother — and Jewish mothers believe their sons capable of anything — that Dietrich had taken it from her own closet.

I believe the story because it wasn't Dietrich's people, it was the son who told it to me.

Actors You Swear Aren't Acting the First Time You See Them

Brando's first Broadway play was *I Remember Mama*, which started the revolution in stage acting he'd complete when he starred in *A Streetcar Named Desire*. He was so natural, so real, people in the audience thought he was a stage hand who'd wandered on stage by accident. I know the feeling, that joy in being completely fooled by greatness. It doesn't happen often, but there have been a handful of film performances that affected me the same way.

Ida Kaminska in *Shop on Main Street*. My God, it's as if some magic camera had caught somebody's bubbie on film. She was one of the great actresses of the Yiddish theater and was one of the first stars of a foreign-language film to be nominated for an Oscar. The movie, a little stagy by today's standards, is absolutely worth seeing. An "Aryan" Pole takes over Ida Kaminska's little button shop on Main Street in their little town. He thinks he's going to be rich. All Jews are rich. It's a great film.

Redd Foxx in *Cotton Comes to Harlem* was another. I couldn't get over this old guy. Where did they find him? I knew Redd Foxx. When I was a kid, every big-city high school boy had heard his party records on the Dootone label. Dirty jokes.

"I'm suing him for breach of promise. He promised to take me to Florida, your honor."

"Judge, I didn't promise to take her to Florida, I said I was goin' to Tampa with her."

And great lines.

"I was in the war. I was running as fast as I could away from the fighting and a general stopped me and said, 'Private! Why are you running?' And I answered, 'I'm running, sir, because I can't fly!'"

I heard those jokes must be forty-five years ago. But I'd never seen Redd Foxx until he played this bum in *Cotton Comes to Harlem*, and I would've bet a trip to Tampa they'd somehow filmed the real thing.

Same thing with Samuel L. Jackson playing a crack addict in *Jungle Fever*. It didn't hurt his cred any that a few months earlier, he'd really been a crack addict. He talks about it. He's one of those people, Anthony Hopkins is another, who you know wake up every morning in love with life, amazed that they managed to escape drinking or drugging themselves to death. Not long after *Jungle Fever*, when Jackson was still fairly unknown, a very attractive African-American woman stopped me at Zabar's. I think it was on a Sunday morning, at Zabar's fish counter. Imagine if the U.S. Mint were selling hundred-dollar bills for ten dollars each — that's what the fish counter at Zabar's is like on Sunday morning. She said hello, let me know she knew who I was, and pointed at this guy elbowing his way to the cash register and asked if I knew who he was. "Sure," I said. "That's Sam Jackson, he's a terrific actor." Then, trying to figure out why she would ask that and, OK, giving her the once-over and thinking I don't think Sam Jackson would mind at all meeting her, I asked, "Would you like to meet him?"

"I already know him," she laughed. "I'm his wife. I just wanted to make sure you knew who he was."

Morgan Freeman in *Street Smart* gave another one of those performances. He played a pimp. The film was based on a true story. He played the perfect sociopath, turning on a dime from hail-fellow-well-met best buddy to murderer. After the screening — I even remember the screening room up on the ninth floor of an old Times Square editing house — we critics couldn't believe what we'd seen. Our reviews got him an Oscar nomination. Riding down the elevator I remembered where I'd seen him before. "Oh, my God," I mumbled, unfortunately loud enough for the other critics to hear (we don't like to give anything away, folks, not anything), "that's Easy Reader from *The Electric Company*!"

A few years later I was interviewing him about *Shawshank Redemption* (great movie, terrible title). I was wearing this very snazzy Nicole Miller movie tie. Popcorn kernels, cans of film, movie marquees advertising *Citizen Kane*. Morgan Freeman liked the tie. I said thank you. He told me again he liked the tie. I said thank you again. Then he said, you know, in some cultures when someone compliments you on an article of clothing you have to give it to them. He really did.

"Are you a Buddhist?" I asked. And he got this caught-with-his-hand-in-the-cookie-jar look; he must have given his mother the same look when he was seven.

I told him that this interview was part of an hour-long Oscar special and I had other interviews to do and I needed the tie for continuity. "But as soon as I'm finished," I said, "I'll mail you the tie. I'd be flattered." He gave me an address. In Mississippi. He'd moved back to Mississippi voluntarily, that's how much America has changed. And when I finished taping the show, I mailed him the tie.

Five years later I'm interviewing Brad Pitt. He and Morgan Freeman had done *Seven* together, and I tell him the story about the tie.

"Funny," Pitt tells me. "He'd wear this great leather jacket he wore in *Street Smart* every day to work and one day I told him I coveted that jacket, so he gave it to me. I didn't want to take it, but he made me take it."

"Wait a minute," I said. "Let me get this straight. You got a leather jacket. He got a tie. What do I get?"

And Brad Pitt said, "You get to tell the story."

22

Rosebud

One reason *Citizen Kane* is the greatest movie ever made is because, if you count 'em up, it has more special effects per minute than *Star Wars* or *Close Encounters* — but nobody thinks of *Citizen Kane* as a "special effects" movie, because the rest of it is so incredibly good. The acting, the camera angles, the lighting . . . what other movie gets you excited about depth of field? And, yes, the story it tells. When Welles died and I was writing his obit, we fast-forwarded through a tape of *Citizen Kane*, and every single shot we stopped the tape on was a masterpiece, starting with the opening shot.

You can almost hear Orson Welles giggle when he came up with the opening: a full-screen sign that reads "No Trespassing." Who *doesn't* want to see what's behind a sign that reads "No Trespassing"?

Then his camera pans up a Cyclone

fence, through a wrought-iron gate with a curved letter "K" at the top, then past an abandoned tiger cage, past two Venetian gondolas Welles found God-knows-where (part of the moviemaking myth is that he used every prop and pieces of every set he could get his hands on when he was creating Xanadu).

David O. Selznick shot *Gone with the Wind* in Culver City and used painted backgrounds, called "mattes," to hide the palm trees. The mattes looked so real that movie fans, especially movie fans in Atlanta, still refuse to believe it when you tell them the whole film was shot in California. But Orson Welles opens *Citizen Kane* with painted mattes of Xanadu that are so blatantly phony he must have wanted them to look that way. It's not realism that makes this the best motion picture. It's the art that makes us suspend disbelief.

Still outside the mansion, we see a light turn off, then on. Welles's mouth fills the screen, and the first word we hear Kane say is his last: "Rosebud." Then he drops the glass snowball he was holding, and we watch it shatter as it rolls down the stairs. We see the door to Kane's room open in an amazing piece of camera work, looking through one of the shards of broken glass.

We see the nurse walk in, fold Kane's arms on his chest, pull the sheet over his face. He's dead.

When Universal rereleased Welles's second-best film, *A Touch of Evil*, which some film buffs had succeeded in getting the studio to recut according to a Welles memo that pleaded, "If you must cut my movie, *please* do it this way," I got to interview the film's stars, Charlton Heston and Janet Leigh. *A Touch of Evil* had been shot in Venice, California, refitted to look like a Mexican border town. (Drive down Windward Avenue a few miles south of the Santa Monica Freeway, and you can still see the stucco columns. It's easy to imagine the set.)

Late one night, after a long day's shooting, Heston told me, he and Welles were accosted by a fan in a Venice bar.

"Mr. Welles, you are the greatest film director who ever lived. I'm a huge fan," Heston let on that Welles was not having a problem with this kind of adulation.

"I just have one question," the man went on. He then described, pretty much shot for shot, the opening of *Citizen Kane.*

"After Kane dies, everybody tries to find out what 'Rosebud' means." And Heston said that Welles nodded. "That's right."

"But," the fan jabbed his finger at

Welles's chest, "the nurse doesn't come into the room until after Kane dies. Nobody heard him say 'Rosebud' — how do they know it was his last word?"

And Heston told me, "Orson grabbed the guy by his collar, pulled the guy's face close to his own and said (and Heston's voice got threatening and menacing), 'Never tell anyone what you told me here today!' "

I met Orson Welles once. It was New Year's Day, I'm not sure what year, 1982, '83. I walked into *Good Morning America*'s green room, which was beige, by the way, and there was Orson Welles. I had no idea he'd be on the air. He was doing some magic tricks, publicizing a charity. He was very big, wearing a free-flowing black suit. He looked like he'd slept in his clothes. I didn't care. I looked at the clock, I had about half an hour to spend alone with Orson Welles.

I didn't ask him about *Citizen Kane*, because I figured everybody asks him about *Citizen Kane*. But I did ask him about his *Othello*, a very low budget version he shot whenever he had the money. He had to shoot some scenes silent because he couldn't afford synch sound, so he directed his cast so that the speakers would have their backs to the camera, or he wouldn't show us the speaker at all but cut together nothing but reaction shots. He'd record the speeches later, separately, when he had more money.

The scene I asked him about was shot in a steam bath. It's the scene where Iago reveals his scheme and the sweat and the steam give the moment a hellish look and feel. The story I'd heard was that he'd run out of money. Again. They'd taken his costumes from him so he had to figure out a way to shoot the scene without costumes.

Welles laughed. His *Third Man* laugh. Just for me. Alive and in person. (The *Third Man* isn't his second best film, because he didn't direct it.)

"I still had my crew and I still had my cast," he told me. "I told everybody on the film to steal the sheets from their hotel the next morning. The sheets were the costumes." Adversity plus genius equals art.

What we spent most of our time talking about was radio. I love radio and have a huge collection of old radio drama, and Welles's stuff holds up.

Welles had played *The Shadow* on the radio.

The weed of crime bears bitter fruit. Who knows what evil lurks in the hearts of men?

The Shadow knows.

I thought he'd been the first Shadow and asked if he'd helped create the character.

"I wasn't the first," he told me. "That was Robert Hardy Andrews."

"The guy who created Jack Armstrong." I said. Welles smiled. I got points for that. One thing I've learned about doing interviews, and that's what this was, disguised as casual conversation. It's important to establish early on that you're not a schmuck.

"That was a great job. I was doing Broadway, they'd have a cab waiting for me, I'd run into the studio, I didn't rehearse, I didn't even see the script before we went on the air."

His "War of the Worlds" broadcast is one of the most famous moments in twentieth-century American history, and rightfully so. It's about the power of electronic media and the power of propaganda.

A little history. Welles was a Broadway boy wonder when CBS offered him an hour of network radio. It didn't cost the network much of anything; the band and the sound effects guys and the engineers were on salary anyway, and the hour was sustaining, which means commercial free because they couldn't find a sponsor, because even as far as CBS could tell, nobody was listening to CBS. The time slot they gave Welles was opposite Edgar Bergen and Charlie McCarthy, the country's number one radio show by far.

Welles did play fair. The program starts with an announcer's read:

The Columbia Broadcasting System and its affiliated stations present Orson Welles and The Mercury Theater on the air in "The War of the Worlds," by H. G. Wells.

Then we hear a band, remote "from the Meridian Room in the Park Plaza in New York City," which didn't exist. "We bring you the music of Ramon Raquello and his orchestra." Which didn't exist.

After a few minutes of 1930s Latin, ANNOUNCER TWO

Ladies and gentlemen, we interrupt our program of dance music to bring you a special bulletin from the Intercontinental Radio News (which didn't exist, either).

At twenty minutes before eight, central time, Professor Farrell of the Mount Jennings Observatory, Chicago, Illinois, reports observing several explosions of incandescent gas, occurring at regular intervals on the planet Mars. . . . We now return you to Ramon Raquello.

More dance music, another interruption. An interview with a "famous astronomer in Princeton, New Jersey."

More dance music, another interruption. A "huge, flaming object" landed in Grovers Mill, New Jersey.

More dance music, this time from the fictional Hotel Martinet in Brooklyn, and one more interruption, this time from Grovers Mill. A huge cylinder, thirty yards in diameter. Something climbs out.

Good heavens . . . that face. It . . . it's indescribable, I can hardly force myself to keep looking at it. The eyes are black and gleam like a serpent. The mouth is V-shaped with saliva dripping from its rimless lips.

And when the on-scene reporter has to move because he has run out of cord for his microphone, more dance music, then another interruption. Welles (Orson) and Wells (H.G.) describe a laser beam setting the field on fire. Then we hear a loud crash, and then, the script reads, "then . . . dead silence."

Wow. Great script. Great drama. But why did people believe this? Why didn't they turn the knob and see if other stations were broadcasting this?

Even in the days of radio and even in the days before remote controls, when you actually had to get up off your couch or out of your easy chair to do it, people changed stations during commercials. Welles had a confederate in the CBS control room listening to a radio tuned to NBC. Whenever Charlie McCarthy went to commercial (for Chase and Sanborn Coffee), the confederate would cue Welles, who'd give listeners a few seconds to tune out Bergen and tune in CBS, and he'd cue the announcer, who'd interrupt the dance music with another bulletin and a live remote of Martians in New Jersey. That's why people didn't tune in to another station to see if the bulletins were true: they'd already tuned to another station to hear the bulletins. Mystery solved.

There's a great photo, taken the next morning, of Welles apologizing for the panic that ensued, telling the American public that he'd never intended anything like that. I told him he looked like someone apologizing for winning a million dollars in the lottery.

(Postscript: This past year, H. G. Wells's great-grandson directed a flop film of *The Time Machine*. In my review, I said, "They should have got Orson Welles's great-grandson.")

I mentioned a summer replacement show he did for Mobil Gas with Betty Grable. Great show, I told him. I had a copy of one and was going to offer it to him.

"Oh, yes," he said. "I remember that. We had a great writer on that show, Lester White." And he went on about what a treat it was to work with Lester White, how funny he was, how he remembers that summer as being one of his most productive because he knew he didn't have to worry about his weekly broadcast because he was in such good hands.

I couldn't believe it. I knew Lester White. His son, Steve, the guy I went to Europe with, is one of my oldest friends. When Welles went on the air, I called Steve at home in LA.

"I know it's six o'clock in the morning on New Year's Day, but I was just sitting in the green room with Orson Welles, who was telling me what a great writer your father is." Steve hung up the phone. And woke up Lester.

Lester, one of the nicest people I've ever met, wrote for Bob Hope for, I guess, forty years. My first introduction to show business was at Steve's house listening to Bob Hope's writers kvetch. About how cheap he was. About how mean he was. About how he'd fold his writers' paychecks into paper airplanes and float them to his writers, making his writers dive for their money. About how he'd keep his writers on call twenty-four hours a day and wouldn't think twice about calling them at home at night. His phrase was, "I need a few things." Which leads to one of the nice stories I've heard about Hope.

One Friday night Lester and his wife, Lorraine, decided to spend the night at home, in bed, reading. About 10:00 the phone rang. It was Hope.

"Lorraine, it's Bob. Is Lester there? I need a few things."

Lorraine looked over at Lester who was curled up in the fetal position, sound asleep. Lorraine said, "Gee, Bob, he's not here. In fact he told me he was going to be working with you tonight."

Without missing a beat, Hope said, "That's why I'm calling, I was expecting him . . . Whoops, I hear a car, that must be him now." And Hope hung up the phone.

And Hope told the story at Lester's funeral. That's two nice stories about Bob Hope.

Lester White had the world's greatest exit line. He had leukemia, he was at Cedars-Sinai, he weighed under 100 pounds, he had just a few days to go. A nurse came in, huge, obese, she bathed him, picked him up, changed his bed, saw to his IV, marked his chart, and as she was walking out, Lester said, "Nurse, excuse me, but could you do me one favor?"

"Anything, Mr. White."

"Whatever you do," Lester White said. "Don't sing."

23

Hitler Was a Nicer Guy

Dear Dylan,
I cried the first time I heard you sing "Sing a Song" from *Sesame Street*. My friend Joe Raposo had written it. I was at Joe's Carnegie Hall studio the day he got a tape of Ray Charles singing another of his songs, "It Isn't Easy Being Green." To hear Ray Charles sing anything is a treat, but to hear that song sung by someone who'd never seen the color green . . . everybody cried.

One of the great perks of my job has been watching songwriters sing their own songs. Nobody sings a song with the same unabashed joy, love, and ego as the guy who wrote it. More than actors, even more than dictators of small Latin American countries, that's the kind of ego the old Tin Pan Alley songwriters had, especially if they went back to the song-plugging teens and twenties, and I interviewed a lot of guys who did.

And as one song leads to another, so does one songwriter.

Tin Pan Alley

These guys had leather lungs. Loud voices. They shlepped from publisher to publisher, singer to singer, pounding out their melodies on bad pianos, shouting out the words. They had to make themselves heard over the metallic din that came from the other 200 guys selling their songs, which was the reason it was called Tin Pan Alley (Twenty-ninth between Fifth and Sixth in the teens and twenties).

Irving Caesar was one of those guys. White hair (when I knew him), deep, loud voice, proverbial Coke-bottle glasses. He wrote "Tea for Two" and "Just A Gigolo," and he loved talking about the composer he wrote "Swanee" with, George Gershwin.

Gershwin wasn't poor, Irving would say. His father owned a chain of cafeterias. But "Swanee" was the first real money either of them made, and George bought his father a 1919 Marmon with his first big royalty check. (A Marmon was a luxury car in the same league as a Cadillac or Packard or Pierce Arrow.) Well, Irving went on, one day George's father got stopped for speeding up on West End Avenue. Doing forty-five in a twenty-five-mile-an-hour zone. This big Irish cop pulled him over, and George's dad proudly said, "Maybe you know my son, George Gershwin" — which, in Pappa Gershwin's thick Yiddish accent, came out more like, "Maybe you know mine son, Judge Gurshvin."

The cop said, "Oh, you're *Judge* Gershwin's father. Well, sir, you'd best drive a bit more carefully."

Kitty Carlisle Hart is a great lady. She's the former head of New York State's art council, the soprano in the Marx Brothers' near-perfect *Night at The Opera*, and absolutely as charming in person as she was on all those early TV panel shows. I interviewed her a few times in her huge East Side apartment. One thing that impressed me: the casual, matter-of-fact way she'd take out a jar of makeup just before the interviews began to cover up the liver spots on her hands. She had a framed, autographed photo of George Gershwin up on her mantle with a very personal inscription.

"George had this song he'd written

where he'd left the girl's name blank," she told me off-camera. "He'd play the song and whoever the girl was, he'd put her name in."

Then there was a pause, a smile, a gleam and a sigh and she said, "Well, it worked with me."

Helen Hayes deserved her title — "First Lady of the American Theater." What a great person she was. I heard her tell this story at the Broadway memorial for Irving Berlin. She met Charles MacArthur, the man she'd marry, at a show business party. He was a struggling playwright and already a notorious figure around Broadway, where she was already a huge star. When they met, he offered to get her a drink, and she shook her head, no. He poured some peanuts into her hand and said, "Miss Hayes, I wish they were emeralds."

He would become a very successful playwright, writing, for one, *Front Page* with his partner, Ben Hecht. He was also a drunk, a womanizer, and a gambler. She really was a nice Irish Catholic girl.

One night she and MacArthur met in her dressing room after a performance and, though very much in love, finally decided to take all their friends' advice and break up. It was sad, it was tear-filled, but it was time to face the music, and they needed someone to tell. Irving Berlin, a notorious insomniac, had soundproofed his apartment so he could write at the piano all night long. Assuming he'd be up, Helen Hayes and Charles MacArthur knocked on his door at 3:00 a.m., and Berlin answered in his bathrobe. Before they could get in word one, Berlin said, "You've got to hear this song I just finished." He sat down at the piano and played and sang "I'll be loving you, always. With a love that's true, always."

The two never told Berlin they'd come to tell him they'd decided to split up. Instead "Always" became their song, and they married. On their tenth wedding anniversary, MacArthur took a small paper bag out of his pocket and poured emeralds into Helen Hayes's hand and said, "I wish they were peanuts."

This is a true story and, in thirty years of covering Broadway, the only nice story I ever heard about Irving Berlin.

Sammy Kahn was probably the last of the old song-pluggers. As my crew was setting up at *his* piano, I said, "It's a coincidence but the last songwriter I interviewed with this crew lived to be a hundred."

"Eubie Blake," Sammy said.

"That's right."

"Irving Berlin lived to be a hundred and one."

"Yeah," I said. "But Eubie was a nicer guy."

"Than Irving Berlin?" There was a pause and not a very long one before Sammy said, "Hitler was a nicer guy."

I hadn't been in New York for very long when I read someplace that Eubie Blake's eighty-fifth birthday was coming up. I knew who Eubie Blake was from a PBS series on ragtime. He'd written "Charleston Rag" in 1899. He wrote, "I'm Just Wild About Harry" and "Memories of You," which I'd learned to play on clarinet, mimicking the Benny Goodman licks. Eubie was the first black composer to write a Broadway musical, which he did back in the '20s. And every five years, until he was 100, we did an interview. His memory was perfect, even at 100.

He'd tell great stories about growing up in Baltimore, about playing piano in, yes, a whorehouse, until he was discovered by an aunt who walked by the parlor and recognized his style of piano playing. "Sounds just like l'il Eubie," he'd say, mimicking the way his aunt told his mother, and he'd laugh and he had one of those laughs that would start below his knees and work its way up until his whole body would shake.

His father confronted him, and li'l Eubie pulled up the oilcloth that covered their dirt floor and showed his father where he'd hidden the gold pieces he'd earned playing piano at a whorehouse. He remembered everything — the names of the hookers, the madam, the pickpockets, everything. On his ninetieth birthday I wanted some new stories, so I tried a different tack.

"You're twenty years older than the airplane," I said.

"What do you mean?" he asked.

"Well," I said, "the Wright brothers invented the airplane in 1903 and you were born in 1883, you're twenty years older than the airplane."

"Let me tell you about that," Eubie said. "I'm going to tell it to you just like it happened. I came home from school — my folks were born slaves, they couldn't read." Then he turned away from me and looked right into the camera and pointed at the lens.

"I say that so you young folks out there know you don't have to be born with a silver spoon in your mouth to make something of yourselves." He pointed again then turned back to look at me.

"I'm going to tell it to you just like it

happened," he repeated. "I told my folks, 'I read it in the paper, white folks gonna fly in the air.'

"And my father said, 'What'd you say, boy?'

"And I said, 'Saw it in the paper, white folks gonna fly in the air.' And my father turned to my mother and said, 'See, send your boy to school, he comes home, tells you nothin' but lies.' "

Eubie did live to 100, but his wife, who was almost thirty years younger, had died the year before, and you could tell he was barely holding on to hit 100; he died a few months after his birthday. His wife, by the way, was the granddaughter of the man who invented potato chips. Her grandfather was a cook at a Saratoga Springs resort. When someone complained that the fried potatoes were sliced too thick, he got angry and sliced them super-thin. On some menus, in some cookbooks, they're still called Saratoga Chips.

I asked Eubie Blake what the most amazing thing was that happened during his 100 years. He was born after the light bulb was invented, four years after, but he'd been here for the phonograph, radio, television, the airplane, the atom bomb, the computer, man on the moon. He answered without hesitation. "Martin Luther King," Eubie Blake said.

(George Abbot, who lived to be over 100, was the great Broadway playwright and director who, when an actor challenged him with "What's my motivation?" Abbot answered, "Your paycheck." When I asked him what the biggest change on Broadway had been since he'd started directing, he answered, "The electric light.")

I was hired by WCBS-TV to cover rock-and-roll music. I was the first TV reporter hired to cover rock and roll, so I was the first TV newsperson to interview Billy Joel, Bette Midler, Randy Newman, Bruce Springsteen. When I was off to interview Stevie Wonder, our show's producer, Ron Tindiglia, a great TV newsperson, demanded that I talk to him about being blind.

"I can't do it," I said. "I just can't do it. I'm not that kind of reporter, I never will be."

"OK," Ronnie said. "Don't say, 'What's it like being blind,' figure out a way to get him to talk about it without asking directly."

Stevie had just turned twenty-one, and his deal with Berry Gordy and Motown was that once he turned twenty-one he could produce his own songs. This was the first Stevie Wonder album that Stevie Wonder produced. The deal was that he'd do one song, and we'd do the interview. The song I wanted was "You Are the Sunshine of My Life."

Stevie apologized. This was so early into the album's life, not only had it not become a hit yet, he hadn't learned the words yet. Instead he sang "Superstitious." Hearing Stevie Wonder in the ballroom of the old Fifth Avenue Hotel down in the Village just doodling on his electronic keyboard, even my super-straight Brit cameraman, who'd piloted a Spitfire during the Battle of Britain, understood he was in a room with a genius.

And, yes, I asked the question. I asked it this way, hemming and hawing aloud so he could hear my uncomfortable body language.

"What's the worst thing about the way people treat you because you're blind," I asked.

He laughed and actually said, "I'm glad you asked that question."

"Just because I'm blind," he said, "I don't know why but people think I'm deaf, too. Every time on an airplane a stewardess will tap my shoulder and shout at the top of her lungs, "OH, MISTER WONDER, IS THERE ANYTHING I CAN GET FOR YOU?"

The Brill Building, at Fifty-first and Broadway, was Tin Pan Alley in the '40s and the '50s. Would-be big shots would give the number of the payphone in the lobby as their office phone and fight with each other when the phone rang. The Brill Building was the model of the Jollity Building in those great A. J. Leibling *New Yorker* stories. It was also the birthplace of the famous "Brill Building Hello," where you shake someone's hand and tell them how glad you are to see them, while you're looking over their shoulder to see who else is in the room. When he first came to America, Sidney Poitier slept on the roof of the Brill Building. He did. He told me that. His first job was in a Broadway deli, washing dishes. He also told me something he still regrets: that he never learned the name of the old Jewish waiter who helped him learn to read. He was never able to thank him, he told me. And he thinks about him every day.

Paul Simon worked the Brill Building when he and Garfunkel were Tom and Jerry. Carole King wrote "Do the Locomotion" there, her Brooklyn babysitter sang it, the record label renamed the babysitter

"Little Eva." Simon and King, singer/ songwriters recording their own songs, changed the music business. Singers don't buy songs from pop songwriters anymore. Simon and King helped put the Brill Building out of business. There's only one publisher left in the Brill Building, the eponymous Elvis Presley Music. A few years ago, Presley Music bought out a very large and very old German publisher. Going through their files, Presley's president found a 200-year-old letter, in German, from a piano player. He had the letter framed and has it hanging in his office. It's from Beethoven, boasting about the surefire success of the piano quartets he just submitted and asking his publisher for an advance. In gold.

Due to Circumstances Beyond Our Control

One of the great rules of making television and making film: the audience doesn't know what they don't see. The Eubie Blake story never got on the air: it took him too long to tell. When Helen Hayes died I wanted to use her telling the Irving Berlin story in her obit. I was sure we had it on tape. But we only had the beginning on tape. The cameraman shut off his camera ten seconds into her speech, and started it again on the applause at the end.

Another great moment missed: I was on-stage during a rehearsal for Carnegie Hall's ninetieth anniversary. They were doing the Bach double violin concerto with Isaac Stern and Yehudi Menuhin, who kind of pranced on-stage showing off a brand-new Stradivarius — well, a very old but brand-new-to-him Stradivarius. He played a bit for Stern, who, of course, knew and rattled off the entire provenance of the violin. Yehudi Menuhin passed the violin to Stern, who did a bit of Bach, nodded, smiled, checked the action. They invited the concertmeister of the New York Philharmonic to try it out. They were like kids trying out somebody's new baseball mitt. Even the piano player got up and took a few licks: Leonard Bernstein.

We missed the shot. My cameraman was up in the last balcony, getting wide shots.

The Ed Sullivan Show

Back in the day, when most cities had just three or four TV channels to choose from, and even New York and LA only had six or seven, stations tried to produce "family programming." The whole family, kids, parents, grandparents, would sit around the TV, glowing like it was a stone-age campfire and we were all members of the same clan. On Sundays at 8:00 p.m., we watched *The Ed Sullivan Show*. Sullivan was a one-time Broadway columnist with, as someone once described him, all the personality of a hotel towel. The Beatles made their U.S. TV debut on *The Ed Sullivan Show*. Elvis Presley made headlines when Sullivan wouldn't let his cameras shoot Presley's swiveling hips. Comics became stars on *Ed Sullivan*. He'd book old-fashioned vaudeville acts like plate-spinners and animal acts and ventriloquists. He was a national institution. I was at CBS when he died, and I did his obit. Here are two stories I had to leave out.

One day, a couple of the guys on his crew told me off-camera on the day he died, Sullivan had booked a bear act. There was never a full rehearsal, because he booked old pros who knew their acts. Instead there was a quick run-through so the talent would know their marks (where they were supposed to stand) and the director could make adjustments. Well you can't do a quick run-through with a bear.

Once he starts, he's got to finish; that's how he learned the act, that's how he was trained. So this Sunday afternoon there is a bear on-stage at the Ed Sullivan theater going through his paces, and Sullivan, standing in the wings, spies this ice cream bar. Looks good, Sullivan thinks. He looks around, no one's there to claim it, so he picks it up, unpeels the wrapping, and starts to eat it.

What Sullivan doesn't know is that this is not only the bear's ice cream bar, it is the bear's salary, it's what he gets for doing his act. The bear sees Sullivan take his ice cream, but the bear is a pro. He goes through his entire act, a watchful eye on Sullivan, and the second the act ends, he runs over to Sullivan and whacks him with the back of a paw. Sullivan ends up in the second row of seats, the bear picks what's left of the ice cream bar off the floor and finishes it, stick and all, in one angry bite.

Sullivan, only slightly injured, was able to do the show that night, and, as far as we know, the bear didn't carry a grudge. But after that, Sullivan would never so much as touch anything he'd find backstage.

Jose Feliciano was a guitar player and singer who was blind at birth. He made his first appearance on *The Ed Sullivan Show* when he was just a kid. Sullivan had booked him on the basis of a big hit record, and had no idea that Feliciano was blind until he showed up for the run-through with his seeing-eye dog.

Sullivan panicked.

"This is a family show," he told Feliciano's manager. "I can't put a kid on the air with a seeing-eye dog, it'll bring down the whole show. Can he work without his dog?"

"I'll ask him," the manager said, "but I don't think so."

"I'll fall down without my dog," Feliciano said. "I need him."

The manager reported that back to Sullivan, who thought for a second and asked, "Does the dog do any tricks?"

PART 6

Lessons for Dylan

Dear Dylan,
These are some of the places I want to take you, some of the movies I want to watch with you, some of the things I've learned that I'd like to share with you, and some of the lectures that, given the chance, I will force you to listen to. Here they are . . . just in case.

24

The Smoking, Drinking, and Drugs Lecture

Smoking

I started smoking when I was kicked out of Hamilton High School. I was sixteen, I'd been senior class president, I was waiting on the corner of Pico and West-wood for the bus to take me to Uni High. I'd published the first underground news-paper in the history of the Los Angeles City School System.

We called it *The Iconoclast*, Dan Pellin and I. It was pretty tame by today's stan-dards. It was even pretty tame in 1959. We made fun of some of the teachers, used a few Yiddish phrases our *goyishe* principal, who ran a school that was two-thirds Jewish, had never heard before. *Goyishe* was one of them. *Bar Mitzvah* was another.

We mimeographed 500 copies. We couldn't figure out how to get a picture on the cover, so Dan, who was a cartoonist, inked up his right hand and used his handprint for the cover of the magazine. With a sixth finger. Not the dirty finger. A sixth little finger. This was 1959.

The principal saw the hand and thought it was the Mafia.

Our case was also not helped by the Boys' Vice Principal, a National Guard two-star general named Homer O. Eaton.

"You're the kind of kids who join the Civil Liberties Union," he muttered at us.

Our case fell apart completely when I pulled out my ACLU card. That year, I noticed with an ironic detachment that General Eaton failed to appreciate, the ACLU student cards were — oddly or prophetically — printed on pink paper.

The ACLU refused to take our case, in spite of my being a member. They insisted that the school system, *in loco parentis*, could assign us to any school they wished.

My father was in the hospital, or he would have fought it with me; he liked to take on the establishment. He had pneumonia; it wasn't life threatening, but to my Polish-born mom, the hospital for anything other than having a baby was pretty scary. And Dan's family was so dysfunctional they made my dad look like Ozzie Nelson and my mom look like Donna Reed.

Dan was sent to LA High. I went to Uni High. On a "social adjustment" transfer. Which is what Chicano street means when they call out to each other, "Hey, Essai!"

A few weeks before, a kid from Uni had transferred into my physics class at Hamilton. When I went to Uni I got his physics book. One of the kids in the class told me he'd been kicked out for punching out the teacher.

Dan went on to become a Hasidic Jew. I started smoking.

There was a newsstand on the corner of Pico and Westwood, a rare sight in Los Angeles. I started reading *Variety* on the bus to and from school. There was a cigarette machine at the far end of the newsstand. Cigarettes were a quarter a pack, and I figured, "If I'm going to be bad, I might as well really be bad," and bought a pack. I sure showed them.

I quit smoking after Jane died. I also lost weight, got my first manicure, got new glasses, trying to coax her back.

The cancer in my lungs isn't related to my smoking, it's just the warm, comfortable place my colon cancer picked as a fallback position to try to make a sneak attack on the rest of my body.

But the treatment's the same. So is the fear.

Here's a number from a 2002 study by the British surgeon-general: 50 percent of people who smoke will die because of their habit.

When I started to smoke, I thought about Humphrey Bogart in a trench coat, his collar turned up, the brim of his hat snapped down, Ingrid Bergman or Lauren Bacall on his arm, one hand cupped against the wind, flipping open a Zippo lighter with the other, and lighting up a Lucky.

I'd rather you carry an image of Humphrey Bogart, too thin and ill to leave his bed, his voice an unlistenable rasp, dying of cancer from smoking.

Or carry the image of those almost symmetrical scars on my back, the two S-curves that look like I was cut up by an astigmatic violin maker. The one on the left, where they took out a third of my right lung, the one on my right where they took out half of my left. And remember the quarter-sized circular scars on my left and right hips where they inserted the glass tube and kept it inside me for a few days so what was left of my lung wouldn't collapse after surgery.

Drugs

This is a lot easier for me to write when you're four and angelic than it would be to tell you alive and in person when you're fourteen and wrestling with the devil. And just maybe that will help me be more honest.

I smoked marijuana for the first time when I was a college senior, listening to Simon and Garfunkel sing "Parsley, Sage, Rosemary, and Thyme." Yes, I inhaled. And I liked it. This was the '60s, and, like they say, if you remember the '60s you weren't there.

Country Joe and the Fish had put out this ten-inch home-pressed LP with sounds of crystal being struck, and when you were loaded, it felt like you were inside the crystal. Or at least inside the speaker.

I did cocaine once. Nothing happened. Nothing.

I flew up to San Francisco a few times during the summer of love — 1967. The difference was I flew in a plane. I stayed with Gene Rosow in Berkeley and Steve White, who'd become the road manager for the Grateful Dead, in the Haight Ashbury.

I went to a love-in at the old Haight Theater on Haight Street. The theater had been closed for years, some hippies had homesteaded it, written LOVE on the marquee, reopened it for music, and ripped out the seats for dancing. The music was loud, though none of the girls had taken their shirts off yet, when I saw someone I knew from UCLA. I'm not sure he saw me. If he'd been British and wearing red he could've walked through the Battle of Bunker Hill, there were no whites of his eyes. I'd never seen anyone like that, not anyone I knew. I never asked what he'd been on, I figured he couldn't remember, but I figured it was LSD. I never even tried it, never even wanted to.

Here's the lecture: you're going to try drugs. Be careful. Don't try them while you're in a life-threatening place — like in a car. And stay away from crazy stuff like homemade pills and sniffing gasoline and paint thinner.

And promise me that if you do drugs, they will never be more than a complement to the things you do. Like having a beer with the guys while you're talking baseball, or sharing a bottle of wine with friends.

It's when the drugs take the place of the talking and the friends that you need to get help. If that happens, I pray you will be around people who love you enough to help you get help. And please, please do.

25

The College Lecture

College is the only time in your adult life when you'll have time to waste. So, for Christ's sake, waste some. Sit up all night bull-shitting about whether there's a God or what truths are universal or whether *Huckleberry Finn* is the great nineteenth-century American novel. Waste time reading books you wouldn't otherwise read, waste time traveling to places for no reason other than you like the name, waste time going to movies to get out of the rain or to the theater because you like that watery orange drink that only the Shubert organization knows how to make. None of that time you waste will be wasted. I don't regret any of the stupid things I did when I was in college, only the stupid things I didn't do.

College is not a trade school. Don't major in theater, journalism, film, advertising, marketing, or that amazing boondoggle called "communications" that allegedly prepares America's youth for careers in broadcasting.

The truth about all of these majors is that you will learn more in one month on the job (as an actor, a copy boy, a go-fer) than you will in four years as a theater or film or communications major. OK, I told you to waste time, but I didn't mean that way.

Take courses in those subjects, see what you like and what you don't like, but if you want to make movies, it's more important that you learn about the human condition than how to backlight a close-up; somebody else will know how to backlight a close-up, and you can learn it later anyway. Study literature, history, psychology. If you want to do TV news, it's more important that you learn what questions to ask about economics, or art, or music than how to face the camera when you're asking them. And having majored in a real subject, like economics, or having mastered the language skills you'd need to study Asian History will impress a would-be employer a lot more than a tape of you reading a teleprompter, anchoring a college news broadcast.

There was no undergraduate journalism

major at UCLA when I was there, but I wrote for the school paper, edited the humor magazine, learned how to proofread and punch a Linotype machine while night-editing the *Daily Bruin*. I always figured — I really did — that I could always get a job on a weekly or a small-town daily somewhere on Route 49 in the gold-rush country. That was my safety net.

Gene Siskel once told me that one of his professors, John Hersey, once told him, "Don't worry about money. This is America. You're smart. The money will be there. Follow your passion." Good advice. I heeded it, and I'd never even heard it.

26

The Money-for-College Lecture

Speaking of safety nets, I'm not a firm believer in working your way through college. I didn't. I was a poor kid, I lived at home, carpooled, paid $200 for a ten-year-old 1955 Buick that took hills at 5 mph (15 mph if you were going downhill). I went to UCLA when it cost $74 a semester plus books, and I earned pocket money playing clarinet and sax at weddings and Bar Mitzvahs. My dad had a conversation with me about money. One conversation. Which is one more than he had with me about sex, for which I will forever be grateful.

He warned me not to expect to inherit anything, because he was going to spend it all before he died.

What he didn't tell me was that he was going to spend it all five years before he died and I was going to have to support him. Which I did. I'm sorry that he didn't live longer so I could have supported him better.

I really don't think anyone should worry about money. You should be conscious of it, be concerned about it, but not worry about it. The U.S. government allowed me to set up something called a UGMA under the United Gift to Minors Act. That's tax-free money I socked away that becomes yours when you're eighteen. There should be enough there to put you through college.

It'll be yours to do with what you want, but if you don't use it to go to the best school you can get into and get the best, broadest education you can stand, I hope you feel guilty as hell.

Every waking moment.

27

Be Anything You Want to Be,
But, Please God, Don't Want to
Be an Actor

"Never tell an actor," a director once told me, "this scene isn't about you."

What he meant was, if you're an actor, it's *always* about you.

What's always about you?

Everything is always about you.

There's a five-hundred-year-old joke about the guy who played one of the gravediggers in the original cast of *Hamlet*.

"What's the play about?" his wife asked him when he came home for dinner, still in makeup, covered with dirt.

"Well," the actor said. "First, I dig up a skull."

Think about it. Is it healthy to want to be a movie star and to want to have millions of people looking at you thirty feet high, you wearing somebody else's clothes and pretending to be somebody you're not? If there were no cameras and it wasn't a movie and you were dressed that way and saying those words, they'd shoot you with a tranquilizer dart and carry you off to Creedmore.

A Joke That Proves the Point

A comedian, playing Vegas, gets a call in his room at four in the morning. A very breathy, sexy woman's voice on the other end says, "I saw your show tonight. You are the best comedian I have ever seen. I want to come over to your room right now and make incredible, fantastic love to you . . ."

And the comedian says, "Did you see the early show or the late show?"

True Story

I love Lena Horne. It's genetic. My father loved Lena Horne. In fact I was named Joel because he loved Lena Horne.

It was the night before I was born. My folks had been arguing over whether to name me *Yossel* after a great-grandfather named Joseph or *Zalman* after a great-grandfather named Solomon. A running gag between my folks was the big crush my dad had on Lena Horne and how he'd leave my mom for her even the night before their first baby was born. They went to the movies that night, to see Lena Horne in *Cabin in the Sky.*

One of the songs from that film is "Happiness Is Just a Thing Called Joe." When my folks heard the song, the story goes, they looked each other in the eye, and both smiled and decided to name me Joel.

I told Lena Horne that story, I think exactly that way. This is a hell of a thing, one would think. She is a great lady and she knew how much I thought of her and how much I admired the way she'd fought racism even in show business, even at MGM. But she's an actress. When I finished the story she got this puzzled look on her face and said, "That was Ethel Waters' song."

Besides, the Odds Are Against You

I have a theory that truly great actors get found: Meryl Streep, Al Pacino, Morgan Freeman. They are so good they'll get work; directors will hire them because they'll make the directors look good, then audiences will discover them and buy tickets to see them because audiences will know they'll see something special. But, my theory goes, one short rung beneath that handful of genius actors are a thousand very good, *almost* great actors, hanging by their thumbs.

You see 'em in national companies of Broadway musicals or replacing the almost-stars who replaced the name-above-the-title actors in the second year of a Broadway hit. I recognize 'em playing the other girlfriend in a Tom Hanks movie, or Jack Nicholson's gay neighbor, or the guys the special effects happen *to* in a Steven Spielberg film. And they're pretty good.

The problem is that there are thousands of these actors, all pretty good, sometimes as good as the stars, sometimes better, all fighting for the same few jobs.

Who gets which role, who gets what billing, who becomes rich and famous, who goes back to waiting tables at Joe Allen's all owes as much to luck as anything else. I really do think that's true. And do you really want your future, your life's work, the decisions as to where you'll live, whether you'll marry, when you'll have children to be decided by the whim of some casting director who has a lunch date or a tooth-ache or is getting shtupped by the guy just behind you so you don't get the part?

"Can't sing, can't act, can dance a little." A note attached to Fred Astaire's first screen test. If RKO hadn't given him a second screen test, we'd never know about Fred Astaire.

George Raft figured he'd played one too many hoodlums and nixed a starring role in the Warner Brothers' film of *High Sierra* and, a few months later, said no to the third remake of *The Maltese Falcon* because the first two were bombs. And Humphrey Bogart became a star.

Max Steiner, who composed the score to *Casablanca*, hated the song "As Time Goes By," most likely, Marvin Hamlisch told me, because he didn't write it. Warners gave Steiner a weekend to write a new song, which he did, but over that same weekend, Ingrid Bergman had cut her hair short for *For Whom the Bell Tolls*, and they couldn't match the shot. That's the only reason "As Time Goes By" is in the movie.

If you do decide you have to be an actor, that there's no other choice, that you've got to at least try, I understand that. But — more advice — give it a real try. With everything you've got, with help from everyone you know.

And give yourself realistic goals in a real time frame.

"I've got till age twenty-five to get a play, get a TV series, get my Equity card, get an agent, start making enough money to support myself." Pick one or two or all of the above.

And, for God's sake, learn something in college so you don't have to be a waiter.

If You Quit School to Be a Kid Actor, I'll Write You Off Without a Cent. It's in the Will.

And it's not just me. I don't know any sane person in the show business who would let their child be a kid actor. Not one.

Most kid actors grow up to be very unhappy adults. The kid actors on *Father Knows Best*, the happiest, fuzziest, familiest TV show on the air when I was a kid, became junkies.

Sarah Jessica Parker and Jodi Foster may be the exceptions, though I don't know either of them well enough to be sure. But their careers were exceptional: raised by single moms, their work helped put bread on the table; maybe that helped the sanity quotient.

Very few kid actors grow up to become grown-up actors. Parker and Foster are two exceptions, but the two most famous kid actors — Judy Garland and Mickey Rooney — could have been poster children for electric shock therapy.

Poster grown-ups, too. I missed Judy Garland, but I've met Mickey Rooney half a dozen times, and he's the craziest person I've ever been with I didn't have to get frisked first for sharp objects in order to talk to. Backstage on Broadway, he told me how every time Louis B. Mayer would see Judy Garland he'd cup his right hand and cop a feel. He cursed Mayer's name, confessed that he was broke, painted a tragic masterpiece of the last years of Judy's life, and I hadn't even asked.

I interviewed him a few years later. He had a new wife he was touring with who seemed to genuinely like him. That might have toned him down. Maybe his MGM pension had kicked in. Maybe he was on new meds. He had nothing but nice things to say about Mayer and wouldn't talk at all about Judy, which had been the reason for the interview.

When the best of 'em go crazy and the worst of 'em become junkies, that's no life for you, at least not as long as your mom and I have any say in the matter.

Another true story: Norman Taurog was directing Jackie Cooper. Jackie was nine or ten, the most famous kid star in America, and Norman, who was dating Jackie's mom and virtually living with him, had given him a puppy when the film started. For one scene they needed Jackie to cry. He couldn't cry. The director, the kid's stepfather mind you, said, "Jackie, if you can't cry for us, we're going to take your puppy behind that van and shoot him."

Jackie still couldn't cry. An MGM cop took the dog behind the van and fired his pistol three times. Jackie cried. The director got his shot. The guard got his raise. He didn't really shoot the dog, the dog was fine. But Jackie wasn't.

28

What to Do When a Bully Picks on You

His name was Mark Koppleman. I never really knew him, we weren't friends, nothing like that. He had red, curly hair and a very loud voice to go with his very brash manner. We interacted exactly once. This was forty-six or forty-seven years ago.

It was at the end of lunch hour, or maybe between classes, at Louis Pasteur Junior High, a few blocks east of La Cienega on a street, for no apparent reason, named Airdrome. There was a bike shop around the corner where the manager sold pornography under the table, a Foster's Freeze, a Mr. Pizza, and Adohr Dairies a few blocks down. Adohr (Rhoda spelled backwards, the owner's wife) was where the legendary fights would take place. Legendary because I'm not sure any ever really went down. But the threat was always in the air.

"Oh, yeah? Meet you at Adohr."

So I am getting a drink of water from a trough-like fountain with three or four spigots when Koppleman and his buddy show up at the fountain to my right. I still remember it was the fountain to my right.

Koppleman was boasting about how he'd learned how to give someone an excruciatingly painful charley horse (about two-thirds of Pasteur Junior High's student body was Jewish, and, yes, even the bullies used adverbs correctly).

He was describing the technique to his friend when he suddenly said, "Wait, I'll show you!"

He turned to his left and kneed me as hard as he could in my right thigh. He didn't know me, didn't know my name, but he was a good enough judge of character to know I wouldn't tell or cry or fight back.

And I didn't.

If I had hit Koppleman back there is no doubt he would have creamed me, as we said back then, a possible reference to the Adohr bottling plant. (For what it's worth, the three bovines pictured on the Adohr milk carton were Linetta of Adohr, Adohr Eldor Pearlette, and their prize bull, Corium Slogan's Oliver.)

But what the kids at Pasteur Junior High

would have been talking about would not have been "Koppleman creamed Siegel" but "Can you believe it? Siegel fought back!"

There is a saying I later learned from people who tend not to use adverbs correctly: If you fight back and get hit, it hurts a little while; if you don't fight back it hurts forever.

29

"Where Do Babies Come From?"

Ask your mother.

30

Something Your Mother Won't Tell You

The Real Words to the Colonel Bogey March (and the reason they only whistle the song in *The Bridge on the River Kwai*):

Hitler,
He only has one ball.
Goering
Has two but very small.
Himmler
Was very similar
And poor old Goebbels [pronounced "Gerbles"]
Has no balls [pronounced "Nerbles"]
At all!
Repeat until VE Day.

31

I'd Give Anything to Take You to Your First Ball Game

I don't mean your very first ball game, or I would've taken you to opening day when you were three months old. I want to be the one who takes you to the first ball game you'll remember. To watch your eyes get big as baseballs when you walk through the tunnel and all your senses are hit simultaneously: you hear the crowd, you smell the grass, you feel the excitement, and, most of all, you see that green. All that green. It's an American thing. You're in the Bronx or downtown Baltimore or surrounded by miles of asphalt parking lot near downtown LA, and you follow a crowd through a turnstile, there's noise and hot dogs and vendors hawking programs and ball caps. You've got your mitt just in case someone smacks a foul nearby. And you turn into a tunnel, and you blink and do a double-take, you've never seen that much green.

It's exciting every time it happens, but it's only the first time once, and I want to be there for yours.

My first ball games were minor league games. LA had two teams in the Pacific Coast League, the Los Angeles Angels and the Hollywood Stars. I was an Angels fan because of their announcer, Bob Kelley, Old Kell', whose voice was described as smooth and smoky as rye. I thought they meant rye bread. What did I know, I was nine.

The Angels played at Wrigley Field, a scale model of Chicago's Wrigley. My daddy took me there to my very first ball game. I can still smell the beer-soaked cement floors. It might have been the first time I smelled beer; we never had it at home. Being first-generation American Jews, there was a bottle of schnapps in the cupboard over the refrigerator that no one could reach without standing on a chair and half a bottle of cherry vishniak that my *zaideh* had fermented himself in Al Capone's Chicago and set aside for my *bris*. I remember the ballpark's smell, I remember looking up at the rivets and the girders — what I imagined the inside of the Eiffel Tower looked like. Then we turned into a tunnel, and on the other end it was like I was mugged by the color green.

We lived a lot closer to Gilmore Field, where Angels' archrivals the Hollywood Stars played. For kids under twelve it was a thirteen-cent bus ride away on the orange and silver Asbury bus. General admission was thirty-five cents, but you could get in free if you had the nerve to ask an adult with a ticket to say he was your father. I never had the nerve. My friend Metzner had nothing but nerve. Once he asked a Japanese guy to say he was his father. How do you say chutzpah in Japanese? I don't know, but the guy admired Metzner's and said "yes." Dustin Hoffman hawked peanuts at Gilmore Field. I might have bought some from him; we were there at the same time.

I love baseball because it's America's common folklore, a history we can share that, like the calendar, is renewed every spring and put to bed every fall. And I love it because baseball, like a languorous August afternoon, which is when games should be played, takes its own time, not in minutes and hours but in innings and outs.

I also love baseball because, like wine and good music and theater and, yes, movies, too, baseball is a serious art form that gets better with age. Your age. The more you know, the more you enjoy it.

I couldn't get a ticket to the first game, but I was there for the second major league game ever played in Los Angeles. The Dodgers versus the Giants and Willie Mays. The LA Coliseum, built for the 1932 Olympics and used as a football stadium, was rushed into use as a ballpark for the new LA Dodgers. The left field wall was 250 feet away from home plate and ninety feet high. If they'd rented out office space in left field, it would've been the tenth tallest building in Los Angeles. The only reason they didn't rent out office space was that Walter O'Malley, who'd brought the Dodgers from Brooklyn for a king's ransom, didn't think of it. (True story: Brooklyn-born writers Pete Hamill and Jack Newfield were at a party and decided to list the ten most evil men who ever lived. They got to three. The same three. Hitler, Stalin, and Walter O'Malley.)

Someone had brought a bugle to the first game. Six notes and the crowd yelled, "Charge!" I'd heard him on the radio and I brought my uncle Bebble's trumpet to the second game. Now they play it through the PA system and a prerecorded crowd screams "Charge!" in synch with light-bulb script on the Imax-sized monitor over the scoreboard. In case we don't know when we're supposed to be rooting. Mine was the only trumpet at the Dodgers' second game. I am, I guess, in part responsible for keeping the streak alive.

We sat up behind home plate. Way behind home plate. Willie Mays looked like an ant we were so far up. I'd been a Dodger fan, a Brooklyn Dodger fan. Because of Jackie Robinson. And I loved the bum. I also loved the word "zany," the adjective of choice in describing the Brooklyns and their fans.

"Three guys ended up on third base, only in Brooklyn."

I don't know what I was expecting when I went to see the Giants and the Dodgers renew their heated rivalry on the other coast, my coast. But I do know I was disappointed. There was nothing "zany" about these guys. Not too much "heated" either. I was never an LA Dodgers fan. I became a baseball fan. A fan of the game and the players, not of a team.

I saw Stan Musial hit a double from his inside-out crouch; he looked like he was trying to hide from the pitcher behind his right arm and his bat. I never saw Ted Williams, wrong league. I did watch Joe DiMaggio, on television. My father wasn't a baseball fan, but even he knew that history was happening on Channel 4 and we watched DiMaggio's last game together on our RCA ten-inch table model.

I was at the stadium the day Reggie Jackson hit three back-to-back-to-back home runs against the Dodgers in the World Series. I saw Yaz play at Fenway. And Willie Mays one more time at an old-timers game at Shea. He bounced a ground-rule double over the right field wall, he was ready to come back at sixty. His hat flew off as he rounded first, not as nearly as wide as he had forty years before, when the only thing faster than him on the Giants was Juan Marichal's fastball. And I realized — my palm hits my forehead as I say, "What a schmuck!" — he *made* his hat fall off all those times. Show business. Say, hey!

When Mays lived in San Francisco, his Cadillacs had vanity license plates: SAY HEY. He'd get one of his license plates stolen once a month. When that story came over the wires, my reaction was: only once a month? If I'd seen one I would've stolen one — and, like I said, I was a Brooklyn Dodger fan. I met Juan Marichal at a movie screening and was so excited to shake his hand I forgot he was a Giant, too, and I hated him.

Steve Greenburg, Hank Greenburg's son, is a good friend. When people ask him how his father would do if he were playing today, Steve says, "He'd probably hit .270, maybe .280, maybe twenty home runs."

The response is always a bewildered "Really?"

And Steve says, "Well, he'd be eighty-three years old."

I worked with a kid named Mike Tanaka who'd grown up an LA Dodger fan although he grew up in Chicago. He was nine or ten, the Dodgers were in town, and at Wrigley the players have to walk by the fans on their way from the locker room. Mike is ready with a baseball to be autographed, and here come Sandy Koufax and Don Drysdale. Together. Talking to each other. Mike holds out the ball and his pen, Koufax takes it and signs it, but Drysdale shakes his head, "No." And Koufax gives Mike the ball back.

Mike is very disappointed. He watches Koufax and Drysdale walk away, talking to each other, and it's obvious that Koufax is arguing with Drysdale, trying to get him to sign the kid's baseball. Drysdale keeps shaking his head. Finally Koufax looks back, Tanaka is near tears, Sandy motions to him to toss him the ball, which Mike does, and

Sandy signs Don Drysdale's signature.

Tanaka still has the ball.

I've only asked one player to autograph a baseball for me, Jimmy Reese. He was ninety, still coaching for the Anaheim Angels. He was the world's greatest fungo hitter — that's where you pitch to yourself, tossing the ball up then hitting it — and Reese could place his hits just about anywhere. Once upon a time he could stand on the pitcher's mound and bat strikes to home plate. Even at ninety I saw him stand at second and wave outfielders to the right or left and hit line drives to where he'd placed them.

The movie *Babe* — the one about Babe Ruth — was coming out, and Reese had not only played with Ruth, he'd been his roommate for a season or two.

"I didn't actually room with him," Reese said. "I roomed with his suitcase. On the road I never saw him."

There is a story you will read, Dylan, every American boy reads it, about the games Ruth missed because he had this horrible stomachache from downing gargantuan amounts of hot dogs. It is not a true story, Dylan. The Babe had the clap.

There is a true story, though, about Jimmy Reese. He confirmed it. He was with the Yankees, and they were playing an exhibition game against the Giants. Harry Danning, who was Jewish, played catcher for the Giants. Another Jewish guy was pitching, and instead of using signals, they shouted at each other in Yiddish. Reese was on third, taking a longer and longer lead. Harry Danning yelled, in Yiddish, for a pitch out. "We'll get that momser," he shouted. As soon as the pitcher started his windup, Reese stole home.

Harry Danning, shaking his head, said, "I didn't know you were that fast."

Jimmy Reese told him, "No, what you didn't know is that my real name is Hymie Solomon."

When You Watch a Ball Game, Learn to Keep Your Eyes Away from the Ball

Watch the manager on the bench and the third base coach passing signs to the hitter, a series of semaphore slaps and tweaks. Watch the pitcher try to hide the way he grips the ball from a runner on third; if he doesn't, the baserunner can tell if the pitch is a fastball or a breaking ball and signal the hitter. If a right-handed batter is up and the shortstop takes a few steps or even leans to his right, that's a giveaway that the pitcher's throwing a fastball, a pitch a right-handed batter is more likely to pull to left field. When a lefty is up at bat, watch the second baseman.

The same thing goes in the theater, good critics know it: keep your eyes off the ball. Don't watch the guy who's talking, watch the guy who's listening. Anybody can talk, but to listen like you mean it is the sign of a great actor.

I learned this stuff sitting in the seats, you might learn it on the field. There's a picture on your bedroom wall of the 1921 New York Yankees your granddaddy Murray sent you. The fifth guy on the left, with his name rubbed off, is "King" Murray, Granddaddy Murray's uncle and namesake, three Yanks away from Lefty O'Doul, Babe Ruth, and Irish Bob Meusel. "King" Murray was all natural talent till he drank it away, Murray told me, but he pitched for the Yankees. On my side of the family we used up all of our athletic abilities running from the Czar.

If you play or if you watch, every time you walk into a ballpark, you'll remember the first time. That's why I want to take you to your first ball game. I'm selfish. Every time you walk into a ballpark I want you to think of me.

32

Movies I Want to Watch with You

Movies are a fraud. Of course they are. From beginning to end. For one, they don't move. They are a series of still pictures that take advantage of an optical trick called the "persistence of vision": We retain an image just long enough that when images are projected in a series past our eyes at twenty-four frames per second, we don't see the lines that separate them.

The source of the images we see isn't "real" either. It's a series of still pictures manipulated in every conceivable way, printed on celluloid, in an edition of thousands. The sound we hear was not recorded when or where the film was exposed. There was no hundred-piece orchestra seated just out of camera range coaxing smiles or tears from the cast and crew while they were filming the scene (though, paradoxically, orchestras did sit just out of camera range

469

to set an emotional timbre when silent films were shot. The first job my clarinet teacher, Leroy Parry, had when he came to LA from Salt Lake City was playing background music for Mary Pickford movies). The sound of footsteps, the buzz a fly makes, the creak of a door opening, the clinking of ice cubes in a glass — these sounds are all added after the fact by a sound effects man called a Foley artist.

The picture we watch is an image of a print of people wearing clothes they don't own, whose breasts have been made larger, whose noses have been made smaller, answering to names that aren't theirs. We'll see them walk into a row house in Baltimore that may or may not really be a row house in Baltimore, but the room they'll walk into will be inside a studio in West LA or, more often these days, a warehouse in Vancouver, British Columbia. They will speak words they did not think up to people who are not there. And if, perhaps, they die, at the sound of the command "CUT!" they will come back to life, only to die again when a different voice yells, "ACTION!"

I am insecure by nature and suspicious by training, yet four or five times a week I will surrender myself for two hours in the dark to someone I have never met whose only interest in me is to tell me two hours' worth of bald-faced lies. And if they don't lie to me, if I am able to pierce their illusions and glimpse the truth, that's when I get pissed off.

Public Intimacy

Walter Murch, who is Francis Ford Coppola's editor, used the oxymoron "mass intimacy" to describe the very personal shared emotions we go to the movies to feel. We read books alone, we enter the world an author creates all by ourselves. But we go to the movies with hundreds of strangers, and the emotional highs and lows are somehow amplified when we experience them with others. Maybe it's tribal. Maybe it's precognitive. But it is the reason neither television nor videos nor home theaters with Dolby surround sound will put movie theaters out of business.

A few years ago, David Selznick's kid released a restored version of *Gone with the Wind*. There was a screening at the Radio City Music Hall, and I realized that although I had seen *Gone with the Wind* probably a dozen times, I'd never seen it in a movie theater with an audience. The scene when Rhett is coming back and Scarlett laments, "I have nothing to wear," and the camera wanders over to the drapes, 6,000 people went "Oooooooooooh!" Movies are better when you watch them with an audience.

And these, Dylan, are the movies I want to show you, to watch you watch them for the first time, as opposed to movies like *The Seventh Seal* and *Seven Samurai* and Dreyer's *Passion of Joan of Arc* and even *Vertigo*, that I do want you to watch but I don't have to be there, we can talk 'em about later. Or movies like *Gone with the Wind* and *Casablanca* that you should see — especially for the first time — with someone who's not your parent.

Head Start

You've already seen a lot of movies, you're a twenty-first-century boy. *Monsters Inc.*, the first film you saw in a theater, and *Shrek*, and *Lilo and Stitch*, each of which you and I have seen at least four times. I'm still not sure how you assimilate all that information or how much you understand. But I'm also not sure how you know to reach into the bag of popcorn, pull out a handful and pop it in your mouth when you're hungry. But I love it when you do. And the way you insist on sitting on my lap.

We've watched *Pinocchio* and *Snow White* and *The Lion King* on video. When we watched *E.T.*, the version where Spielberg CGI'd the guns into walkie-talkies (thank you, Steven, it worked perfectly), you shrieked and jumped and almost flew as high as E.T. did when the bicycles took off.

When I showed you the *Wizard of Oz* for the very first time, I was talking to you through the black-and-white part, trying to get you excited about what you were going to see next.

"Oh, oh, the tornado's coming. It's a twister. Dorothy bumped her head! Look out! There's Auntie Em! And look, there's Miss Gulch!"

You were sitting on my lap and you turned your head to face mine and said in a very conspiratorial way, "She's just dreaming."

Stalag 17

I was eleven. We were on a summer trip to Yosemite National Park. We were in a town called Sonora, California, in the heart of the gold rush country when my father said, "Let's go to a movie," and this was the only movie that was playing.

It was the 1950s, so there was no cursing. There were also no women in the film, so there wasn't any sex, though I remember Harvey Lembeck looking pretty cute in drag, but that was probably a memory from a later viewing.

Stalag 17 was the first film that got me. Snookered me. I was had. I was sure, I would have bet everything I owned, had I owned anything, that I knew who the villain was. I was wrong. I loved it. I still carry some of that wonder with me to every movie I see.

Double Indemnity, The Apartment, Some Like It Hot, and Sunset Boulevard

Four more great films from the same great director who made *Stalag 17*, Billy Wilder. In order they are: one of the best ever films noirs, a great romantic comedy, the screwball comedy the American Film Institute and I voted Hollywood's best, and the very best movie about movies ever made by anybody. Watch them with me. Let me tell you about Wilder living in the men's room of the Chateau Marmont when he came from Germany. About how

Jack Warner burst into Wilder's office when he was under contract to Warner Brothers.

"Schmucks with Underwoods," Jack Warner called writers. An Underwood being a brand of typewriter. A typewriter being . . . ah, hell, Dylan, look it up in the dictionary.

Jack Warner would walk by "Writers' Row" on his backlot and listen for the sound of typing. If he didn't hear it, he'd figure he was being cheated and he'd pay a surprise visit to the writer, which is how he happened to find Billy Wilder asleep on his couch, his newspaper unfolded over his face to keep out the bright Burbank sunlight.

"I'm paying you ten grand a week!" Warner fumed. "Why aren't you writing?"

"I am writing," Wilder said. "Later I'll be typing."

I don't know of any other director who made so many great films in so many different genres. I even loved *Five Graves to Cairo*, which has one of the movies' great lines: "There is no 'G' in Egypt!"

I met Wilder. It was at Mr. Chow's, a restaurant in Beverly Hills. He was in his nineties, in a wheelchair, and his food had to be cut for him. I introduced myself and told him I did not know any other director who made so many great films in so many different genres.

Here's my version of the story Wilder would tell about Marilyn Monroe. When she started dating Arthur Miller, Miller invited her to his mother's small apartment in the Bronx. Monroe was charming, she was deeply in love with Miller, and Miller's mother was charmed.

Halfway through dinner Marilyn excused herself to go to the bathroom, which was just off the dining room in this neat, efficient Bronx apartment. To mask the sounds, Marilyn turned the water tap on.

The dinner went very well, and the next day Arthur Miller called his mother.

"Well?" he asked. "What did you think?"

"Arthur, she's charming, she's wonderful, she's even more beautiful than she is in the pictures. But she pees like a racehorse."

Someone older than Arthur Miller heard me tell this story and told me it was an old Jewish joke. The punch line, in Yiddish, *Zi pished a zai vy a ferdl!*

"Nobody's perfect," as Billy Wilder might have said. In fact he did.

Citizen Kane

Yes, the greatest film ever made. If you can't watch it with me, watch it with Roger

Ebert. Either in one of the classes I hope he's still teaching or with his audio commentary track on the DVD. Learn to watch *Citizen Kane*, and you'll learn to watch film. Example: What is one thing you see throughout *Citizen Kane* you almost never see in any other movie? Answer: ceilings.

Richard III, Hamlet, and Romeo and Juliet

Ian McKellan's Richard, Zeffirelli's *Hamlet* with Mel Gibson and Glenn Close, and Baz Luhrman's Romeo, set in modern-day Miami.

Beautiful films with exciting, involving stories — *and* they happen to be written by William Shakespeare.

The stage version of Ian McKellan's Richard was your mommy's and my first date.

When you visit the Globe Theater in London, check the tiles in the courtyard for the one with my name on it. I had to make a donation to get it there. But Shakespeare was the reason I was able to make a living sitting inside watching people act instead of standing outside digging and shlepping, so I figured I owed him.

The Black Stallion and The Little Princess

The 1979 *Black Stallion*, directed by Carroll Ballard, and the 1995 *A Little Princess*, directed by Alfonso Cuaron, are two of the most beautiful, most magical films about childhood I know. On your seventh birthday, watching them with you will be your present to me.

Field of Dreams and To Kill a Mockingbird

I want to watch these with you on Father's Day. That would be wonderful. And it would be even better if you chose them.

If I'm not around, tell whomever you're watching *Field of Dreams* with that your daddy said the movie would have been better had Jackie Robinson been one of the players who came. After Kevin Costner built it.

Billy Crystal told me a story that when he was a kid in New York — this was long before he was Billy Crystal — he was crossing Sixth Avenue when he heard a familiar-sounding voice ask, "Excuse me, but could you help me across the street?" It was Jackie Robinson, so racked with the effects of diabetes that he couldn't see well enough to cross the street by himself. What are the odds?

In *To Kill a Mockingbird*, that's Robert Duval as Boo Radley, his motion picture debut. But it's when the woman tells Scout, "Stand up, your daddy's passing," that makes this a great Father's Day film.

The Red Balloon

After the movie I'll ask you what language you heard people speaking.

Singin' in the Rain

This was the first movie I ever saw alone. It was a revival at the old Waverly in Greenwich Village. Going to the movies in LA was always a social occasion. Also, you had to drive there, which meant that, as a kid, I had to be driven.

But my first summer in New York, there I was, alone on Sixth Avenue, the matinee prices were in effect, I walked in, and, watching *Singin' in the Rain*, I kept turning to my right, turning to my left, looking for somebody to talk to, somebody to tell how great this movie made me feel. That's the downside of going to the movies alone. Not that I recommend sitting next to strangers at the movies and telling them how great the movie makes you feel. Especially in Greenwich Village.

It was your first trip to Disney World, you were four and a half. It was a beautiful, sunny day, not a cloud in the sky, but, for some reason, you burst into song, smiling and singing, "I'm singing in the rain, just singing in the rain . . ."

"Dylan," I said, smiling even wider than you were. "Where did you learn that song?"

"In school," you said.

Thank you Beginnings Pre-School. Worth every penny.

A Hard Day's Night

There was a joke making the rounds in the '50s when Israel was a poor country (we'd send clothes and toys to our family there; one of my first jokes was "We were so poor my family in Israel planted trees in our backyard." Nobody got it then, either). Two Jews were trying to scheme Israel into prosperity when one shouted, "I've got it! We'll declare war on America!"

480

"But we'll lose," the other Israeli says.

"Of course we will, that's the whole idea. And what happens when America loses a war? They bring in food, they build schools and hospitals, their GIs come and spend millions of dollars, it'll be heaven on Earth!"

And the other Israeli says, "Our luck, we'd win."

Somebody turned the joke into a book called *The Mouse That Roared*. Walter Shenson, who ran publicity for United Artists, thought it was a great idea for a movie and optioned the rights, fully expecting UA to make the film.

"It is a great idea," his boss told him. "You're fired."

So Walter Shenson became a reluctant film producer, which may be why, when I met him, he was such a nice guy. And more than a little afraid. And I don't think I'd seen an adult this fearful before.

It was early 1964, and he had just finished filming *A Hard Day's Night*. He was a friend of Steve White's dad, Lester, and Steve and I visited him when we were in London on our trip to Europe on $100 a month. That really was our budget, and we visited anybody we could in hopes they'd buy us lunch. Shenson didn't buy us lunch. It was before the movie came out, and I think he was broker than we were. He did show us the Tiffany clock on his desk, engraved John, Paul, George, and Ringo. And he confessed that he didn't think these guys would still be stars three months later when the movie would finally come out.

They were. I was exactly the wrong age to view this film critically. It was so much fun it wasn't until I did start to review film critically, ten years later, that I understood that this is one of the great movie musicals of all time. Richard Lester redefined the genre for a new generation. The Beatles were great. Naturals. The quick cuts and visual non sequiturs created music video technique that is still cutting-edge almost forty years later. Plus I know all the words to the songs.

The second best Beatles movie is *I Wanna Hold Your Hand*, a movie about the Beatles so smart it doesn't have one Beatle in it. Stephen Spielberg, who produced it, perfected that kind of movie sleight of hand when he made *Jaws*. The shark didn't work. It looked phony. Spielberg understood that if he showed the audience the shark early in the movie they'd laugh the movie off the screen. So he didn't show the shark until we were so scared we couldn't tell what it looked like, because we were holding our hands over our eyes by then anyway. Interesting how the most gripping scene in *Jaws* has no effects at all, it's the scene where Robert Shaw tells the story of the *USS Indianapolis.* Being able to force your audience to imagine: that's great filmmaking.

John Sayles's film, *Alligator,* is another film where having no budget becomes money in the bank. It's a story about the baby alligators New Yorkers supposedly flushed down their toilets, now grown huge and haunting the sewers and the subways. But Sayles didn't have enough money for a whole giant alligator, so all you see is this huge alligator tail flapping around a corner.

The Princess Bride

There is a picture of me up on the bookshelf standing between André the Giant and Mandy Patinkin. I really did meet these guys.

The Adventures of Robin Hood, Beau Geste, and The Man Who Would Be King

Ah, the Brits. Loyalty. Devotion. Knowing right from wrong. Viking funerals. The things we learn at the movies. You can watch the others without me, and I think you'll love 'em, but I really do want to be there when you watch *The Adventures of Robin Hood*. The Errol Flynn *Adventures of Robin Hood*, of course.

So I can tell you about left-handed staircases and right-handed staircases and show you why the archery scenes looked so real. The secret is they were. Olympic archers were just off camera. Stunt persons wore balsa wood chest plates backed with stainless steel. Slow-mo or stop action the DVD, and you can see the arrows actually going into people's chests instead of just bouncing off and popping out the way other films do it. And what a way to learn about justice, about fighting for what you believe in, about teamwork, about love, about how Basil Rathbone was Jewish.

This was MGM movie-making, big Hollywood fantasy at its Technicolor best. Adolescent values? To be sure. Which is exactly why I want to watch this film with you when you're an adolescent.

Many years later, Sean Connery and Jean Simmons were perfectly matched in a beautiful love story called *Robin and Marian*. Robin returns from the Crusades, bitter and disillusioned. Marian has become an abbess at a nunnery.

"I always loved you," Robin says.

"Why didn't you write?" Marian asks.

"I don't know how to write."

When you were three, running through the loft, tipping things over, stopping to scream nonsense at the top of your lungs, then laughing as hard as you could, I wondered how and when you'd ever be able to feel that free as a grown-up. Then I thought: watching the Marx Brothers.

Day at the Races

Groucho, as Dr. Quackenbush, taking someone's pulse.

"Either this man is dead or my watch has stopped."

A Night at the Opera

"Thank youuuuuuu."

"Thank youuuuuuu."

"Tootsie frootsie ice cream."

"That's the sanity clause."

"You can't fool me. There is no Sanity Clause."

Duck Soup

The incredible ballet between Harpo, disguised as Groucho, who, very believably, breaks a mirror and is caught on one side of the empty frame by the real Groucho on the other. Beat for beat, move for move, Harpo convinces Groucho that he, Harpo, is Groucho's reflection. And the inevitable, hysterical topper you'll have to watch the movie to see.

There's Some Television I'd Like to Watch with You, Too

Lucille Ball and Harpo reprised the mirror gag on *I Love Lucy*, which I'd love to watch with you. You can catch old TV shows on cable, and *Lucy* and *The Honeymooners* and Sid Caesar and Uncle Miltie's classic episodes are also on video and DVD. Of course I watched them live with my dad. Or, because we lived in LA, on something called a kinescope; movies taken off a TV screen and rushed by propeller-driven airplane to the left coast and broadcast a week later. The kinescopes are pretty much all of what survives of early TV; the shows went on the air live and were only intended to be seen once. In the '50s when the network was up, the LA stations would film the live feed from New York and broadcast the kinescopes they made three hours later to compensate for the time difference. (A Fred Allen joke: The time difference. It's so confusing. When it's nine o'clock in New York it's 1947 in Los Angeles.)

We got our first television in 1949. My dad, you know he was an electrician, had also been a radio amateur when he was a teenager. We actually woke up early to watch test patterns, to stare at the Indian. It was that amazing to us: a picture in your living room.

The living room, at 3320 Pomeroy Street, filled up when a little girl named Kathy Fiscus fell in a well. She was my age. It was covered live.

The first TV I ever saw was on a Tuesday night; this might have been 1948. My mom's brother, my Uncle Muttie, won a TV in a raffle, a Pilot table-model television with a three-inch screen. I know it was Tuesday, because we all went over to watch Milton Berle. My memories of the evening are so vivid that I thought they were wrong: I remembered looking up at the TV through parallel, vertical towers. Yes, I finally realized, I was five. I was short. I really was looking up at the TV. Through peoples' legs.

Some of my best memories of my father are of him laughing while he and I watched TV. We didn't go to the movies much; most families didn't in the early '50s.

"How do you get folks back in the theaters?" Herman Mankiewicz, who wrote *Citizen Kane* with Orson Welles, asked a room full of Hollywood moguls.

"Show your films in the streets!"

Sid Caesar

Milton Berle doesn't hold up — he plays more as history today than comedy — but I'd love to watch Sid Caesar with you, and you'd love it, too. *Aggravation Boulevard*, about the silent movie star making his first talking film who sounds like he's inhaled helium. The foreign film parodies. *The Bicycle Thief* in pidgin Italian. The Kurosawa film in double-talk Japanese with a few Jewish words thrown in; one of the characters was named Gansa Mishpucha, another called Chaza Ri. And *This Is Your Story.* Howie Morris's Uncle Goopy grabbing onto Sid Caesar's leg and not letting go.

I hadn't seen these sketches in almost

fifty years, but I remembered the punch lines, I remembered the jokes and, most of all, I remembered hearing my father's laugh.

Caesar saved the original kinescopes, and fifty years later put the best of his bits out on DVD. I did an interview with him. When I told him some of my best memories of my dad were of the two of us watching his show, he started to cry. For him, remembering his father, sitting in his audience, are some of his best memories of his dad.

I hope you remember me, Dylan. And, most of all, I hope you remember me laughing.

Laurel and Hardy

The Music Box. I saw this first on TV, the one where they play movers shlepping a piano up a never-ending flight of stairs. It is their funniest short. *Big Business*, where they play Christmas tree salesmen who tear someone's house apart, is a close second. It is such a fine line between civilization and another fine mess you've gotten me into.

The steps are still there. Not far from

where your Aunt Phyllis used to live in Echo Park, not far from Hollywood.

Time for Beanie

Live TV 1949. Monday through Friday at 6:00 p.m. on Channel 5, KTLA, your Paramount television station in Los Angeles. And I don't think I ever missed it. This was the TV I watched when I was a kid. So how can I complain when you watch too much Sponge Bob or Scooby Doo? You have other choices. I didn't. When I was a kid, this was all that was on.

Korla Pandit was on every day, maybe all day every day. An Indian who played an organ and wore a white turban with a huge crystal in the middle. Sometimes the camera showed the keyboard, sometimes it showed the crystal. That was it.

Ina Ray Hutton and her All-Girl Orchestra was a big KTLA nighttime show. A remnant of the days, not too far from 1949, when desperate people took desperate measures to try to save the big band era. "Ina Ray Hutton and her All-Girl Orchestra, seventeen pieces and they play music, too" was a joke I did in high school that I didn't understand in 1949.

490

I came across some video of these shows. They're on a three-quarter-inch tape labeled KTLA. The Museum of Broadcasting has copies, too. I gave 'em to 'em. You'll know everything you need to know about early television in your first thirty seconds of viewing. Trust me.

There are a couple of old *Time for Beanies* there, too. The show was so popular that kinescopes were made and sent back east, where they watched *Beanie* a week late. Later it became an animated Saturday morning show, but the *Beanie*s I watched were done live. The characters were hand-puppets, and two very funny men — Stan Freberg and Daws Butler — crouched in a box doing all the voices: Beanie, Cecil the Seasick Seaserpent, Dishonest John, and Cap'n Huffenpuff of the old Leakin' Lena. Watching the tapes I was shocked it was as crude as it was. But no one had done television before, so by 1949 standards it was *Star Wars*.

I watched *Beanie* with my dad. The show made so much fun of the La Brea Tarpits I was shocked to learn later that they were a real place. I didn't miss many episodes, and I wasn't the only one.

Stan Freberg, who looked like my uncle Bebble even though he wasn't Jewish

(Freberg, not my uncle Bebble), was another childhood hero. His parody records and hysterical commercials made him to records and advertising what Harvey Kurtzman was to comic books. Freberg once ran a contest between a power mower and a sheep. "Yes, this proves it beyond any doubt our mowers are faster than sheep!" He also bought time on LA radio's two leading morning shows, Bob Crane and Dick Whittinghill, to announce in stereo Butternut Coffee's entry into the LA market. I could still hum you the jingle. Be glad I don't. But I did hum it for Freberg when I met him. Albert Einstein was a *Time for Beanie* fan, he told me.

Einstein was at Cal Tech and, once, during a symposium, he looked down at his watch, stood up at his desk and announced, "Six o'clock, Time for Beanie." And left the room.

Yes, Einstein had a sense of humor. On his twenty-fifth wedding anniversary, when asked to what he attributed his happy marriage, Einstein said, "When we got married we decided I would make all the major decisions and my wife would make all the smaller ones. And in twenty-five years we have not been faced with one major decision."

My favorite Einstein story: When he devised the theory of relativity, he said, "If I'm right, the Germans will say I'm a German and the French will say I'm a Jew. And if I'm wrong, the French will say I'm a German and the Germans will say I'm a Jew."

Well, actually, that's my second favorite Einstein story. He loved music, played a left-handed violin, and enjoyed playing chamber music with whoever might be around. Artur Rubinstein, the great pianist, perhaps the greatest of the first half of the twentieth century, was playing a little Mozart with Einstein, who kept coming in on the wrong note. Finally, in desperation, Rubinstein slammed the keyboard shut and glowered at Einstein, "Albert, can't you count?"

Grandmommy Charleen

Did you know that your Grandmommy Charleen, Ena's mother, met Einstein? She was a teenager, still in high school, when she won a church scholarship to a choir camp at Princeton University. Charleen was learning to conduct, all five feet of Carolina chutzpah, when an elderly man walked into the hall, everybody stirred, and Charleen missed her cues. The old man — it was Einstein, though Charleen didn't recognize him — felt responsible and asked her if she would walk with him. They spent an hour together, Einstein and your grandmother, and what she remembers most is the aura of kindness he generated, the soft way he spoke, and the ten minutes they spent watching a spider spin her web.

"I think it's some kind of language," Charleen said.

"I think so, too."

"Can you understand it?" Charleen asked.

"No," Einstein said, "but maybe one day we'll be able to."

33

On Friendship

Jane died in January 1982, just before the Super Bowl, about which I remember nothing. Except that Jeff Greenfield ordered in some deli and invited a group of us over to watch it. The idea was to watch the game, but the hidden agenda was to give me someplace to go. They knew Jane, they liked her a lot, they were devastated by her death, they knew I needed someplace to go.

Greenie suggested we meet for lunch during the week. Jerry Imber was a big fan of pelmeny, a lamb- and beef-filled Russian *kreplach* served in chicken broth with sour cream and a mustard-based dill sauce on the side. Wednesday was pelmeny day at the Russian Tea Room, one of New York's great dishes at one of New York's great restaurants, so Wednesday it was.

There is an alternate theory. There had been a Thursday lunch group, freelance writers who showed up at an East Side saloon, writing being a lonely profession. Andy Bergman and Greenie had been regulars at this lunch. Michael Kramer had come and gone. I'd been there a couple of times myself, invited along by Bob Christgau and Richard Goldstein, who wrote for the *Village Voice* and whom I'd known in LA. But the real reason the Pelmeny Club happened was to keep me from committing suicide.

Between us we've written more than a dozen books (even Imber the doctor has written three books), done more than a dozen movies, and had two plays on Broadway. Part of the deal was we've promised each other we'd never write about us. So I'll keep it short.

The Cast:

ANDY BERGMAN. Watch *The In-laws*, which he wrote, and *Honeymoon in Vegas* and *The Freshman*, which he wrote and directed. His youngest son, Teddy, who was born on my fortieth birthday, is the kid who's ice-skating with Marlon Brando.

JEFF GREENFIELD. CNN's political analyst, formerly with CBS and ABC News.

"I don't know what's wrong," he confessed one Wednesday. "I've been grumpy for weeks."

"Big deal," Imber said. "I've been 'Doc' for years."

DR. GERALD IMBER. Plastic surgeon. His connection: I'd gone to junior high and high school with his first wife, Eileen. Once he removed stitches from Della Femina's wrist curbside on Seventh Avenue while we were waiting for a cab.

MICHAEL KRAMER. One Sunday night in 1992 I channel-surfed past Diane Sawyer, who was then with *60 Minutes*, interviewing the first George Bush, then Vice-President of the United States, soon to be President of the United States. Michael had coined the phrase "wimp factor," in a column questioning Bush's political spine. When Diane asked him about it Bush asked her, "Do you know Michael Kramer?"

(He was writing cover stories and political commentary for *Time*; now he's one of the people who puts the *Daily News* together.)

"Yes, I do," Diane answered. She did.

"Well," Bush laughed that half laugh of his. "He'll never play linebacker for the Chicago Bears!"

The Vice-President of the United States of America insulting one of my closest friends, the best man at my last wedding, live on network television!

A few days later Bush sent Michael a Dick Butkus retro-jersey and a tongue-in-cheek apology stating he'd changed his position.

Safety? Left back?

JERRY DELLA FEMINA. The advertising guy who, among his other triumphs, created the singing "Meow Mix" cat. Jerry was a late addition to the lunch group. When he married Judy Licht, long a friend of Andy's and Michael's and mine, she asked if he could join us. All the males he knew were business associates, people who wanted something from him. All his friends were female, and Judy figured male friends might help keep their new marriage together. It worked. Since we started having lunch on Wednesdays we've been through a cumulative eight marriages, but Judy and Jerry (and Andy and Louise, still on their first marriage) are still together.

One Wednesday Jerry was going on about how he had so many affairs before he was married to Judy, he had a secretary whose only job was to keep his social life straight.

"I was sleeping with so many women, when I would come I'd shout, 'Oh, Jerry!' "

In a rare burst of self-restraint, I waited a full week. The next Wednesday, I said, "I followed your advice. I got laid last night, and when I came I shouted, 'Oh, Jerry!' She almost killed me."

We are funny.

When Jerry sold his advertising agency to a French conglomerate and was set to clear $4,000,000, we knew the place and time the contracts were going to be signed. I actually talked to Alan Funt, who created *Candid Camera*, and tried to get him to be sitting in the office when Jerry walked in. He wasn't well enough to fly, he said, or he might have done it.

One day I was going on about how all that really mattered was what they say over you at Riverside Memorial. Andy said, "I know exactly what I want them to say over me."

"What?" we asked.

"Look! He moved!"

When I got sick I got no phony sympathy from these guys. I don't remember getting any real sympathy from them, either.

These are good friends, Dylan. Almost like family. Better than family, because they aren't the family we were born into and had no say about; they are part of the family we chose.

If you need serious advice or a serious favor or a serious loan, ask these guys. And if it comes to pass that one of them or one of their kids asks you, don't say no.

34

Why Don't You Live with Me and Mommy?

Oh. Dylan, I was afraid you were going to ask that question.

A few months before I met Ena I had a long conversation with my friend, Michael Kramer, and told him I was sure I was going to end up alone. And without children. I was in my late forties, I hadn't had a serious relationship since Melissa and I split up, and, though I joke about how many times I've been married, I hadn't had many serious relationships before that.

I met Melissa a year and a half after Jane died. She was alone for the Jewish holidays, and our first date was to my friend Larry Raphael's *shul* on Yom Kippur. She lived in my building. And worked at ABC. As a page.

There is a great joke where you tell someone, "You know what the most important thing in comedy is? Timing. Go ahead, ask me what the most important thing in comedy is."

And when they get out "What's the most. . ." you interrupt them. You say, "Timing."

As in "What's the most . . ."

"Timing!"

That's the problem Melissa and I had. I was forty-one. She was twenty-one. Forty and twenty just don't work. Fifty and thirty can work. Sixty and forty can work. But forty and twenty don't work.

We got married, and she had never lived alone. She graduated from college while we were married. ("The Joel Siegel scholarship fund," the Wednesday lunch guys called it.)

I didn't help matters. Funny how I never do. On our honeymoon we went to Italy, where I'd been with Jane. Saw the same sites, even stayed in some of the same hotels.

Melissa was terrific. She is terrific. Still funny. Still gorgeous. We're still friends, close, serious, good friends.

Timing.

Funny how it took me longer to start dating again, to be interested in women again after Melissa and I split than it did after Jane died. And, until I met Ena, I wasn't seriously interested in anyone at all.

As much as I thought I wanted a partner, and a family, and kids, I always found a way to avoid getting involved. And not the commitment-phobic boomer cliché way of keeping people on the hook for years and years. I avoided getting involved in the beginning of a relationship. Andy Bergman used to call me the world's greatest magician. I'd introduce him over dinner or up in the country to a woman I was seeing, and, abracadabra, she'd disappear: he'd never see or hear about her again.

I was finally able to accept this, I told Michael. I'd made my peace with it, I said. It was OK.

Then I met Ena.

You know where we met, Dylan. I pointed it out to you, and the last time you came to see me at ABC, you pointed it out to me. "That's the wall Ena painted."

She had become a decorative painter, a painting contractor, hand-painting walls with a varicolored kind of faux marble to earn a living while she supported her real painting.

She worked with architects and decorators, did Richard Gere's apartment and Marlo Thomas and Phil Donahue's New

York ceiling and Connecticut house and had been hired by ABC to decorate two floors of conference rooms and the Columbus Avenue lobby of the ABC News building that *Good Morning America* was about to move into.

The building wasn't quite finished when we moved in, and each morning for the first few mornings I'd look up at two very attractive young women in very tight Levi's and paint-splattered combat boots standing on a portable scaffold, dabbing at twenty-foot walls, making them glisten like mother-of-pearl.

One was blonde, and the other was a redhead; not a copper, strawberry-blonde redhead, but an almost auburn redhead. She was the one who turned around when I stopped and asked what they were doing, and she was beautiful. Not cute. Not pretty: She had an almost otherworldly kind of glow-from-the-inside beauty. And her southern accent didn't hurt, either.

I thought she was ten years younger than she was — she looked ten years younger than she was — and, though I sensed some interest on her part and knew I was interested on mine, I didn't want to ask her out. I was sure she was too young. One Wednesday after lunch, Jerry Della Femina came by my office to pick up a piece of video and met her.

"Go ahead," he said. "She's beautiful. Ask her out."

"She's not too young?"

"Of course she's too young. So?"

He convinced me. It didn't take much.

Ena tells the story that she had no idea I was on television, couldn't remember my name, wasn't sure if I had a mustache, and had no idea why I would stop and talk every morning.

She had told me she was an artist and, as the job was finishing up, asked me for an address so she could put me on her mailing list for her next show. I said, sure, if I could take her to a movie.

We made a date that would have been our first except that I got sick. I was home with a cold or the flu or something. I had no idea how to reach Ena by phone. I made someone at *GMA* find her painting the hallway and break the date for me. Ena got my address and dropped off a Louis and Ella CD to make me feel better. It did.

Our first real date was a few days later, to Ian McKellan's *Richard III* at the Brooklyn Academy of Music. What a thing to fall in love over. Shakespeare's most evil villain, transformed by McKellan into

Adolph Hitler. Very romantic.

On the way home from Brooklyn, just over the bridge into Manhattan, I kissed her for the first time.

She lived on Eighth Street between Avenues B and C. In New York we call it Alphabet City. Her street looked like Dresden after the firebombing. Like shots you'd see of the south Bronx or the south side of Chicago when AP or ABC wanted to illustrate a fertile breeding ground for drug addicts and gangs. And this beautiful woman, who barely spoke above a whisper, lived there. And somehow survived. She'd homesteaded the place with a group of other artists, bought the building from the city, built her own apartment.

Wow. I'd never met anyone like that before.

She didn't invite me upstairs to see her place, because there was a guy named Richard who was living there. With her, I found out a few days later. I'd never met anyone like that before, either.

She had this New York bicycle that could fold in half. You ride it to where you're going and fold it up and carry it with you so it doesn't get swiped. She rode it from Eighth Street to Eighty-sixth Street, where I lived. And it was watching her ride it back home, watching this fragile-looking angel with bright red hair and bright red Converse All-Stars pedaling down Broadway, my heart gasping for air, that I knew I'd fallen in love.

"Oh, my God," I remember thinking. "For the very last time."

I introduced her to the Wednesday lunch guys over dinner at Le Cirque. It was my birthday. She gave me a Nancy and Sluggo tie as a gag gift, and a painting for a real gift.

We loved each other so much that we got married. And loved each other so much more after we got married that we decided to have a baby together. There was no other way, nothing else we could think of to show each other how much we loved each other.

When we realized that we weren't getting pregnant but were getting older, we went to New York Hospital for help. The *in vitro* process is so hard on the woman. Shots every day. Surgery to remove the eggs. More surgery to replace them after they've been fertilized. They give the fathers a two-week dose of heavy-duty antibiotics, allegedly to keep them infection free because the mother's resistance is so low. But I'm convinced the real reason for the antibiotics is to make us sick so we get a taste of what our partners are going through.

The process was painful. And it didn't work. But we loved each other so much, and wanted you so much, we did it again. And a few weeks after we started, I got cancer. And had surgery. And did chemo and radiation that mutated any sperm I had left. And, during much of your first three years, left Ena a single mother.

I don't know if you can understand this, but Ena wanted to have another baby because she loved you so much. She was afraid if anything would happen to you, she wouldn't be able to survive. She started *in vitro* but didn't finish the cycle. By that time, we had started to see how difficult our lives together would be.

It was the opposites that attracted us to each other. I think it was how much alike we are that made things so hard. Two control freaks, defined by our work — she an artist, me a TV guy, our work dominated by our personalities. She filled in every inch of every canvas she painted her own way. I wrote my stories, every word, filled each frame of film with pictures I picked. It was hard for us, both of us, to learn to trust each other enough to bend and give. And the cancer made it impossible.

I got sick so soon after we got married, we never had the time couples need to develop a net, a bottom line the relationship can't crawl beneath. We never learned to argue or to discuss or disagree. Every argument we had avalanched into a horrible, marriage-threatening fight. We love each other, but we never learned how to live together.

A few days ago, in a cab on our way home from the dinosaurs at the Museum of Natural History, you asked me why I don't live with you and mommy anymore.

It wasn't a grown-up, give me a serious explanation why these things have happened question. It was an invitation: Why don't you live with me?

I asked you if you remembered how much mommy and daddy would fight and argue. You said you did, and, although I wish you didn't, I'm afraid you do.

"Daddy gets mad and mommy gets sad," was the rhyme scheme.

We've done our best, Ena and I. We still love each other. And we look forward to seeing each other. And, finally, we trust each other, too. All because of you, Dylan. There isn't anything either one of us wouldn't do for you, and there isn't anything each of us wants more than what is best for you. And the best way to do that is to live apart.

35

Dylan Says the Darndest Things

Your mother is convinced that your first words were "William H. Macy" — as in the actor.

I wasn't there, and, as you were only six months old at the time and didn't say another word for another five months, it just might be that she read something into a cough or a gurgle or a burp.

Flower

You were just a year and a half old, it was an August afternoon, you were playing on our deck in Connecticut and didn't know I was watching you. You were backlit by the sun behind you, and I saw some spittle fly out of your mouth and that caught my attention. You were standing next to a box where we grow dahlias, and I watched you point at one and teach your-self a word. "Flower," you said, once, then said it again. "Flower."

Your Vocabulary Grows

When you were just four, we were watching *Lilo and Stitch*, me for the fourth time, you for the third (I had to make sure it was good enough and not too violent before I let you see it). The character Binkley came on-screen, an alien with four tiny legs like a coatrack and one huge eye in the middle of his forehead. You turned to me and said, "He's a Cyclops."

Your First Joke

We were making Mickey Mouse pan-cakes. You were about three. I sat you up on the kitchen counter, and you poured the milk and flour into the bowl after I measured them, and you helped beat the batter. We'd first seen Mickey Mouse pan-cakes at Disneyland, and I copped the recipe: pour one round pancake, add three-quarter-circles of batter at 10 o'clock and 2 o'clock, and, after it bubbles, flip very carefully. The hard part is spelling out *copyright Walt Disney Productions* in maple syrup.

I flipped the first pancake, put it on a plate, spread some butter, poured some maple syrup, and asked you, "Who does that look like?"

You thought and thought and thought, moving your head and scrunching your brow so I would know you were thinking, and finally brightened up into a big smile and shouted, "Donald Duck!"

That's a real joke.

It's only funny if the audience (me, in this case) knows you know the answer is Mickey Mouse. And by the look on your face, the pretend puzzlement, I knew you knew. And what's the best punch line, the funniest character you would confuse Mickey Mouse with? You got it. I was so proud.

Say Goodnight, Gracie

You were almost three, just two months away from your third birthday, and we took you to visit Santa Claus around the corner at the ABC Carpet Company, where, we had been told, they have a great

Santa Claus. And they do, a Santa who wears a nineteenth-century Thomas Nast "Night Before Christmas" kind of costume. That year, you were obsessed with vacuum cleaners, and that's pretty much what you wanted for Christmas. A blue one, I think; your favorite color that year was Day-Blue.

After your visit with Santa, we went next door to a Spanish restaurant for brunch. It was neat. There were fountains, guitar music, the waiters were Spanish, the menu was in Spanish. You wanted pancakes, and when the waiter came, I asked you, "Dylan, can you say pancakes in Spanish?"

And you looked right at the waiter and said, "Pancakes in Spanish."

I Lied

It was just after Christmas, you were almost five, I was watching you trying to piece a puzzle together when you looked up and asked me, "What language do they speak in Los Angeles?" We hadn't been talking about Los Angeles, we hadn't been talking about languages, I have no idea where this question came from, but a thousand punch lines must've crossed my mind.

After careful thought, I answered, "English."

I lied.

Cell Phones

I don't know why it is or where it comes from, but from the ages of three and a half to four and a half you have been obsessed with cell phones. You take one with you wherever you go. At least one. You know how to use them, and at four and a half you know exactly which buttons to push to get you into the phone's directory, then which buttons to push to scroll up or down the list, and you taught yourself to read enough to find the name of the person you want to call: Ena, Joel, your Godfather Roberto, your old nanny Marina.

When you meet someone new, you ask if they have a cell phone, then you ask if you can see it. It is tough to say no to you at four and a half, and almost no one does. You identify the phone by maker — Nokia, Motorola — and by provider — Verizon, Sprint, AT&T. Then you change the ring to one you like, identifying various classical themes by title and composer — Beethoven's Fur Elise, Tchaikovsky's Swan Lake.

One day when you were four you asked Ena, as kids will, why we made you. Ena was telling you how much we love you and how much fun we have together and how wonderful it is to be with you, and you said, "Yes, but you didn't know I'd be obsessed with cell phones!"

What Does This Mean, Dylan?

It was one month after your fourth birthday. Ena's studio takes up the north third of our Flatiron loft. Her desk and computer are there, a painting wall, scaffolding, a flight of huge canvasses, and a bookshelf.

Punk poet Richard Hell is a friend of Ena's. Twenty years ago, I interviewed him in front of CBGB's on the Bowery. I was doing a piece on this new kind of music, which I was smart enough to describe as the first music since rock and roll that wasn't for or about me or my generation.

Hell gave me one of the best sound bites any interview subject has ever given me. I asked him if he could describe "punk." He said "Yes." And he hit me.

I was working at my desk and Dylan was sitting on the floor nearby playing with

some small toys. I heard him saying some-
thing to himself as he held Richard Hell's
Hanuman book and looked through it. I
quickly wrote it down, as he said it to him-
self in a sing-song rhythm.
                    Ena Swansea, March 10, 2002

THE EDUCATIONAL PROPHETS

The edge-ing-cational walk down the hill
Then he walks on the ceiling to be 90-40
Head to the ceiling
Head to the cross
Head to the killer
Head to the 98-40

The heads cross the ceiling
They dive off the water
To Sony
And they lived happily ever after
                              Dylan Siegel, 2002

Were you channeling Richard Hell?
Were you repeating random words you'd
heard, recited for the rhythm? Is this a
glimpse inside the intense mind of children, which somehow gets diluted as we
grow up? Does it mean anything at all?
Did you know the word "cross"? Where

did you learn the word "killer"?

You've never said anything else like this. [*Eerie music comes in softly and builds to a crescendo.*] As far as we know.

Some Hebrew Gets Through

There was this PBS kids' show called *Zoom* you were addicted to when you were three and a half and four. Preteens out of Boston would introduce segments: "And this recipe comes from Judi S. of Philadelphia, PA."

You learned that PA was Pennsylvania, MA was Massachusetts. You'd read the hack license in the back of taxicabs, "NYC TAXI & LIMOUSINE COMM."

"New York City Taxi and Illinois Colorado."

And you'd make up names and places. "And this experiment comes from Sidney Z. of Elohanu, New York."

Elohanu, New York? Where did you learn that word? I asked.

"Chanukah," you answered.

We'd light the candles and say the *brochas*, the blessings.

I was giving a speech at the synagogue in Nantucket. It's not really a synagogue —

they meet in the basement of the Unitarian Church, but it is a real congregation of a few hundred families. I began my talk, "I truly hope that someplace — in Brooklyn, in Tel Aviv, on the Lower East Side — there are a group of Unitarians meeting tonight in the basement of a *shul*."

Sitting through the service (and you were very, very good) when we sang the *kaddish*, the prayer over wine, you nodded knowingly and said to yourself, "Chanukah."

July 27, 2002

When you were little you called me Joel and called your mom Ena. It was what everybody else called us. Once when you were about three and I was home from one operation or another and feeling especially vulnerable, I asked if you could call me "Daddy."

"Anybody can call me Joel," I told you. "But you're the only person in the world who can call me 'Daddy.'"

To no avail. It was Joel. Until . . .

It was breakfast time, cherries were in season, and you asked me to take the pits out for you. I only know one way to do that: bite the cherry in half, bite the pit, spit it out, and then give you both halves of the cherry. It is not a foolproof method.

I was wearing a white sweater. A bright, white sweater. The pit, newly freed, popped onto my sweater. I tried to catch it with the hand that had the half cherry in it and ended up with a half-dollar-sized blot of cherry juice in the middle of my chest.

I looked down at the big red blot, looked up at you, grabbed my chest with both hands and started to shout, "Dylan! I'm bleeding! I've been shot!" I grabbed you and we fell onto the floor, me pretending to writhe in pain. "Help! Help! I've been shot! Call the police!" I think I got a few tickles in, too.

"You're a silly daddy," you laughed.

The first time.

I'll take it.

Dylan's Phone Call

It was August 2002. You called me on my cell phone from your cell phone. "I can't wait for you to come over so I can give you a hug," you told me.

No one had ever said anything like that to me before.

Prognosis

Dr. Tepler was very excited after my latest batch of tests. My blood work was clean. My CAT scan was clean. My colonoscopy was clean.

There was a graduation of sorts. I had been getting scoped and scanned every three months. Now, he told me, we can wait a year between tests. I'm not sure that's a good thing. If it's going to find the stuff while it's small and treatable, I wouldn't mind getting tested every day. Some days I'm so nuts I wouldn't mind getting tested twice a day. Besides, the last time I heard Dr. Tepler that excited about my prognosis, six months later they took out half my lung.

It's been over five years since my initial diagnosis, and five years is a benchmark for colon cancer survivors. According to the American Cancer Society, five years means you're cured. Five years without a reoccurrence.

Remember "Never ask a question unless you really want to know the answer"? I didn't listen to my own advice. I asked: My lung metastases count as reoccurrences. According to the American Cancer Society, I'm back to year one.

I heard a story on National Public Radio that 50 percent of people with colon cancer survive. That was good news. The next sentence: 85 percent of people with lung cancer don't survive.

I didn't ask. I don't want to know the answer. I feel great. That's enough.

Besides, I don't think anyone is ever cured of cancer. The pain might stop, your life might no longer be threatened, but the scars never go away.

I call myself a recovering cancer patient. And I hope to be one for a long, long time.

P.S.

You weren't quite four. You dialed my cell phone on your cell phone and asked me to come over.

"I'd love to, Dylan, but I'm working."

"What are you doing?"

"I'm writing a book."

"Oh, come over and play. We'll watch a show."

"But I'm writing a book for you."

"I have a lot of books."

I really do want to come over and play. This book is just in case I can't.

Acknowledgments

If writing a book were like winning an Academy Award, this would be the time I would romp on to the stage, pull a very long list out of my tux's inside pocket, confess that I didn't want to forget anyone so I made a list "just in case," and start reading.

And if reading a book is anything like watching the Academy Awards, this is a very good time for you make a pit stop or hit the fridge.

I'd like to thank my publisher, Peter Osnos, for allowing a TV guy the privilege of becoming an author. And my agent, Esther Newberg, for her confidence that I could. This project began as a series of letters and lessons for Dylan. My wonderful editor, Lisa Kaufman, organized and architected the pieces into a coherent whole.

Tamara Walsh was Dr. Tepler's nurse whose infectious optimism made my chemo not exactly fun but far less an appointment in Samara than it might have been. Ditto Dr. Minsky's radiology team at Memorial Sloan Kettering. I have to thank Georgain Yurtian, the colostomy nurse at New York Hospital for making me feel and helping me to believe, at least a little, that I really could live with this (and I have to thank Harrison Ford who, when I explained how much of a fan she was of him and how much of a fan I was of her, signed an autograph for her, something he rarely does).

I am grateful, too, to Dylan's caregivers, Marina Williams and Kristie Terrebon and Wendy Martinez and especially to Ena who is one great mom.

Dr. Paul Glasser of the Yiddish Institute of Folk Research (YIVO, go know?) vetted the Yiddish for me. My good friend (and ex-wife) Melissa De Mayo vetted the recipes. Cari Strassberg, Patti Neger, Charlie Gibson, Terry Gilliam, Shelley Ross, Dorothy Johnson, Susan Silver, Steve White, Eric Siegel and the Wednesday lunch guys read and reacted to various pieces of the manuscript in progress, painstakingly Xeroxed and collated by Maria Licari and Meg Kettel. Frank Lalli's very gentle suggestions were, as Spencer Tracy once described Katharine Hepburn's curves, "few but *cherce*." I also have to thank the Lalli's, Frank and Carole, for seating me next to Ellen Levine their New Year's Eve dinner, 1999. We couldn't get a baby-sitter, we had to bring Dylan, cute as a bug, and Ellen suggested I write a story for *Good Housekeeping*'s Father's Day issue on being an older dad; that story, restructured a bit, became the introduction to this book. Bob Meadows, a fine writer and reporter for *People* turned the kind of interview TV people call a "talking head" into a very moving story, the title of which became the title of this book.

I have to thank the crews, the floor managers, the camera people, the stagehands, make-up and hair, all the behind-the-scenes people at *Good Morning America* and *Eyewitness News* for not gasping, or shaking their heads or tearing up when I'd stumble into the studio — at least not so I could see.

Bart Feder, a former WABC-TV news director, summed it up after one broadcast shortly after my colostomy was reversed. I wore a diaper, the *kegel* exercises I had just begun hadn't yet taught my new muscles to contract and I told Bart, "I was shitting while I was on the air."

"You're not the first guy on *Eyewitness*

525

News to do that," he said. "Just the first guy who knew."

I have to thank those I can no longer thank in person: mentors Blanche Bettington and Bill Randall, friends Glenn Steinfast and Michelle Cossack and Johnny Robinson and Steve Meyers and, of course, Jane.

Finally, a few months ago on a flight from JFK to LAX, one of the stewardesses told me her daughter, Meaghan, Meaghan Lehrer, had watched me and Dylan on *Good Morning America* and added my name to her prayer group's list at her Catholic School.

Of all the worthy things in all the world to pray for, I am truly humbled she chose me.

As my Grandma said, "I need all the help I can get." As her grandson has learned, we all do.

Thank you.

DATE DUE

AT APR			

DATE DUE
